Whatsoever things are **true** ...**honest** ...**just** ...*pure* ...**lovely** ...of good report if there be any **virtue** and if there be any *praise*

Think on These Things

Philippians 4:8

from ***Grandma's HeartPrints***
by Velma Beavon

TEACH Services, Inc.
P U B L I S H I N G
www.TEACHServices.com

World rights reserved. This book or any portion thereof may not be copied or reproduced in any form or manner whatever, except as provided by law, without the written permission of the publisher, except by a reviewer who may quote brief passages in a review.

This book was written to provide truthful information in regard to the subject matter covered. The author assumes full responsibility for the accuracy of all facts and quotations as cited in this book. The opinions expressed in this book are the author's personal views and interpretation of the Bible, Spirit of Prophecy, and/or contemporary authors and do not necessarily reflect those of TEACH Services, Inc.

This book is sold with the understanding that the publisher is not engaged in giving spiritual, legal, medical, or other professional advice. If authoritative advice is needed, the reader should seek the counsel of a competent professional

---

Copyright © 2011 TEACH Services, Inc.
ISBN-13: 978-1-57258-705-2 (Paperback)
ISBN-13: 978-1-57258-706-9 (Hardback)
ISBN-13: 978-1-57258-707-6 (E-book)
Library of Congress Control Number: 2011932572

All scripture quotations, unless otherwise indicated, are taken from the King James Version Bible.

Scripture quotations marked (ERV) are taken from the Holy Bible, English Revised Version (1885).

Scripture quotations marked (NIV) are taken from the Holy Bible, New International Version®, NIV®. Copyright © 1973, 1978, 1984 by Biblica, Inc.™ Used by permission of Zondervan. All rights reserved worldwide.

Scripture quotations marked (NLT) are taken from the Holy Bible, New Living Translation, Copyright © 1996, 2004, 2007 by Tyndale House Foundation. Used by permission of Tyndale House Publishers, Inc., Carol Stream, Illinois 60188. All rights reserved.

Scripture quotations marked (TLB) are taken from *The Living Bible,* Copyright © 1971 by Tyndale House Publishers, Wheaton, Ill. Used by permission.

Published by

www.TEACHServices.com

The following titles were written by Ellen G. White and are quoted in this book:

- *The Acts of the Apostles*
- *Christ's Object Lessons*
- *The Desire of Ages*
- *Early Writings*
- *Education*
- *The Faith I Live By*
- *The Great Controversy*
- *In Heavenly Places*
- *Life Sketches of Ellen G. White*
- *Messages to Young People*
- *Mind, Character, and Personality*
- *The Ministry of Healing*
- *Patriarchs and Prophets*
- *The Review and Herald*
- *Steps to Christ*
- *The Signs of the Times*
- *Testimonies to Ministers and Gospel Workers*
- *Testimonies for the Church*

Dedication

This book is lovingly and prayerfully dedicated
to our sons, Eric, Fred, and Ted, their families,
and to all others who are seeking spiritual growth.
My prayer is that your response will be to pass on the torch!

Think on These Things is a follow-up to *Grandma's Heartprints*, my personal memoir. It is written from my heart. It is my spiritual heritage. Each of us must individually choose our own spiritual direction, be willing to grow during our journey, and be fully persuaded in our own mind. We should also be willing to lovingly accept others' choices though different from ours. Scripture provides a yardstick to measure our character: "By this shall all men know that ye are my disciples, if ye have love one to another" (John 13:35).

About the Author

Velma Beavon is an 84 year old great grandmother with the motivation, energy, and spiritual vision of one just beginning their career. Back in the '40s, she studied Bible Workers Training as a major at Emmanuel Missionary College and has joyfully made rewarding use of it all her meaningful life. She married a young minister, Fred Beavon, and faithfully worked by his side. The couple was blessed with three sons in fourteen months. The family lived a simple life in rural environments. Nature, music, God's word, work, and play were all first priorities for them.

Very early in Fred's career, he was called into Conference M.V. (youth leadership) where Velma fit in whole-heartedly by working with Pathfinders, teaching nature at youth camp, working with college students, including several who lived with them while attending school.

For several years while working in Montana, she conducted a Neighborhood Bible Club in a Catholic neighborhood with a dedicated Catholic helper. As Food Service Director at Mount Ellis Academy in Bozeman, she had the pleasure of rubbing shoulders and hearts with academy student workers.

While in Alaska, she worked with a Vacation Bible School among the Eskimos on St. Lawrence Island, just 40 miles from Siberia. Her bi-monthly bulletin to the pastor's wives was much appreciated.

Retiring after 40 years of service, she and her husband have gone on several Mission Projects and Maranatha Volunteer trips abroad, building churches, schools, clinics, and hospitals, as well as holding seminars. When at home, they keep busy visiting shut-ins and nursing home patients, holding a small group Bible study, and hosting youth groups at their property on the shores of beautiful Flathead Lake, south of Kalispell, MT. A favorite outing for their gusts is to be taken by boat over to Wild Horse Island to hike and view the Rocky Mountain Big Horn Sheep, wild horses, and other wildlife.

Velma's pen is often found writing notes of love and encouragement to family and friends. She is willing. God made her able!

Acknowledgement

Much of the material included has been collected over many years from a variety of sources. I have sought permission from numerous places for the use of this material. Some of the letters I sent were returned to me. These authors may be deceased. Some writers gave permission to rewrite their thoughts in my own words. Throughout the writing of this book, I have used the word "men" to be an inclusive term meaning "mankind"—just as the older versions of the Bible did. So, every reader, sit back and feel that what is written here is for all—including me, the author!

In the chapter, "Mining for Gold," I am indebted to the authors of two small books for ideas gleaned from their fascinating tour through the sixty-six books of the Bible—*From Genesis to Revelation*, by Theodora S. Wangerin, and *My Bible Notebook*, by Phyllis Bailey. I have used ideas from these books, along with personal thoughts and pertinent texts from Scripture.

Also, there are some descriptive thoughts from *Jesus, A Heart Full of Grace*, a 2007 devotional by William G. Johnsson, and *Old Testament Grace* by Jon Dybdahl, published by Pacific Press. When queried as to the use of quotations from the Adult Sabbath School Bible Study Guide, Editor Clifford R. Goldstein, replied, "Help yourself." Other help is mentioned in the script. Thank you all!

I have tried at great effort to be an honest compiler of other authors' thoughts. I am deeply grateful to them. I have confidence that they would agree with the following quotations: "Do not be concerned over the authorship . . . but put the thoughts into your heart and life," and "It's amazing how much good can be accomplished in this world if we don't care who gets the credit."

I wish to express my deep gratitude to a faithful friend, Audrey Neuharth-Ponaski, who through her computer skills transformed my handwritten script into readable printed material. Thanks to my husband, Fred, for his editing and polishing. Most of all, I thank God for the thoughts given to me . . . to Him be the glory!

Velma Beavon

Foreword

The book is laid out and has been written in three distinct and different sections. The first section deals with a variety of struggles that come to people who are trying to live a Christ-like life. The author is a long-time pastor's wife who has had much experience in helping people through these experiences. A series of topics are covered with down-to-earth solutions and suggestions of ways to overcome these issues when they arise. Each topic is covered using the Bible, Spirit of Prophecy, and experiences of others who have had similar concerns.

Section two is a succinct description of the whole Bible, an overview of the parts of the Bible including a time line. Each book is described including the authors and their backgrounds. It is very well written and the reader will have a new respect and appreciation of the Bible and what it meant to God's people throughout the history of the world.

Section three is a meaningful description of the ways we can and do worship God. Among the numerous ways included are such topics as music, our dress, and our deportment. It tells how God reaches out to us over and over. One can not read this without having and experiencing an overwhelming desire to serve God for what He has done for us and wanting to prepare for His soon coming.

—Don L. Weatherall
Assitant Director of Education, Retired
North American Division

Table of Contents

Introduction 11

1. A Dangerous Neighborhood 17
2. Copycat or Genius 20
3. Joy on the Journey 24
4. Don't Trip Over Yourself! 37
5. Choosing at the Crossroads 39
6. Taking the High Road 45
7. The Blame Game 47
8. M-A-P to Abundant Life 55
9. Mother's Regret 65
10. More than a Ride 67
11. Mining for Gold 71
12. Take Time to Remember 163
13. We Can All Be Winners 168
14. A Revolutionary Challenge 174
15. It Pays!—To God be the Glory 185

Introduction

Think On These Things

What you think means more than anything else in your life. More than what you earn, more than where you live, more than your social position, and more than what anyone else may think about you. Paul told us, "whatsoever things are true . . . honest . . . just . . . pure . . . lovely . . . of good report; if there be any virtue, and if there be any praise, think on these things" (Phil. 4:8; see also Prov. 23:7).

There are several levels of conversation that express our thoughts. The first is *chitchat*, which even includes the weather! Next is talking about people and events. Unless unkind gossip is included, these two types of conversation can be worthwhile, pleasant, and quite harmless. The final type of conversation, which gives most people deep satisfaction, is to converse about values, ideas, and beliefs. Deeper yet, is to talk about personal feelings.

It has been said, to be safe with your friends, don't talk about politics or religion. For some people, speaking on these subjects often brings more heat than light and leaves the conversationalist either angry or still with their own opinion. Sir Walter Raleigh said, "A man convinced against his will is of the same opinion still." For others, this level of conversation brings a great deal of hope, comfort, courage, and enlightenment. No doubt it's one's attitude while conversing the depth of communication and the tone of voice that determines whether this type of conversation is satisfying. Maybe it's the motive in the heart that makes the difference!

God has given us keen minds, yet using them superficially is the curse of our age. People's intelligence and talent can be a blessing, but there's a desperate need for deep-thinking people. Jesus' thoughts were deep. Of Him it is said: "Never man spake like this man" (John 7:46), and "they were astonished at his doctrine: for his word was with power" (Luke 4:32). We are to have the quality of His humble mind (Phil. 2:5-8).

We all need friends to whom we can feel safe speaking our deepest concerns. Rich are we whose spouse is a kindred-spirit and with whom communication can be carried on in depth from our hearts.

There are some thoughts that go far deeper than expressing them in conversation. Some are so sacred, so special, so spiritually personal that one wonders if anyone else would understand them. Jesus' mother, Mary, had these thoughts: "But Mary kept all these things and pondered them in her heart" (Luke 2:19). On occasion, Jesus used what could be referred to as *time speech*. "I have yet many things to say unto you, but ye cannot bear them now" (John 16:12). In another *time speech* experience, Jesus said things to His disciples they didn't understand. It was hid from them, "neither knew they the things which were spoken" (Luke 18:34). No doubt they *got it* (the meaning) as they witnessed the fulfillment of His words later (Luke 18:31-34).

On another occasion, some of Jesus' followers did not recognize the resurrected Christ who had joined them on their way to the village of Emmaus. These disciples were sadly pondering over the events of the crucifixion—which left them discouraged and questioning. In response, Jesus expounded the Scripture concerning Himself from Moses through the prophets. After their "eyes were opened," they recognized Him and then He vanished from their sight. These beautiful, encouraging words were meaningful to the disciples, and they testified, "Did not our heart burn within us, while he talked with us by the way, and while he opened to us the scriptures?" (Luke 24:32). This beautiful story is recorded in Luke 24:13-35. Such words can burn within our own souls.

There are such deep thoughts of emotional heartbreak that the human brain can't put them into words. God has a solution for our prayers during these times. "Likewise the Spirit also helpeth our infirmities: for we know not what we should pray for as we ought, but the Spirit itself maketh intercession for us with groanings which cannot be uttered" (Rom. 8:26).

The moving, beautiful words of many hymns are the result of deep thinking and feeling. Often hymns of depth impress me with messages I believe were inspired.

A dedicated mother once said to her hymn-composing son that she would rather have him write a hymn to the glory of God than be the president of the United States! She knew that the value of his deep thinking would be a blessing to people the world over when they thought of the words as they sang his song.

On one occasion, I noticed a hymnal on the bedside table of our son and daughter-in-law, Ted and Donna. I understand the blessing they receive from reading the soul-filled poetry of hymns for their last thought before retiring.

Other things we read, hear, or see, including the Bible, require great depth of thought. "O LORD, how great are thy works! and thy thoughts are very deep" (Ps. 92:5). Yet, there is awesome simplicity in the great depth of God's love for us. Even a child can understand it. Our depth of thought should lead our hearts to a deeper love relationship with God, and a more meaningful worship of Him.

On the other hand, thinking and talking about things in depth should *not* include ideas and thoughts that lead to fanaticism or sensationalism. Perhaps these two areas could be classed under the warning given in 1 Timothy 1:4: ". . . nor to occupy themselves with myths and endless genealogies which promote speculations rather than divine training that is in faith" (RSV). See also Colossians 2:8: "Beware lest any man spoil you through philosophy and vain deceit, after the tradition of men, after the rudiments of the world, and not after Christ."

Solomon had an unusual way of describing fanaticism: "Be not righteous over much; neither make thyself over wise: why shouldest thou destroy thyself?" (Eccl. 7:16). This unbalance in the spiritual and mental life will leave us a poor witness for God and *too heavenly-minded to be of any earthly-good.*

Another descriptive thought on Solomon's warning is that it has been said that *to live with the saints in heaven—that will be glory; but to live with the saints on earth—that's another story*!

Depth of thought is also reflected in the way we live our lives and accept our personal responsibilities. These values are as important to share as are the experiences of day-by-day living stories. In fact, values make life's events meaningful and they positively affect our attitudes toward life.

You may be blessed by reading more modern versions, but I treasure the poetic beauty of the Kings James Version and its accuracy. My memory work of Bible verses from childhood was from the King James Version; however, I am blessed by the use of modern translations, which—in many cases—clarify the meanings.

Both the King James Version and the new modern translations are a blessing. One thing I appreciate about the modern translations is that they capitalize the personal pronouns referring to Jesus and God. The ancient worshippers of God felt that His name was too sacred to utter. No doubt words like Yahweh, Lord, etc., came to be used with this thought in mind. And I feel that the modern translations treat God and His name with the respect He deserves by capitalizing personal pronoun references.

One of the reasons I write such personal thoughts is for my own benefit. This writing is meant to be a tribute to God who loves and understands me better than I understand myself. Being the kind of person who gets excited over a good product, I often purchase extras to share with others. I feel the same about the things I read and learn through the years. Consider this book as a gold mine that I am sharing untold riches with you!

Each day I see more of the full, big picture of life. This knowledge, when applied, has helped me make *no regret* decisions. My personal goal—and for those reading—is to encourage a strong sense of belief, love, and loyalty to the God of creation and salvation, and to His inspired Word.

Writing this material has been an awesome challenge; yet, I consider it a great joy to share spiritual gems that have helped me through the years. You may find some repetition of thoughts and Bible verses, but remember, *repetition adds emphasis and is the mother of all learning.* For my family and others to be blessed will be the answer to my prayers.

It is difficult to restrain and refrain from writing on and on about this grand and glorious theme. But my primary objective in writing this book is to stimulate readers to do their own digging and to find their joy and trust in God. I am giving you the *skeleton* but you, the reader, can study and put on the *meat*; then you can join me in your joyful testimony (John 5:39; Acts 17:11; Hebrews 5:13, 14; 2 Peter 1:19-21).

"No sooner does one come to Christ than there is born in his heart a desire to make known to others what a precious friend he has found in Jesus; the saving and sanctifying truth cannot be shut up in his heart" (*Steps to Christ,* p. 78).

Chapter 1

A Dangerous Neighborhood

I have heard it said that the mind is a dangerous neighborhood. Contrast the two different mindsets: "For to be carnally minded is death; but to be spiritually minded is life and peace" (Rom. 8:6). This brings these other verses to my thoughts: "and you, who once were estranged and hostile in mind, doing evil deeds, He has now reconciled in His body of flesh by His death in order to present you holy and blameless and irreproachable before Him provided that you continue in the faith, stable and steadfast, not shifting from the hope of the gospel which you heard…" (Colossians 1:21-23, RSV). That's good news!

Here are words of spiritual wisdom for persons in all generations: "By the indulgence of impure thoughts, man can so educate his mind that sin which he once loathed will become pleasant to him" (*Patriarchs and Prophets,* p. 459). Here are some tips on how to have our minds reconciled! "Thou wilt keep him in perfect peace, whose mind is stayed on thee: because he trusteth in thee" (Isa. 26:3). "Let this mind be in you, which was also in Christ Jesus" (Phil. 2:5). "And the peace of God, which passeth all understanding, shall keep your hearts and minds through Christ Jesus" (Phil. 4:7). This peace comes by what we see, read, and think on (Phil. 4:8).

There may come a time in your life, as it has in mine, when you feel a civil war going on in your heart with conflicting thoughts. In my case, the civil war occurred for me when a series of unfair, unjust treatments happened from persons who did not take their responsibilities serious when doing maintenance work at our home. And they refused to come to a reasonable and fair agreement to make their wrongs right. We tried to return good for evil by suggesting a positive, kind, Christian way to settle the matter, but we were rebuffed by being ignored.

I continued to go over and over in my mind the injustice done to us until I was a sleepless, nervous wreck. Though I shared my misery with just a very few friends, I even felt guilty doing that, knowing that they also had problems, perhaps larger than ours.

God brought to my attention this thought, which helped me to heal. The way to overcome a feeling of hurt is not to go over and over the hurt but to go over and over and over again the things God has done for you, especially His leaving an adoring heavenly host to come to this earth where His own received Him not, to die for the sins of the human race. I had to ask for God's forgiveness and thank Him for His gift and remember that an *attitude of gratitude* is contagious to others who need healing!

My civil war dissipated as I gained control of my confused mind. Now when such disturbing thoughts come to my mind, I find it a bit easier to sweep them aside. I am slowly learning that when I get upset at others' failures, I am making their problem my own. And here's another important thing to think on, which is found in 1 Corinthians 6:7: "Why do ye not rather take wrong? why do ye not rather suffer yourselves to be defrauded?" That should settle it! I must remember present problems are so temporary. God is eternal! How much better it would be to praise God and have victory. "Oh that men would praise the LORD for his goodness, and for his wonderful works to the children of men!" (Ps. 107:8).

The battle for the mind, and victory over it, is also described in Romans 7:22-25. God has made a promise to those who will ask and receive it: "I will put my laws into their mind, and write them in their hearts: and I will be to them a God, and they shall be to me a people" (Heb. 8:10). "Casting down imaginations, and every high thing that exalteth itself against the knowledge of God, and bringing into captivity every thought to the obedience of Christ" (2 Cor. 10:5). "Let the wicked forsake his way, and the unrighteous man his thoughts: and let him return unto the LORD, and he will have mercy upon him, and to our God, for he will abundantly pardon" (Isa. 55:7). Here's a bonus thought on the mind: "And be not conformed to this world; but be ye transformed by the renewing of your mind, that ye may prove what is that good, and acceptable, and perfect, will of God" (Rom. 12:2).

Enoch had a *transformed* mind and was fully surrendered to God. He practiced the presence of God (Gen. 5:24; Heb. 11:5, 6.) Many people down through the ages have also practiced this beautiful gift. It is my own goal to do the same. This is no doubt also your desire. There is a price to pay for this experience, for no prize is won without it. We achieve it by our desires, choices, effort, perseverance, and surrender to God. It is further developed as we share with like-minded believers, for "out of the abundance of the heart the mouth speaketh" (Matt. 12:34). This experience doesn't come immediately, but let us not get discouraged with what we might call *spiritual failure*. We can begin anew with a joyful spirit: "Looking to Jesus 'till glory doth shine; Moment by moment, O Lord, I am Thine," wrote Daniel Whittle.

Yes! *The mind can be a dangerous neighborhood*, and the battle does not bring a one-time victory—but an every-day challenge! But the foregoing encouraging thoughts are matched with these for daily warfare and victory: "(For the weapons of our warfare are not carnal, but mighty through God in the pulling down of strongholds;) . . . and bringing into captivity every thought to the obedience of Christ" (2 Cor. 10:4, 5). I can visualize the victorious soldier with the "armor of God" described in Ephesians 6:10-18. Oh, glorious victory! We have it in Christ, with a transformed mind! ♥

Chapter 2

Copycat or Genius

I do not recall the subject we were discussing one morning in our Bible study, but I do remember that the response to my contribution during the discussion made me silent. Perhaps we were discussing the fact that *no man is an island* in this world of interaction. I remember expressing the fact that all through my life, I have been greatly blessed by the ideas and thoughts of others. I guess I'm really a *copycat*.

Our discussion leader then said, "That's not being a copycat; that's being a genius!" I was too puzzled and embarrassed to ask for his explanation. However, his thought was interpreted for me in an article I read later that very day.

The author of the article told of people who were so in love with their own ideas that unless the thought was from their brain, it wasn't worth repeating, and certainly not worth writing about. Wow! That didn't describe me! But, to be a genius for appreciating other people's thoughts? It may put us on the road to wisdom, but to be a genius would certainly include not only valuing an idea but living it out and allowing it to enter our lives to cause a new, good habit to be born.

Though I'm definitely not a genius, I do use other people's thoughts to help me form goals to aim for. "For none of us liveth to himself, and no man dieth to himself" (Rom. 14:7). Mankind is interdependent for knowledge, fellowship, and learning. There is no such thing as a self-made man. Our personal decisions do determine our destiny; yet the lives and thoughts of many others make a marked contribution for good or for evil.

Other people's ideas can make a positive difference. A tip from a friend started me on a habit of drinking a quart of water during my morning devotional time. I am also indebted to a young man who shared the thought that because our bodies are God's temple physical exercise is as much a part of our personal worship as Bible study and prayer. So another habit was formed. My heart benefits from both my spiritual and physical exercise!

I use and enjoy healthful *ideas* from cookbooks, as well as wholesome recipes. Though I appreciate and use many ideas from others, I am grateful for the ideas and thoughts God has given to me, especially spiritual insights that are a direct answer to my prayers for guidance.

For some reason, the first thought that came to my mind regarding a genius using other people's ideas to spur activities was what does the Lord want me to do? Micah 6:8 flashed the answer: "He hath shewed thee, O man, what is good and what doth the LORD require of thee, but to do justly, and to love mercy, and to walk humbly with thy God?" (see also Deut. 10:12, 13). No doubt the dictionary would not include a genius walking humbly with God, but it made a lot of sense to me.

Here are some definitions of humility that also make a lot of sense to me: "Humility does not mean thinking less of yourself than of other people. It means freedom from thinking about yourself one way or the other. Being occupied a great deal about yourself and saying you are of little worth is not Christian humility. It is one form of self-occupation and a very poor and futile one at that. Anything we accomplish is a gift from God," wrote William Temple. Not thinking less of yourself, but thinking of yourself less. The genius part of humility is to remain teachable no matter how much one learns.

"There can be no true humility without some sense, explicit or implicit, of one's relation to God—and acknowledgement that man lives out his existence under a power and a goodness which are above him; that man must depend on God for everything he is and has," said Paul Ramsey. W. R. Beach adds this: "In short, true humility puts us in our place—that is, in a proper relationship to God and to our fellowmen."

Mahatma Gandhi (1869-1948), Indian nationalist leader who established his country's freedom through a non-violent revolution, had this attitude: "I claim to be a simple individual liable to err like any other fellow-mortal. I own, however, that I have humility enough to confess my errors and to retrace my steps." Sir Isaac Newton (1643-1727), English mathematician and physicist, developer of calculus and laws of motion and universal gravitation, confessed: "If I have seen further than others, it is by standing upon the shoulders of giants." Newton was a firm believer in God and His creation of the world. To sum it up: "The fear of the LORD is the instruction of wisdom; and before honour is humility" (Prov. 15:33).

He is wise who profits by the wisdom of others; yet, we should be thinkers and not always a reflector of other people's thinking. Even so, we must not worship or be proud of our own thinking. "Be not wise in your own conceits" (Rom. 12:16; see also Jer.9:23, 24 and Prov. 27:2). The very best advice of all is recorded in Proverbs 3:5-8: "Trust in the Lord with all your heart and do not rely on your own insight. In all your ways acknowledge Him, and He will make straight your paths. Be not wise in your own eyes, fear the Lord, and turn away from evil. It will be healing to your flesh and refreshment to your bones" (RSV). Good thoughts are a gift from God. As we go through life, it takes *wisdom* and *modesty* to grow from our own thinking and that of others.

However, much care and responsibility should go with our accepting thoughts, for "we henceforth be no more children, tossed to and fro, and carried about with every wind of doctrine . . . but speaking the truth in love, may grow up into him in all things, which is the head, even Christ" (Eph. 4:14, 15). These verses remind me of the saying "if we don't stand for something, we may fall for anything." And to refuse to take a stand for a truth that is not popular fits the quote that "none are so blind as those who refuse to see." We need to be aware of Bible standards before accepting ideas and thoughts from others or forming our own conceptions. The Bible gives us this warning: "Beloved, believe not every spirit, but try the spirits whether they are of God: because many false prophets are gone out into the world." (1 John 4:1). If we know the genuine from God's Word, the fake will be obvious when we see or hear it.

When I told my husband, Fred, I wanted to title this chapter "Copycat," he was opposed. He reasoned that the news media often uses the term *copycat* to describe the behavior of those following a similar pattern in the commission of murderous or other heinous acts that blanket our world. Naturally, Fred's protest is far from my idea for this title. My definition goes like this: "by beholding, we become changed" (see 2 Cor. 3:18). We change for the better or for worse—depending on what we behold and what choices we make.

No doubt there are other titles that may come closer to describing the ramblings of this section, such as "Smorgasbord of My Soul" or "From the Depths of My Heart." How about "A Vote for Christianity" or "From a Satisfied Customer"? Yes, each of these titles might do a pretty good job of describing what I want to share. But I've settled for "Copycat or Genius," since these words are what first gave me the idea for this chapter. In this and the following chapters, I will share some of the thoughts and concepts I have gleaned from others and the thoughts God has given to me. ♥

Chapter 3

Joy on the Journey

"Let the righteous be glad; let them rejoice before God: yea, let them exceedingly rejoice" (Ps. 68:3).

From a daily devotional, *Light from God's Lamp,* by W. R. Beach, I read this caption: *Can You Laugh?* The author went on to share wise words on false and real joy: "Much of the laughter we hear is really not laughter at all. It is simply the hollow guffaws of a comedian doing a stunt, or the studied smile of actors having a lifelong habit of looking happy in public (for a huge salary, I might add). This laughter ends in a sickly whimper . . .

"The life of Jesus with His disciples, on the other hand, is a scene of men filled with the delight and abundant joy of closeness to heaven . . . He (Jesus) loved the comradeship of people and lived in the joy of taking joy to others. 'Thou wilt show me the path of life; in thy presence is fullness of joy; at thy right hand there are pleasures for evermore' (Ps. 16:11).

"The idea that pleasure is sinful is not in harmony with Christ's wish for us . . . His endorsement of happiness is emphasized throughout the New Testament: 'Be of good cheer;' 'Let not your heart be troubled;' '…that your joy may be full.' Yet, some of us have forgotten these words. We appear to equate goodness with sadness, and in so doing, we certainly offer no inducement for others to accept Christ. Salvation is a matter of affirmation, not negation—fullness, rather than emptiness. Pleasure can be good or evil. It is good when it can be used for the upbuilding of character; it is evil when directed toward destruction. The laughter ringing through the house as a result of joy in the Lord is pleasing to heaven indeed."

Alden Thompson has this to say when testing *fun*: "When foolishness threatens the sacred or when fun undermines our values, then it is indeed time to 'sigh and cry.' This 'fun' is sin" (*Gleaner*, Mar. 1, 1993). He quotes: "the joy of the LORD is your strength" (Neh. 8:10).

Proverbs 17:22 has good advice: "A merry heart doeth good like a medicine: but a broken spirit drieth the bones." Some versions use *cheerful*, and I like that! Acceptable humor is very beneficial to our positive attitudes and our overall health. From it we can grow more accepting and understanding of people and life in general. Good humor puts a smile on our face and some good thoughts in our mind. Over the years, scientists have discovered the inseparable link between the mind and the body—what impacts one, impacts the other. A good frame of mind actually produces endorphins! Acts of kindness, gratitude, rejoicing, and trusting in God's love and care are the greatest benefits to health—just like medicine!

However, jokes and funny stories can be unacceptable if they are unkind, sacrilegious, impure, or uncouth. A gathering of men were enjoying some frivolous humor when one of the men wanted to tell a smutty story. He clued his listeners in by looking around the group and asking, "Are there any ladies around?" One man replied: "There are no ladies, but there *is* a gentleman here!" The joke was never told.

A good source of humor can be found by laughing at our own mistakes. It's much better than becoming angry or hurt. I remember an incident when I was far too young to blame it on a *senior moment*. I was backing out of our garage, aiming the car at a large gas tank so I could fill up. I steered toward the tank before I was completely out of the garage—thereby hitting the wall and knocking it right off the foundation! I don't recall that I laughed, but I *do* remember my great relief when Fred pushed the wall nicely back onto the foundation. Maybe then, we hugged and laughed!

During a recent event, when perhaps a *senior moment* could be blamed, my husband gave me a big helping of laughter. We have two garage doors with two separate door openers. We use our sedan to go most places, so we've gotten in the habit of pushing the particular button that opens the door for it. One day Fred pushed the button for the door for the sedan, and then hopped in our VW van to take the garbage cans and trash to the dump, backing right into the unopened door behind it! After our laughter, we were grateful that with a good push the door popped back into its normal place (almost)—at least from all outside appearances.

"Blessed are they who can laugh at themselves, for they shall never cease to be amused," was written by an unknown author who had a rather good insight.

> "Laughter sort o' settles breakfast better than digestive pills.
> Found it, somehow in my travels, cure for every sort of ills . . .
> Like to start the day with laughter;
> when I've had a peaceful night, an' can greet the sun all smilin'!
> That days goin' to be all right," wrote Edgar Guest in his poem *Laughter*.

The following are other beneficial thoughts, quotes, and stories I've collected or heard over the years from various sources:

> "Springtime recipe: Halve your food, double your drinking water, triple your intake of fresh air, and quadruple your laughter."

> "The most wasted day of all is that one which all have not laughed."

> "Anyone without a sense of humor is at the mercy of everyone else."

> "The ability to see the bright and humorous side, even in adversity and hardship, is priceless. Some people can find something to be amused at in almost everything."

> "Having a sense of humor in family living is a good thing! Humor lubricates the machinery of living, helping to reduce stress and strains . . . humor should not be used to minimize or bypass issues that need serious attention."

> "Humor should never be used to hurt someone's feelings. Humor, tact, wisdom, and kindness should all go together."

> "When choosing your attire for the day, be sure it includes a happy face because a smile is a curve that can set a lot of things straight, and people smile in the same language."

> "The chief function of our bodies is to carry the brain around."

"A young minister decided to use a visual demonstration for his Sunday sermon. He placed three worms into jars. The first worm was put into a container of alcohol. The second worm was put into a container of cigarette smoke. The third worm was put into a container of good clean soil. At the conclusion of the sermon, he reported these results:
- The first worm in alcohol: DEAD
- The second worm in cigarette smoke: DEAD
- The third worm in good clean soil: ALIVE

"Then the minister asked the congregation, 'What can we learn from this demonstration?'

"A little, old woman in the back quickly raised her hand and said, "As long as you drink and smoke, you won't have worms!

" '…abstain from fleshly lusts which war against the soul' (1 Peter 2:11)" ("Missed the Point"). No doubt we all, at times, miss the point! But, we can also use humor to help remember good points such as this one.

"An older gentleman, at the time of his own physical, discussed his concern over his wife's hearing problems with his doctor. The doctor made a suggestion to him in order to gage the hearing loss of his wife, he should ask his wife the same question at different distances. The wife was in the kitchen and the husband about twenty feet away called out: 'Honey, what are we having for supper?' No answer. The same question at fifteen feet, then at ten. No answer. Finally, standing right in front of his wife, he hugged her and said: 'Honey, what are we having for supper?' She answered, 'For the **fourth** time—potato soup!'" (See Rom. 2:1).

"The hardest thing to keep to yourself is an opinion."

"Opinion is that exercise of the human will which helps us to make a decision without information," wrote Josh Erskine.

"He who is green with envy will soon be ripe for trouble."

"It is better to give than to lend—it costs about the same!"

"I always prefer to believe the best of everybody—it saves so much trouble."

Think on These Things

"The congregation was pleased with the first sermon their new pastor preached. They told him so. The next week, he preached the same sermon. Those who were absent the first week told him that his message was a blessing to them. The next week the pastor gave the same message. Perhaps some wondered at his sanity. Then some brave member said: 'We hired you to be our pastor, but we don't want the same sermon every week.' Whereupon the pastor replied, 'When you start living this sermon, I'll give you another one'" (See James 1:22-25) ("The New Pastor").

"A happy heart makes a face cheerful."

"There's nothing lost by discarding your faults."

"A honeybee is never complimented for making honey . . . it just gets criticized for stinging."

I am lost. I have gone out to look for myself. If I should get back before I return, please ask me to wait! (Some do not know they are lost. See Matt. 18:11; Luke 15:8-10) (poster at a Sear's Repair Shop).

"This is an age in which one cannot find common sense without a search warrant."

"Character is what you do with your fast food garbage when you're driving along a deserted road at night."

"How much better to grow **better** than **bitter!**"

"Joseph remained true to God in Egypt. Daniel was loyal in Babylon. But Adam fell in Paradise."

"Persecution and tough times in life can be a blessing for some by building faith, courage, and loyalty. '. . .knowing that tribulation worketh patience'" (Rom. 5:3).

"The minister was preoccupied with thoughts of how he was going to—after the worship service—ask the congregation to come up with more money than they were expecting for repairs to the church build-

Joy on the Journey

ing. Therefore, he was annoyed to find that the regular organist was sick and a substitute had been brought in at the last minute. The substitute wanted to know what to play: 'Here's a copy of the service,' he said impatiently. 'But you'll have to think of something to play after I make the announcement about the finances.'

"During the service, the minister paused and said, 'Brothers and Sisters, we are in great difficulty; the roof repairs cost twice as much as we expected, and we need $4,000 more. Any of you who can pledge $100 or more, please stand up.'

"At that moment, the substitute organist played *The Star Spangled Banner*. And that's how the substitute became the regular organist!" ("The Substitute Organist").

"God loveth a cheerful giver" (2 Cor. 9:7).

"A farmer, who was very thrifty with time, said to his hired hand at the breakfast table, 'You know, we really waste a lot of time leaving the field of labor to come in for our noon meal. Why don't we eat our noon dinner right after breakfast and save that time for work?'

"So, dutifully, they ate their dinner. With this success, the farmer went further by suggesting they also eat their supper before they went to the field to work. Mission accomplished! The farmer, as he arose from the table, ordered: 'Now, we are ready to go to work.'

"Whereupon the hired man replied, 'I don't work after supper!'"

("The Thrifty Farmer").

"Be temperate in all things" (see 1 Cor. 9:24-27).

"Let me tell you about little boys. They are like camels. They can play all day and never think about a drink of water. They can run around out in the hot sun, and a drink of water never enters their little minds. But at night, as soon as their head hits the pillow: 'Can I have a drink of water?'

"One night my three-year-old and I went through our regular bedtime routine. I read him a story, listened to his prayers, gave him a good-night hug, answered a dozen questions, and finally after the fourth or fifth 'good-night,' I slipped out of the room.

"Finally, after a long, hard day, I could sit down and relax. It was nice and quiet for all of five minutes, when suddenly, 'Daddy, can I have a drink of water?'

"I knew he was not thirsty and was just wanting a little more attention before going to sleep, so I said, 'Son, get quiet and go to sleep!'

"It was silent for a couple of minutes, then just a little louder than before, 'Daddy, can I please have a drink of water?'

"'Son, hush up in there and go to sleep!'

"He was quiet again, but it did not last any longer than before. 'Daddy, please can I have a drink of water?'

"I could see we were not getting anywhere. 'Son, if I hear one more sound out of that room, I am going to spank you!'

"You could hear a pin drop. The silence was thick. But suddenly he called out, almost as sternly as I had, 'Daddy, when you come in here to spank me, would you bring me a drink of water?'

"This story was compared to a parable that Jesus told in Luke 18:1-7. It was 'The Parable of the Persistent Widow.' I encourage you to open your Bible and read this short parable and may it be a reminder of an all-caring Father who asks us to *'always pray,'* and not give up. He hears the prayers of His chosen ones and He will answer those prayers—that's a promise!" (Jim Forrest, "Daddy, Can I Have a Drink of Water?", *The Grape Vine*).

"Patience is peace under pressure."

"The middle of the road—a good place to get run over by vehicles going in either direction."

"A smile will go a long way but you will have to be the one to start it on its journey."

"The Scots kept the Sabbath and everything else they could get their hands on.

"The Welsh prayed on their knees, and also on their neighbors.

"The Irish don't know what they are fighting for, but they fight anyway.

"The English consider themselves self-made people which relieves the Almighty of an awesome responsibility" (tongue-in-cheek motto in a Scotland gift shop).

It's refreshing when people can write humorous stories or thoughts about themselves. It makes one laugh and yet think seriously about a matter. (See Mark 7:6, 13 and James 1:22-24.) Following are a few more funny quotes:

"Really, there's only one race—the human race."

"The main thing is to keep the main thing the main thing!"

"We can't run away from our problems. Jonah tried and you know what happened to him. He was supposed to preach in Nineveh and he procrastinated himself into a whale of a fix. So do **now**, what you've been putting off."

"Often the best way to win is to forget to keep score."

"Resentment is like taking poison and waiting for the *other* person to die."

"All Christians should speak in such a way that they would not be afraid to sell the family parrot to the church gossip."

"Who was the world's greatest financier? Noah. He floated stock while the rest of the world was in liquidation."

"It's awful to be indecisive—you're like a centipede that's told to put his best foot forward. Would Ephesians 4:14, 15 go with this problem? Check it out."

"Only a fool tests the depth of the water with both feet."

"Reading his well-worn Bible one day, a farmer saw the great truth of God's ownership.

"Falling on his knees, he prayed: 'I'm sorry God—I thought I owned this farm. Now I see you really own it—I'm just the manager. So, I'm going to give it back to you. But, I hope you'll forgive me 'cause we do things a bit strange down here. You see, I'll have to keep my name on the deed, but you and I know who really owns this farm!'

"Down in the village, neighbors thought he'd been out in the sun too long when he told them he had given land back to the one who owned it—especially when they found out it was God!

"But—not allowing their jests to disturb him, he expressed that this took all the worry from his shoulders. 'I just get down on my knees each morning and ask God to show me how He wants His farm run, and that's the way I run it—just as good as I can.'

"Then one day plagues of grasshoppers ate across neighbors' farms, then they got to his.

"They didn't stop, roll over on their backs and die; they swept across his field too. Neighbors could hardly wait to see him: 'We'll bet this changes your mind about God owning your farm,' they greeted.

"'Why not at all,' calmly replied the farmer.

"'We don't get it,' replied the neighbors.

"'It's simple—God owns the farm and He owns the grasshoppers. If He wants to pasture His grasshoppers on His farm, it's all right by me.'

"There is security in such trust in God" ("<u>God's the Owner</u>").

(See Hab. 3:17-19.)

"The bigger a man's head, the worse his headaches."

"Being told things for our own good seldom does us any. (See Prov. 1:22, 24, 25; 2:13.) The book of Proverbs has much to say on the life-long benefits of listening to good advice!"

"Life wouldn't be so hard if we didn't expect it to be so easy. It's not ever going to be easy. When someone says 'life is hard,' I ask them 'compared to what?' Would Psalm 30:5b give any light here?"

"A Montana University professor made the following observation regarding political correctness in gender equality:

"Woman has 'man' in it,
"Female has 'male' in it,
"Person has 'son' in it,
"Human has 'man' in it,
"Lady has 'lad' in it,
"And Eve had Adam's rib in her!"
(See Gen. 2:21-23 and Gal. 3:28, 29.)

"Just be sure your brain is in gear before your mouth is in motion."

"He who throws dirt looses ground!"

"Looking for faults? Use a mirror, not a telescope."

"Sooner or later, every person quotes their mother."

"No one became a man of the hour by watching the clock!"

"He who buries his talent is making a grave mistake" (see Matt.25:14-30).

Joy on the Journey

"One of the best things about not saying anything—it can't be repeated or misunderstood."

Some readers may think I am encouraging humor and comical stories during the sermon. This is not my intention. It is true that one can get across a sensitive issue or serious thought with well-chosen humor. It is like using tact to build a fire under people—sharing what can be beneficial to them without making their blood boil! (see Rom. 2:20, 21).

The best humor is meant to make people have a desire to make changes in their character by growing more like Jesus. There is no question regarding the sacredness of what is said during the sermon. It may be the only sermon some people ever hear. Jesus should be the foundation of all that is said. The prayer of the speaker is, no doubt, that those who hear the message will respond to Christ's love with their willing, joyful, and loving obedience and service.

As profitable and pleasant as good humor can be, we need to keep a good balance. There can be too much of a good thing! In our conversations as well as our presentations, we must be realistic and present both sides of the picture.

Jesus was happy in bringing the joy of healing to others. His pleasant mannerisms made Him attractive to mothers and little children. Yet, Isaiah 53:3 says of Him: "He is despised and rejected of men; a man of sorrows and acquainted with grief." The whole of this beautiful chapter tells us that "He bore our griefs and carried *our* sorrows" and that *our* sorrow shall be turned to joy! We will find in this balanced Savior both sorrow and joy; His goal was to "shew me the path of life: in thy presence if fullness of joy; at thy right hand there are pleasures for evermore" (Ps. 16:11). God's pleasures are true pleasures.

Robert Browning Hamilton penned "Sorrow's Wisdom":

> "I walked a mile with pleasure
> She chatted all the way
> But left me non the wiser,
> For all she had to say.
>
> I walked a mile with sorrow
> And never a word said she
> But oh! The things I learned from her,
> When sorrow walked with me!"

King Solomon wrote the following about sorrow in Ecclesiastes 7:3: "Sorrow is better than laughter; for by the sadness of countenance the heart is made better."

The Living Bible version translates this verse as follows: "Sorrow is better than laughter, for sadness has a refining influence on us. Yes, a wise man thinks much of death, while the fool thinks only of having a good time now" (Eccl. 7:3, 4).

Who hasn't sat in the quietness of deep sorrow to note the pain and grief of others? "I was dumb with silence. I held my peace, even from good; and my sorrow was stirred" (Ps. 39:2). It is in decisions of what we can do to help others that our "heart is made better."

Consider more of God's balance—the same compassionate nature of Him who will by no means clear the guilty yet whose glory it is to be "merciful and gracious, longsuffering, and abundant in goodness and truth, keeping mercy for thousands, forgiving iniquity and transgression and sin" (Ex. 34:6, 7).

Because God is responsible for vengeance, He frees His followers to return good for evil! (Rom. 12:17-21). God's discipline and punishments are meant to be redemptive (2 Peter 3:9). He sends the sun and rain and abundance of other blessings on the just and the unjust! (Matt. 5:45).

In the days of Noah, because every principal of right-doing was violated and iniquity became so deep and widespread that God could no longer bear with it, the decree went forth: "I will destroy man whom I have created from the face of the earth" (Gen. 6:7). To have to destroy what He created and said to be *"very good,"* was a tragic time for God. I've often thought that the raindrops of the Flood could represent His tears of grief. Yet, God saved the only righteous ones and gave them a rainbow of promise (Gen. 9:13). Later, He said, "I am with you always, even unto the end of the world" (Matt. 28:20).

Jesus, living on this earth, was a balanced man. His example of time management is worth emulating. He got done what He needed to do with His time. In the early morning, He spent time with His Father in prayer, often after a hike into the mountains. In His leisure time ("come apart and rest awhile"), His mind was on pleasing His Father. His weekly habit was to seek fellowship and blessing in the synagogue. He spent much time with others who needed Him for healing of body and soul. His physical exercise came with walking wherever He went. He was neither a workaholic nor a time-waster. Jesus took seriously the thought found in Psalm 90:12: "So teach us to number our days [time], that we may apply our hearts unto wisdom."

Jesus is balanced in His heart toward us, for He is merciful and full of grace—yet He renders justice to the human race. There is balance in God's Word. "Mercy and truth have met together; grim justice and peace have kissed" (Ps. 85:10, TLB). Peace and security are the rewards of being balanced in all we think and do.

Purposely living a balanced life and choosing to think and live in its perimeters is to escape the great tendency—the great trap—to go overboard on either side of any issue. Avoid extremes—develop harmoniously. God wants us to keep balanced—yet to be deeply passionate about Him and serving Him with our "whole mind and heart" (Matt. 22:37-40; Deut. 6:5). We need a balanced mind in a balanced body—with a balanced heart.

The teachings of Christ make radical, life-changing demands. However, "heavenly focus brings earthly fulfillment." It's encouraging to know that our victory is the result of cooperation between our choices and God's power! (Jude 24). Revelation 2:10 also promises that if we are "faithful unto death ... I will give thee a crown of life."

Every genuine doctrine (Jesus' teachings) has a counterfeit (Matt. 24:24). A person who studies God's Word, with a balanced perspective, is protected from being led astray by false doctrine. Those who claim Christianity yet become fanatical and cultish demonstrate imbalance. We need to heed the warning in Matthew 24:24 for even the "very elect" could be deceived.

Although life consists of joys and sadness, humor and serious times, the balance we are seeking is a balance in our value system. We should accept the balance of God's teachings from Genesis to Revelation. The gospel commission commands us to teach all things He has told or taught us. More than we realize, this command was radical. Going into all the world and making disciples involved "teaching them to observe [obey, TLB] all that I have commanded you" (Matt. 28:20, RSV). That's a tall order! The foundation, of course, is love, mercy, grace, etc., but a good foundation is prepared and meant for further building. Another of the many benefits of *balanced thinking* is a willingness to accept and cling to God's solid instruction as taught all the way through the

Bible (2 Tim. 3:16, 17).

Balanced Christians have a living knowledge of their responsibility to God and their accountability for their decisions. Love makes pleasing and serving God a pleasure in our lives, and it is not burdensome (1 John 5:3, 4; Gal. 2:20). If we would remember that we, as Christians, can either bring glory or dishonor upon His name, we might be inspired to make every effort to live to bring glory to His name. We have God's reputation in our hands—by our actions in all circumstances. Let us pray daily to our Father in heaven for help in representing Him aright. We would, no doubt, have some sincere apologies to make on some occasions. A good conscience can make us free to enjoy our journey! ♥

Chapter 4

Don't Trip Over Yourself!

Often when I went to visit a dear older friend, Bessie, she would tell me "God must really love me, I've never smoked, I've never drank liquor, I've never committed adultery. He must really love me." Was Bessie tripping over herself?

By our own choices, and the grace, protection, and strength of God, others could also make the same claim. But I had to remind her that every living being is a sinner. It may be true that being free of these vices result in fewer scars, but I'm sure it wouldn't make God love us any more than any other sinner.

God IS love! No matter what mankind does, His love for us is not altered. However, we can add to His joy and satisfaction: "joy shall be in heaven over one sinner that repenteth" (Luke 15:7); "He shall see the travail of his soul, and shall be satisfied; by his knowledge shall my righteous servant justify many; for he shall bear their iniquities" (Isa. 53:11). Taking time to form a deep relationship with God brings Him pleasure. Let us live so as to increase God's joy.

I've not heard of anyone boasting about the fact that they were never jealous, never angry, never covetous, never gossiped or found fault, never judged another unjustly, or never harbored other sins of the heart. These sins often cause heartbreak. Let us never forget: "All have sinned, and come short of the glory of God" (Rom. 3:23).

There is no earthly human being alive who does everything right all the time. We've tripped ourselves up and been bruised. To change our focus, we must "walk not after the flesh but after the spirit" (Rom. 8:1). Our victory is by the grace of God. Grace is both pardon *and* power to overcome. Grace means there is nothing we can do to make God love us more or love us less. Grace, *unmerited favor*, was God's idea, not ours. It was our need that made it necessary.

"Behold, I was shapen in iniquity; and in sin did my mother conceive me" (Ps. 51:5). Yet, we have loving and comforting thoughts recorded in God's word (Ps. 22:10, 71:6). The problem is solved by Christ, our *Problem-solver*. "Purge me with hyssop, and I shall be clean: wash me, and I shall be whiter than snow. . . . Create in me a clean heart, O God; and renew a right spirit within me" (Ps. 51:7, 10).

Let me share some encouraging thoughts on the results of our choice to be free from those "sin[s] which doth so easily beset us" (Heb. 12:1). "That the righteousness of the law might be fulfilled in us, who walk not after the flesh [our natural self], but after the Spirit [our born-again experience]. . . . For to be carnally minded is death; but to be spiritually minded is life and peace" (Rom. 8:4, 6). "For it is God which worketh in you both to will and to do of His good pleasure" (Phil. 2:13).

For Bessie, and all of us for that matter, the entire eighth chapter of Romans is full of gems of encouragement. "For I am persuaded, that neither death, nor life, nor angels, nor principalities, nor powers, nor things present, nor things to come, nor height, nor depth, nor any other creature shall be able to separate us from the love of God, which is in Christ Jesus our Lord" (Rom. 8:38, 39). What promise could outdo this?

Throughout the entire Bible, we find words of love and obedience. "We love him, because he first loved us" (1 John 4:19). "For this is the love of God, that we keep his commandments: and his commandments are not grievous [not disagreeable to our thinking]" (1 John 5:3). "That ye might walk worthy of the Lord unto all pleasing, being fruitful in every good work, and increasing in the knowledge of God" (Col. 1:10). Truth and love transform!

I appreciate the testimony: I'm a Christian, saved by the blood of Jesus. In love, respect, and thanksgiving, I choose to represent the One I love. Obedience from love is the only obedience that counts. Let us all *put the cross in our hearts. That's where it belongs.* Bessie would agree. ♥

Chapter 5

Choosing at the Crossroads

Because my friend Bessie had never indulged in the evil habits of the world, she felt God must love her in "a special way." I've thought of innocent Bessie's boast, especially when I heard the story of a man whose family had been murdered during Hitler's reign of terror. He was to be interviewed on the national news. Suddenly he burst out in uncontrollable tears. His interviewers were sympathetic to what they thought he was remembering of those horrific scenes. When they asked him why he was weeping, he surprised them by saying, "It could have been me [doing those wicked deeds]!"

When one considers the world news, some reports blow our minds. We find it difficult to believe that someone who is involved in worthy causes turns out to be a very wicked criminal. I think of the verse: "The heart is deceitful above all things and desperately wicked: who can know it?" (Jer. 17:9). No wonder we are told in God's Word to have the same attitude as that man who was interviewed on national television.

Socrates said, "The unexamined life is not worth living." Paul put it this way: "Examine yourselves, to see whether you are holding to your faith. Test yourselves. Do you not realize that Jesus Christ is in you?—unless indeed you fail to meet the test! I hope you will find out that we have not failed" (2 Cor. 13:5, 6, RSV).

Some people do not like to be invited to "examine" themselves. They say they already are defeated knowing how sinful they are. They miss the point. "In order to receive help from Christ, we must realize our need. We must have a true knowledge of ourselves. It is only he who knows himself to be a sinner that Christ can save. Only as we see our utter helplessness and renounce all self-trust, shall we lay hold of divine power" (*The Ministry of Healing,* p. 455). Isaiah 64:6 says, "All our righteousness are as filthy rags." "All our good works are dependent on a power outside of ourselves; therefore there needs to be . . . a constant, earnest confession of sin and humbling of the soul before Him" (*The Ministry of Healing,* p. 455). No change occurs without a struggle and contemplation. "For when I am weak [in my own strength], then am I strong [in Christ's strength]" (2 Cor. 12:10).

The charge to "examine ourselves" has a great purpose. In God's eyes "all have sinned" (Rom. 3:23); yet, we are "the apple of his eye" (Deut. 32:10). When we examine ourselves, we realize our need of a Savior and His atoning sacrifice on our behalf. We become aware of our need of His forgiveness and the power of His Spirit to help us finish the good work He has started in us and proceed on in a victorious life (John 3:16, 17; 2 Peter 3:9; 1 John 1:7, 9; Jude 24; and Hebrews 12:1, 2.)

Jesus has promised to go and prepare a place for us and take us there (John 14:1-3). To me that's a terrific exchange for "examining ourselves." Incidentally, I have discovered that to spend time examining myself (not other people), is profitable for me—not only for my relationship with God, my Creator and Redeemer, but also in the daily life lived right here and now as I relate to family and friends. Having examined ourselves, we would all surely be nicer to live with and more likely to live worthy of a life forever! So, no matter how we look at it, examining ourselves is a *win-win* experience.

The closer we get to God and see His majesty, wisdom, power, and righteousness the more we will feel like the great prophet Isaiah: "Woe is me! for I am undone; because I am a man of unclean lips, and I dwell in the midst of a people of unclean lips: for mine eyes have seen the King, the LORD of hosts" (Isa. 6:5). Isaiah saw his need, which resulted in being forgiven: "and thine iniquity is taken away, and thy sin purged" (verse 7). Now he was ready! "I heard the voice of the Lord, saying, Whom shall I send, and who will go for us? Then said I, Here am I, send me. And He said, Go" (verses 8 and 9).

To be aware of our sinful condition is not meant to make us feel hopeless or helpless, but instead to know where the source of our help lies. We are to know of our value and worth to God and of His great love for us. "For I know the thoughts that I think toward you, saith the Lord, thoughts of peace and not of evil, to give you an expected end [future and a hope, RSV]. Then shall ye call upon me, and ye shall go and pray unto me, and I will hearken unto you. And ye shall seek me, and find me, when ye shall search for me with all your heart" (Jer. 29:11-13). God is eager for a relationship with us—He stands at our door and knocks (Rev. 3:20).

"If we say that we have no sin, we deceive ourselves, and the truth is not in us. If we confess our sins, he is faithful and just to forgive us our sins, and to cleanse us from all unrighteousness" (1 John 1:8, 9). The Bible is filled with encouraging thoughts of God's love for us. Here's another one I could repeat and repeat, for it's a winner: "If God be for us, who can be against us? . . . Who shall separate us from the love of Christ? shall tribulation, or distress, or persecution, or famine, or nakedness, or peril, or sword? . . . For I am persuaded, that neither death, nor life, nor angels, nor principalities, nor powers, nor things present, nor things to come, nor height, nor depth, nor any other creature shall be able to separate us from the love of God, which is in Christ Jesus our Lord" (Rom. 8:31-39).

The following are testimonies of those who examined self—and God. One of the most popular preachers of his day, Henry Ward Beecher (1813-1887) had a list of 100 great fundamentals a Christian should hold to. However, on his deathbed, the list had dropped to one: "The doctrine that I am a great sinner and Jesus a great Saviour."

The use of chloroform in preparing patients for surgery was discovered by Sir James Young Simpson in 1847. It was a fantastic contribution to medicine and has saved millions of lives since its introduction. In his old age, one of his former students asked him what he considered the most valuable discovery of his lifetime. Without doubt, he expected Simpson to tell of his chloroform discovery. Instead, the great doctor replied: "My most valuable discovery was when I discovered that I'm a great sinner, and Jesus Christ is my Saviour."

John Wesley, the founder of the Methodist Church, revealed this deathbed assurance: "I can remember only two things: I am a great sinner, but Jesus is a great Saviour." The founder of the Lutheran Church, Martin Luther, had this to say: "When I look at myself, I don't see how I can be saved; but when I look at Jesus, I don't see how I can be lost." The founder of the Presbyterian Church, John Calvin, said with great trust: "Upon a life I did not live, upon a death I did not die, I hang my whole eternity."

John Bunyan (1628-1688) was the author of *Pilgrims Progress*, one of the most famous religious allegories in the English language. He gave this testimony: "It is the greatest truth in the universe that the righteousness that is in a Person in heaven should justify me, a sinner on earth." What a God! "We love him, because he first loved us" (1 John 4:19).

Ellen White, one of the founders of the Seventh-day Adventist Church, wrote much on the spiritual needs of sinful man and the love of God—who supplies that need. "The world's Redeemer was treated as we deserve to be treated, in order that we might be treated as he deserved to be treated. He came to our world and took our sins upon his own divine soul, that we might receive his imputed righteousness. He was condemned for our sins, in which he had no share, that we might be justified by his righteousness, in which we had no share. The world's Redeemer gave himself for us" (*The Review and Herald,* March 21, 1893). These thoughts gave her great confidence in her salvation. In peaceful calmness on her deathbed, Ellen White lovingly fastened her eyes on her son and whispered softly: "I know in Whom I have believed." "God is love." "He giveth His beloved sleep." (*Life Sketches of Ellen G. White,* p. 449). (See 2 Tim. 1:12 and Ps. 127:2.)

These spiritual giants saw man's condition of sinfulness, but they also had assurance that our Creator is the Friend and Savior of sinners. They saw the doctrine of grace in every promise of God and experienced the personal knowledge of Christ's earthly ministry as *God with us.* Each had the personal assurance of salvation! Many other great inventors, scientists, and world-renowned thinkers and writers—from age to age—have made this their testimony, too. Wise men will always seek Him!

Often I read a story in the Bible or elsewhere and ask myself what I would have done in the same situation. Would I have made a wise decision that obeyed and pleased God? Would I have seen the need in someone else's life and met the need in caring love? Or would I have been just like the person who violated his free choice? These are scary questions for me to think about. Whatever happened—good or bad—I too might have said, "It could have been me!"

Because of God's love, His creatures will always have free choice. He never forces obedience—it must come from a love relationship with Him.

Even in heaven, those who are saved will continue to exercise free choice. Since God will put an end to sin, it will never rise up a second time (Nahum 1:9). There will never be another Lucifer in heaven again. All the saved will know that God's way is the only way that brings love, joy, peace, and security. They will be *safe to save*.

Every choice of life should be made on the basis of principle rather than of convenience. Life in this world is really only a choice of difficulties: he who chooses the right way is not promised release from further hardship, but he who chooses wrongly is certain to have trouble, for ultimately "the way of transgressors is hard" (Prov. 13:15). We are often confused by the choices we need to make. Our prayer should be "give me first a conviction of what is right, and then give me the power to act upon that conviction." Convictions from God will be consistent with His written Word.

Yes, it could have been me if I had chosen to live apart from God and existed in a troubled, disappointing life. But I have chosen to accept His invitation of eternal life and the promise that one day I will live with Him in a place He has made ready for me where there is no more sin and suffering. Jesus asked the question: "When the Son of man cometh, shall he find faith on the earth?" (Luke 18:8). I have asked Him to keep me loyal and faithful to the end, and I can trust Him to "keep [me] from falling, and to present [me] faultless before the presence of his glory with exceeding joy" (Jude 24; see also Heb. 6:11, 12).

Without thorough study, we often read verses in the Bible, or in other spiritual books, that we feel make our salvation seem impossible. Take heart! Here's the secret of our fearless assurance through God's power: "We should not make self the center and indulge anxiety and fear as to whether we shall be saved. All this turns the soul away from the Source of our strength. Commit the keeping of your soul to God, and trust in Him. Talk and think of Jesus. Let self be lost in Him" (*Steps to Christ*, p. 72).

God wants us to have assurance of our salvation—that's what the gospel is all about. "I write these things to you who believe in the name of the Son of God so that you may know that you have eternal life" (1 John 5:13). Don't wait for a *feeling*. Believe it by faith because God has promised!

These thoughts have been very encouraging to me: "The character is revealed, not by the occasional good deeds and occasional misdeeds, but by the tendency of the habitual words and acts" (*Steps to Christ*, pp. 57, 58). "We shall often have to bow down and weep at the feet of Jesus because of our shortcomings and mistakes, but we are not to be discouraged. Even if we are overcome by the enemy, we are not cast off, not forsaken and rejected of God. No; Christ is at the right hand of God, who also maketh intercession for us" (*ibid.*, p. 64). "These things write I unto you, that ye sin not. And if any man sin, we have an advocate with the Father, Jesus Christ the righteous" (1 John 2:1). Each day, at my own crossroads, I have chosen to be saved. The final salvation is given when Jesus comes again to take us home! ♥

Chapter 6

Taking the High Road

Comparing can be helpful or harmful. We would do well to compare our own daily decisions and choices with the ultimate outcome to ourselves. This is important in regard to health—mental, emotional, and spiritual. If we would think ahead to the *pay-off later*, we'd make wiser decisions. There are many positive reasons for comparing.

However, comparing can be dangerous. Paul warns us against comparing with people (2 Cor. 10:12, 13). Comparing ourselves with others may make some feel proud of themselves, or on the other hand, some may feel inferior or worthless. One of my favorite books of the Bible is Philippians. Paul gives much counsel on getting along with others and thinking positively of them: ". . . but in lowliness of mind [humility] let each esteem others better than themselves" (Phil. 2:3). (See the rest of the section for further counsel: Phil. 2:1-8.) When we love, we are thankful for the success of others.

The fire of jealousy arose in King Saul when the singing women of Israel compared him with David. When the army came home from battle, they sang: "Saul hath slain his thousands and David his ten thousands" (1 Sam. 18:7). The displeasure and anger of Saul, at hearing this comparison, made him envious of David. From that day forward, Saul made much of David's life that of a fugitive.

What a vast contrast to Saul was Jonathan, his son! Jonathan avoided the comparing and the hatred of his father to become David's trusted and best friend. Though Jonathan stood in line to follow his father as king of the Israelites, he humbly succumbed to the plans he knew God had for David. Their love and trust for each other is a model for everyone. Jonathan's unselfish life makes him one of my Bible heroes.

Parents, teachers, and others may—without thinking—compare youth and hurt their tender hearts. Would that we all would grow up into the stature of Jonathan who basked in David's successes because he was filled with God's love. Sometimes we, as adults, have forgotten if we have—in the long ago—said hurtful, comparing words to those we love. If we have, we pray that those who heard them have forgotten too—with forgiveness. Often words are not meant for how some people take them. This shows the value of communication. And the sooner, the better!

My slogan has long been: "Don't compare people!" Each person is cut from a different pattern. Each is valuable to others, to our Creator, and to those who love them. Our own attitude determines our happiness or lack of it. God will help us control it, if we remember by faith that "with God all things are possible" (Matt. 19:26).

It is possible to waste precious hours, weeks, months, even years without a peaceful, joyful life of love and acceptance by hanging on to a misunderstanding of the past. Again, I stress, we need communication laced with humility of spirit to shake off the heavy heart. Let's take the high road and let the Son shine in! Truly, this is something to think about. ♥

Chapter 7

The Blame Game

A news item told of a young man who was in prison and blamed his parents, who he thought were "too easy" on him. They allowed him too much freedom, so he said. No doubt others in prison would blame parents who were too hard on them and lacked tact and love in their childhood training. It sounds like people know how they should have acted, but it is easier to blame others.

I read that one prisoner said, "Blessed be prison; it allowed me time to think and to make lasting choices and decisions for Christ." This prisoner did not hamper his positive thinking by practicing the *blame game*. Christ is the only One able to bring about a change in our lives. Life is not based on chances, but on choices. "I can do all things through Christ which strengtheneth me" (Phil. 4:13). Someone once said: "If you are not satisfied with your first birth, try being *'born again'*!" A little humor, but so true.

It is a human trait to blame others for one's problems and excuse ourselves—to find fault elsewhere, anywhere, but in ourselves. We've all done our share of blaming. Sometimes we fail to accept responsibility for our poor choices and taking the blame.

Consider this thought: "The root problem in nearly all depressions [unhappiness] is pent-up anger, either toward ourselves . . . or toward others. . . . These grudges are usually unconscious (that is, we are unaware of them), because we are ashamed or afraid to admit them to ourselves" (Frank Minirth, *Happiness is a Choice: The Symptoms, Causes, and Cures of Depression*, p. 52). Many know this to be true from experience.

As to blaming our genes: "Heredity is not fate—what we have received from our parents does not weave around us a net of guilt and misery through which we can never break—if it be true that we belong to God as well as to the past," (James Denney, *Studies in Theology*, p. 90).

I was impressed by a letter written by a teenaged girl to Ann Landers and signed "Freedom Unlimited." The teenager wrote that she envied other teenagers whose parents were strict. She felt that it showed that their parents cared about them, knowing that their teenager needed rules to follow. She wished her parents were caring parents who set boundaries for her, not just people who lived in the same house and paid the bills.

Ann Landers responded: "Dear Unlimited: You've got a smart head on those seventeen-year-old shoulders. I hope your message gets through to teenagers and parents. Thanks for writing."

Though my heart ached for this young lady, I had a lot of admiration for her. She wrote from a lonely heart. In spite of her feelings, it appears she will do what is right. For this decision, she will have no regrets. I can picture her making a great caring mother some day. Her sensible attitude is what is needed in *bringing yourself up*.

If the *blame game* is allowed to be part of our character and is played continually in our hearts, the fruit will be bitter, resulting in animosity, revenge, hatred, smoldering resentment, and unforgiveness, which will ultimately negatively affect our self-worth and self-respect. What woe we can bring on ourselves and we have only ourselves to blame.

The author of the following quote is unknown, but it speaks to the heart: "Perhaps we can't help it when the hurts come, but we can help it if the hurts last. When hurts come, don't curse them, don't rehearse them, don't nurse them, but disperse them and reverse them, and under the miracle-working power of God, the hurts may be halos, the scars may turn into stars."

Some of the preceding thoughts may seem cold and without compassion, but they are meant to give hope and courage to those whose inherited tendencies have given them a great challenge. We do reap the consequence of Adam's fall. We have inherited a sinful nature, and we commit sin by choice, not by birth. We face the condemnation that sin brings. We may be tempted to complain against God by saying, "We inherit the fallen nature of Adam, and are not responsible for our natural imperfections" (*The Signs of the Times*, August 29, 1892). Adam couldn't make that complaint, but look at what he did with his perfect condition! Though some may have reasons for their unfortunate lives, reasons must not be blamed or given as excuses. For great encouragement, see the loving words found in *The Desire of Ages*, chapter 4, which is titled "Unto You a Saviour."

To attempt to live a Christian life by human effort is a dead-end street. "When the goodness and loving kindness of God our Saviour appeared, He saved us, not because of deeds done by us in righteousness, but in virtue of His own mercy, by the washing of regeneration and renewal in the Holy Spirit; which He poured out upon us richly through Jesus Christ our Saviour so that we might be justified by His grace and become heirs in hope of eternal life" (Titus 3:4-7, RSV).

I have read books on the lives of people—beginning with their infancy—that made my heart ache and tears flow due to their poor and sad upbringing. Eventually some of these people chose to serve God. This turnaround took time—but it came! One such individual testified that his choices have made him the happiest man in the world. That's what Christ did for him and forgiveness made it possible.

A forgiving spirit does not come naturally to a sinful, human heart. It's a gift from God worth seeking and accepting. Remember, forgiveness of others precedes God's forgiveness to us. See the Lord's Prayer in Matthew 6:12.

Most normal parents take seriously their parental responsibilities and try to do their best. Yet, most parents would have done some things differently if they were to do it over. Forgiveness opens the door to a new beginning to both parents and offspring, or whoever might need forgiveness. "Therefore if any man is in Christ, he is a new creature: old things are passed away; behold, all things are become new" (2 Cor. 5:17). A forgiving person is in Christ and allows the forgiven to be a new creature too. Stumbling blocks can be stepping stones to a satisfied, meaningful life if we let them be.

Lack of a forgiving spirit means that we are holding on to a grudge. What a tragedy to hold on to a grudge. It is said that no matter how much you *nurse* a grudge, it will never get better! How destructive to the entire being—physical, emotional, and spiritual.

I think of an article I read titled "Eating Worms." It reminded the reader of a song that was popular many years ago. The lyrics were sung, in humor, by a disgruntled, offended person. The song taught a lesson. The words went: "Nobody likes me, nobody loves me, guess I'll go eat worms." The article stated that many people are offended by parents, family members, organizations they belong to, their boss, or coworkers. The man in question had been offended by his church and pastor. To get even with the church, this individual sought to hurt the church by becoming involved in all the evil habits he had been taught to avoid.

When we hear stories of this kind (and they are not rare), we are saddened by this type of reaction and question the intelligence of that person's decision. Truly, this is a result of playing the *blame game*.

Another church member left the church because he thought the church had failed him in its teachings. When it was brought to his attention—in a kindly Christ-like way—that he had failed himself by not taking personal responsibility to see what the church taught, he re-studied the teachings of his church and discovered that it had not failed him in any way. He saw himself as he was. He was blessed by the visit and his personal study, and he returned to church a changed man. What a blessed, good ending.

Because I tend to be a sensitive person, I was surprised when I read that a *super-sensitive* nature is sinful! My eyes were opened! Embarrassed, I had to admit to myself that when I get hurt, I have a tendency to misjudge the one who offended me. Undoubtedly, most of the time this happened, *no* offense was meant. When counsel was needed, I should have sweetly thanked the one and grown by the reminder instead of taking offense. I now try to use my sensitive nature positively by shielding others people's feelings. "A word fitly spoken is like apples of gold in baskets of silver" (Prov. 25:11, ERV).

There are times when our problems are undeserving and seem insurmountable, but with God all things are possible. God can give us the gift of courage and help us stand true in our unfair world. We must rise above the crowd. Some people pay the rest of their lives for poor decisions while others benefit throughout life by making good choices.

The following verse is an apt description of how we pay for or benefit from our choices: "Do not be deceived; God is not mocked: for whatever a man sows, that he will also reap. For he who sows in his flesh will from the flesh reap corruption; but he who sows to the Spirit will from the Spirit reap eternal life, and let us not grow weary in well-doing, for in due season we shall reap, if we do not lose heart" (Gal. 6:7-9, RSV).

If one has a sincere desire to change the course of a *blame-game* life, he must hate what he is doing to himself and to others. This goes along with the desire to *bring yourself up positively!* We must realize that our lives are too valuable and worthwhile to allow ourselves to live and act in a way we hate and cannot respect. We must cultivate the proper kind of self-love and self-worth. I like this definition of self-love: "Self-love is having a feeling of dignity, a feeling of belonging, a feeling of worthwhileness, a feeling of adequacy—yet a healthy sense of humility," wrote Dr. Robert H. Felix.

Also, we are to love others as we love ourselves. This love includes helping those who need a big dose of the proper kind of self-love! It's not hard to find people to minister to, and helping them proves very rewarding. Sad to say, some people grow up with no sense of what real love is all about as is shown in 1 Corinthians 13. They need the example of a living sermon in shoes. Loretta Girzartis describes it this way: "If someone listens, or stretches out a hand, or whispers a kind word of encouragement, or attempts to understand a lonely person, extraordinary things begin to happen." They show they really care.

God cares too—His love at Calvary was shown while we were yet sinners (Rom. 5:8). Each one of us is so valuable that Christ would have come to die for just one of us! Realizing this great love for us and our great value to God prompts us to make changes. Though we acknowledge we are sinners, we must not keep our eyes on that fact, but rather on Jesus' righteous life for it has been credited to us! It is ours if we truly receive it. What more awesome news could there be for the sinner?

We can hardly fathom the beauty of God's love. "I have graven thee upon the palms of my hands [the nail-scarred hands]" (Isa. 49:16).

We can do much to help ourselves by our choices. Healing the mind can be found by feeding the soul on things we read, listen to, and think about. We must pray for strength to control our thoughts. We should remember that our thoughts can change *our* world.

I've heard it said: "If you are not satisfied with how you are brought up, you can, with God's help, bring yourself up—prayerfully." Choose a godly mentor who takes balanced marching orders from God's Word. Invite this person to keep you accountable for your choices and desire to change. Don't expect instant results, and don't get discouraged if there are setbacks. Keep looking at your Guide and keep pressing on. You'll be thankful you made the changes needed.

There are some things we may not see the necessity to change; however, if not changed, they could negatively affect morale. An example could be a lack of neatness. Living with a mess, inside the house or outside, can bring on a feeling of depression. At times, circumstances cause all of us to make our homes unsightly. From my own experience, I can testify what a morale-builder it is when the mess is cleaned up! Jesus was neat. He even folded His grave clothes when He rose from the grave! Another example can be found in making a habit of always being late, causing much inconvenience to others. We should make every effort to be neat and on time. Days will then be brighter and more pleasant for everyone. We all have areas in our lives to conquer, and we will have a feeling of victory when we do.

As we contemplate the ways of the world, we realize many reasons why people's lives become a great challenge and often a disappointment and disaster. I agree with Sally Huss who said, "We are all the way we are for a lot of reasons, and for all these reasons and more, we are worthy of being loved."

Through no fault of our own, we are born with a sinful nature (Ps. 51:5). However, we must take into consideration that "whoever knows what is right to do and fails to do it, for him it is sin" (James 4:17, RSV). God is so gracious that He distinguishes between sins done unknowingly and those done deliberately; yet to purposefully be ignorant of what is right or wrong so as not to be held accountable to God is sin. Instead of blaming our fallen nature for our sins, we can willfully choose to do God's will. Our free choice is a gift! We can actually override our sinful nature with God at our side.

Physical and mental changes can come as a result of hormonal imbalances. Accidents, at times, cause brain damage. Many, if not most, accidents and crimes are caused by people who are intoxicated. The example of drinking often results in weeping at a gravesite following an accident that took one or more lives. There are alcoholic mothers who give birth to infants and pass on their *alcoholic syndrome,* which challenges their children's lives with near hopeless addition. We have ministered and been friends to people facing this

The Blame Game

challenge in their lives.

What a tragedy that people who bring children into the world do not consider the horrific burden they place on an innocent child through bad habits. Thankfully they are in God's merciful hands. "Righteousness and justice are the foundation of thy throne; steadfast love and faithfulness go before thee" (Ps. 89:14, RSV). God will see that all mankind will eventually receive fairness, mercy, and justice.

Handicapped children can be born into any family. I've often thought that perhaps the Holy Spirit or their guardian angel (or both) must do a special work for them. Many of these little children have a helpful, sweet disposition. I find great comfort trusting God to make it up to these individuals by their experiencing God's world someday. The population of heaven will be a mix of people who are *safe to save* despite the mental and physical condition they had on this earth. The saved are those who will live thankfully, contentedly, loyally, and happily in heaven.

My greatest heroes are those who maintain a personal love and trust relationship with God even while going through experiences where their world seems to be turned upside down. These survivors become the best mentors. It usually takes time to crawl out of the pit of discouragement. Some people who have done so turn their effort, time, talent, and love into helping others who have similar problems. Those who help others actually feel their own problem was a blessing to them. It made them compassionate and gave them a mission in life.

It's a *given*—we will admit—that we all need the Lord. "I've struck it rich," said one man to another. When asked if it was gold, he replied, "No, it's God." No longer is he lonely for he has the companionship of a Friend that "sticketh closer than a brother" (Prov. 18:24). All of us who have a Friend like that have struck it rich! God also gives us earthly friends whose faces we can see and touch. I've heard it said this way: The right kind of friend is the first person who comes in when the whole world has gone out. A close friend is one who desires to be truer to us than we are to ourselves and inspires us to be all we can be. So, people do need people and we must be aware of the kind of people we need.

> "A friend is one to whom one may pour out
> all the contents of one's heart, chaff and grain together,
> knowing that the gentlest of hands will take and sift it;
> keeping what is worth keeping and with a breath of kindness
> blow the rest away" (Arabian proverb).

One feels safe in confiding their emotional and spiritual needs to God and a friend like that! It is also important for us to be a friend to others like the description above. By focusing on others, we find a cure for the negative feelings produced when focusing on self.

If one looks in the right places, he will find encouraging instruction and compassionate help from people who care. These mentors, who cost us nothing, will show by their own example that a satisfied life requires responsibility and accountability. Our part then is to absorb this help and make use of the information given. Consider it a gift from God! He will help us put these helpful thoughts in our hearts to be acted out.

In addition to mentors, a safe Christian counselor may help us heal by not dwelling on blaming others for our problems. We need to concentrate on the positive and exercise forgiveness to those who may have wronged or abused us. Those who have practiced these principles can testify that it works wonders even though it may take time. However, forgiveness doesn't always automatically mean that the damage is undone. Many times it is not. How careful we must be to always be in God's hands. We can't trust ourselves without Him. Incidentally, true forgiveness never leaves us as a doormat or in a dictatorial role.

I recall a popular song of long ago written by Johnny Mercer that gave good advice. It went like this: "Accentuate the positive, eliminate the negative, latch on to the affirmative, and don't mess with Mister In Be-tween!" Let me emphasize again: think positively, shun the *blame game,* and forget the negatives of past and present times.

Let's follow the admonition of Paul found in Philippians 3:13 and 14: "... forgetting those things which are behind, and reaching forth unto those things which are before, I press toward the mark of the prize of the high calling of God in Christ Jesus." ♥

Chapter 8

M-A-P to Abundant Life

Our God of love desires His creatures to live an *abundant life*. Satan, on the other hand, is determined to bring ruin. If one considers material wealth, power of authority, pride of accomplishments, or popularity to be the definition of an *abundant life*, the essential point has been missed. John 10:10 describes it this way: "The thief cometh not, but for to steal, and to kill, and to destroy: I am come that they might have life, and that they might have it more abundantly." What a revelation of the *great controversy between Christ and Satan* over the destiny of the human race. God was so sure about His part in this controversy that He gave us Jesus who could say, "I am the good shepherd; the good shepherd giveth his life for the sheep" (verse 11).

During the construction of our home by our son Eric and his father, a friend wanted to go on a walk-through. He was enjoying what he saw, but his main remark has stayed in my mind. He said in Latin, "Liquenda," meaning "I must leave it." Though we are most grateful for whatever material blessings God has chosen to give us, we have learned to put this bonus in its place and share it with others. God is more interested in building *character* in us than in giving us material comfort. This text came to my mind when I heard *liquenda*: "For what is a man profited, if he shall gain the whole world, and lose his own soul? or what shall a man give in exchange for his soul" (Matt. 16:26).

As I considered the true meaning of the *abundant life* that God wants to give us, I began to consider the method the human race must use to receive it. An acrostic with the initials **M-A-P** came to my mind. The purpose of a map is to help a traveler find the way—just so this one leads to the gift of *abundant life*.

M stands for *motive*. There are innumerable reasons (motives) for doing good deeds. This is a good time to "examine ourselves." Do we do our good deeds to glorify ourselves? Or do we do them to *get squared up* because we *owe* someone? Or do we want to bring God glory?

The following is a story from the October 2004 issue of *Signs of the Times* by David Zimmerman:

Fanatical Forgiveness

"A frail black woman and a white police officer named van der Broek faced each other across a South African courtroom. Mr. van der Broek had just been found guilty of murdering the woman's son and her husband. He had come to her home a number of years earlier, shot her son, and burned his body while he and some other officers reveled in the act. Several years later, Mr. van der Broek returned and took away her husband as well. For two years, she heard nothing of him.

"Then the man came back and led the woman to a place beside a river, where she saw her husband bound and beaten, lying on a pile of wood. The last words she heard him say were, "Father, forgive them" as the officers poured gasoline over his body and set him aflame.

"In time, however, justice caught up with Mr. van der Broek. He had been found guilty, and it was time to determine his sentence. The judge asked the elderly woman, "What should be done to this man who so brutally destroyed your family?"

"The woman said, 'I want three things. First, I want to be taken to the place where my husband's body was burned so that I can gather up the dust and give his remains a decent burial.

"'And because my husband and son were my only family, I want, second, for Mr. van der Broek to become my son. I would like him to come twice a month to the ghetto and spend a day with me so that I can pour out on him whatever love I still have remaining within me.

"'Third,' she said, 'I would like Mr. van der Broek to know that I offer him my forgiveness because Jesus Christ died to forgive me.' Then she walked across the courtroom and embraced Mr. van der Broek.

"The police officer fainted, overwhelmed by the widow's response. Then quietly, friends, family, and neighbors—all victims of similar oppression and injustice—began to sing *'Amazing grace, how sweet the sound.'*"

Going on with our **M-A-P** to *abundant living*, we come to **A** for *attitude*, defined as "a state of mind or feeling with regards to some matters" in

The American Heritage Dictionary. The following quote is taken from *Strengthening Your Grip* by Charles R. Swindoll and is surely worth thinking seriously about:

Attitudes

"Words can never adequately convey the incredible impact
of our *attitude* toward life.

"The longer I live, the more convinced I become that life is
10% what happens to us and 90% how we respond to it.

"I believe the single most significant decision
I can make on a day-to-day basis

Is my choice of *attitude*.

It is more important that my past,
my education, my bankroll,

my successes or failures, fame or pain,

what other people think of me or say about me,

my circumstances, or my position.

"*Attitude* keeps me going or cripples my progress.

It alone fuels my fire or assaults my hope.

"When my *attitudes* are right, there's no barrier too high,

No valley too deep, no dream too extreme,

No challenge too great for me."

(*All rights reserved. Used by permission of Insight for Living, Plano, Texas*)

When I first read Charles Swindoll's comments on attitude, I was convinced of its truth and value. I have shared it many times and matted it in frames as gifts for young people, considering what better time than in their youth to help them realize the importance of having the right attitude. Our granddaughter, Jessie, told us she put it by her door as a *motto* so she would be reminded of it as she left the house. It has been a big help to me personally, and I strive to make it one of my daily goals.

Some have accused God of pride when they consider that the Bible, especially in the book of Psalms, requires us to thank and praise Him. Actually, all of God's requirements are for our benefit. God knows who He is, so He's not in need of our praise, but we certainly are in need of developing a thankful attitude. It is medicine for our soul and body, and it lifts us above life's daily trials. Come to think about it, our relationship with God grows deeper when we thank and praise Him for life's blessings. It's a way of giving *hugs* to our heavenly Father.

By letting *gratitude be my attitude*, I can personally testify to its benefits to me. It puts my heart on *cloud nine*. Now, no human being rides on cloud nine at all times, nor should we expect to! If we take seriously the emotional, physical, and spiritual pain of others and our own, we'll have a mix of being on the cloud to coming down to lower ground. But this variance of emotions never takes away the peace we have within. We experience more ups than downs. Let's not be fearful of being human.

A health segment broadcast during the national news revealed how damaging a negative attitude can be on one's health, both physically and mentally. Unfortunately, many suffer unhappiness due to a poor attitude toward themselves and others. They fail to see what there is for which to be thankful. "Reflect upon the present blessings, of which every man has many, not on past misfortunes, of which all men have some," wrote Charles Dickens. Thank God for the thorns as well as the roses. "O joy that seekest me through pain, I cannot close my heart to Thee; I trace the rainbow through the rain, and feel the promise is not vain, That morn shall tearless be." These words are from the hymn "O Love That Will Not Let Me Go" by George Matheson.

When frantically rushing about for many good causes, I often think of this verse and it pierces my conscience: "Do everything without grumbling or arguing, so that you may become blameless and pure, 'children of God without fault in a warped and crooked generation.' Then you will shine among them like stars in the sky as you hold firmly to the word in life" (Phil. 2:14-16, NIV). It is possible to take on too much, even in *doing good*. But balanced, rejoicing Christians are one of God's best advertisements.

I have chosen to surround my thinking with positive, loyal thoughts by reading, thinking, and sharing with positive, loyal people. We should believe our beliefs and doubt our doubts and speak about what we are for—not what we are against—always progressing toward more of God's advancing light. "But the path of the just is as the shining light, that shineth more and more unto the perfect day" (Prov. 4:18). I have discovered that the right attitude keeps me from playing the *blame game*. As Christians, we must take responsibility to encourage fellow Christians with our conversations and our influence. We may make good choices, but moment by moment we need God to keep us faithful to those choices.

Consider these beautiful examples of attitudes in the version of the Paradoxical Commandments by Dr. Kent M. Keith known as the poem "Anyway" as it appeared on the wall of Mother Teresa's children's home in Calcutta:

Anyway

"People are unreasonable, illogical, and self-centered,
LOVE THEM ANYWAY

"If you do good, people will accuse you of selfish, ulterior motives,
DO GOOD ANYWAY

"If you are successful, you win false friends and true enemies,
SUCCEED ANYWAY

"The good you do will be forgotten tomorrow,
DO GOOD ANYWAY

"Honesty and frankness make you vulnerable,
BE HONEST AND FRANK ANYWAY

Think on These Things

> "What you spent years building may be destroyed overnight,
> BUILD ANYWAY
>
> "People really need help but may attack you if you help them,
> HELP PEOPLE ANYWAY
>
> "Give the world the best you have and you'll get kicked in the teeth,
> GIVE THE WORLD THE BEST YOU'VE GOT ANYWAY."

(Copyright Kent M. Keith 1968, renewed 2001. Included by permission. Reported in *Mother Teresa: A Simple Path*, compiled by Lucinda Vardey [New York: Ballantine Books, 1995], p. 185).

P stands for *priority*, which is defined as "in order of importance and urgency" in *The American Heritage Dictionary*. Thoughts on *priority* make our **M-A-P** complete in our search for *abundant life*.

We all feel the need of a friend we can trust to open our heart to, knowing we'll be understood. Jesus wants to be our *Best Friend*. He is the best friend we can trust, confide in, and share our life with. How do we go about making this kind of friendship? Getting to know God should be our first priority. "But seek ye first the kingdom of God, and his righteousness; and all these things shall be added unto you" (Matt. 6:33, see also Matt. 6:24-34). "We do not segment our lives, giving some time to God, some to our business or schooling, while keeping parts for ourselves. The idea is to live all of our lives in the presence of God, under the authority of God, and for the honor and glory of God. That is what the Christian life is all about," wrote R. C. Sproul.

Knowing God will prompt us to love Him and others. Knowing God will make us desire to use our money as a blessing to those who need it and for spreading news of the kingdom of God. Our friendship with God will make us choose to study His Word and be responsible for what we know by applying it to our lives (James 1:5).

It was a challenge for me to form a permanent habit of prioritizing a special time and place for getting to know God in a personal way; however, it is a necessity if we wish to take part in the *abundant life*. Granted, it is easier to find time when one's family has left for their own homes and responsibilities; yet, before we had an empty nest, I profited by establishing the habit of getting up early for devotions. I'm encouraged as I observe the early morning devotional habits in others of all ages, but especially as I see it in the youth.

I like how Ralph Spaulding Cushman says it:

> "I met God in the morning,
> When the day was at its best,
> And His presence came like sunrise,
> Like a glory in my breast.
>
> "All day long the presence lingered,
> All day long He stayed with me,
> And we sailed in perfect calmness
> O'er a very troubled sea.
>
> "Other ships were blown and battered.
> Other ships were sore distressed.
> But the winds that seemed to drive them,
> Brought to me a peace and rest.
>
> "Then I thought of other mornings,
> With a keen remorse of mind,
> When I too had loosed the moorings,
> With the presence left behind.
>
> "So, I think I know the secret,
> Learned from many a troubled way:
> You must seek Him in the morning
> If you want Him through the day."

Early morning may not be the best time for all, but if one is seeking the *abundant life*, it is imperative to set aside some time each day. No Christian should leave home without communion with God, which will give them the spiritual inspiration that will help them throughout the day.

God has created us to worship Him. We can spend time with Him, any place or any time, when we focus our thoughts on Him. Time spent with God creates sweet fellowship that we each can enjoy with Him.

Coupled with prayer and devotions is action. Paul makes this plain in

Think on These Things

Philippians 2:12: "Wherefore, my beloved . . . work out your own salvation with fear and trembling." These words depict seriousness on our part, and they trouble some for we have been taught that salvation is a free gift and we have nothing to do with it. But Acts 4:12 tells us: "And there is salvation in no one else, for there is no other name under heaven given among men by which we must be saved." Is there a discrepancy here? Not at all—God is gentle. He never forces His way with His creatures.

Notice Revelation 3:20: "Behold, I stand at the door, and knock: if any man hear my voice and open the door, I will come in to him, and will sup with him, and he with me." God is eager for fellowship—what an invitation! The door knob is pictured as being on the inside for us to open by our free choice and willing desire. So, man's part is to open the door to being available for sweet, nurturing relationship times with Christ. The result will be finding pleasure in obedience. We choose to be with God and stay there—that's what it means to "work out your own salvation." We are invited to ask for the Holy Spirit to be our daily guide. We do not use the Holy Spirit. He uses us. God is eager to give us this gift (Luke 11:13; Gal. 5:22-25). If we fail to have this blessing, could it be because we haven't asked for it? (James 4:2, 3). Are we willing to be emptied of *self* to receive the Holy Spirit and be led by Him? He convicts us of sin, guides us into all truth, brings things to our remembrance, and gives us power to overcome sin and power to witness for Him. If we sincerely ask, we will receive. This choice is part of our *working out our own salvation.*

My husband had a precious experience that show how the Holy Spirit convicts people of their sins. He often pricks the conscience. This experience happened when Fred was the youth leader of a four state area. I'll let him tell his story:

"I shall never forget an experience I had while conducting a week of prayer at Wisconsin Academy. During one evening meeting, I emphasized the importance of making everything right with others and with God. I urged that if the students wanted to have true peace, they must have a clear conscience.

"After the meeting, I retired to the guest room in the boys' dormitory and was ready to crawl into bed when there was a knock on the door. I opened the door to one of the students who quickly said, 'Elder Beavon, I need to talk to you.' I invited him in, and without delay he expressed in deep concern, 'I did something to a faculty member that was just terrible. If he, or the rest of the faculty know about it, I would be kicked out of school. I feel terrible about it, and I can't sleep at night over it, but if I tell about it, I'm out of here. My folks really sacrificed to send me here, and I can't disappoint them. I know I should make it right, but what can I do? My folks would be devastated!

"I replied, 'John [I'll call him that], I'm not so sure about your being expelled. Regardless of the consequences, you need to make it right, or you'll never have peace in your heart.'

"Then he surprised me by saying: 'Elder Beavon, if I go tonight to make it right, will you go with me?'

"What could I say? 'Yes, just let me get dressed, and we'll go right away.' Soon we were walking over to the faculty member's house. I could see John was very frightened. When we reached the house, John very gingerly rapped on the door. 'You'd better knock louder than that or he will never hear you,' I said. He knocked louder and soon the professor came to the door. Without any introduction, John blurted out a confession and said, 'Will you forgive me?'

"'Of course I'll forgive you, if you have also asked God to forgive you. You just go back to your dorm determined never to do anything like you did again and live for Jesus. We won't tell anyone else about it.'

"The next morning I was headed for the cafeteria, which was in the girls' dormitory. I was halfway there, rounding the flagpole, when I heard a voice behind me. 'Elder Beavon, wait up.' It was John. He came running up and jubilantly said, 'Elder Beavon, I had the best night's sleep I've ever had.' He could sleep again!

"The Holy Spirit had been working on his heart the previous night and had convinced him to do something about his problem. He finally responded and acted, whatever the cost. He could not only sleep again, but he could look people in the eye again. He had peace!"

We put God first and are willing to act as the Holy Spirit moves our hearts, demonstrated in the previous story.

As a person begins to spend time in God's Word, especially if the Bible is being read through from cover to cover, there will be many times when discipline is needed. Don't get discouraged; don't give up; "and let us not be weary in well doing: for in due season we shall reap, if we faint not" (Gal. 6:9).

Think on These Things

As we consider the Bible a manual for a life inspired by God, we will feel compelled to thank Him for it and pray for His blessing each time we read it. The prophet Jeremiah got to the place where he could say: "Thy words were found, and I did eat them; and thy word was unto me the joy and rejoicing of mine heart: for I am called by thy name, O LORD God of hosts" (Jer. 15:16). This degree of fellowship is so sweet that it will linger with us in thoughts through each day and night. One friend described it this way: "At first we read because we know we should, for our own good. It's dry like shredded wheat. Soon it becomes like peaches and cream—it is our delight."

Following the M-A-P leads us to abundant life, but just what IS it? You may wonder at my choice of a verse that struck me as describing abundant life and you may discover one you like better. Here's mine from Habakkuk 3:17-19: "Though the fig tree do not blossom, nor fruit be on the vines, the produce of the olive fail, and the fields yield no food, the flock be cut off from the fold and there be no herd in the stalls, yet I will rejoice in the LORD, I will joy in the God of my salvation. God, the LORD, is my strength; He makes my feet like hinds' feet, He makes me tread upon my high places" (RSV).

The *abundant life* is having a beautiful relationship with the heavenly Family so that even when material and physical loss come we still maintain a peaceful, thankful, rejoicing, forgiven heart. "And this is life eternal, that they might know thee the true God, and Jesus Christ, whom thou has sent" (John 17:3). ♥

Chapter 9

Mother's Regret

Though it was always a pleasure to visit with my dear mother, one of her regrets in her golden years still rings in my ears. I wonder if it applies somewhat to most of us—at any age? After reading some noteworthy article or book, she would comment, "I often wonder what good it does to read this, for I don't remember what I read." I reassured her that reading to strengthen our faith is like eating good food for physical strength. Though the food may not still be in our mouth or stomach, it is beneficial to our body. As we read or study, our courage, loyalty, and peace of mind are enhanced as our faith is strengthened. It will surely help us to be faithful to the end as our love for God and His Word increases.

In my younger days, while reading or in prayer, my mind was often interrupted by thoughts about my busy day ahead. A godly friend gave me an idea that is still very helpful when my mind wanders. Keeping a pen and paper close at hand, I stop my reading or prayer and free my mind by writing all my thoughts down so that I don't have to mentally remember my chore list. It takes those thoughts off my mind, and I can then concentrate on my reading or prayer. Often, I am impressed during this *note break* that my *plate is too full* with *things* that really don't matter, and I am convinced to let go of the truly non-essentials. Now when I share in my *mother's regret*, I stop and try to think of something in the passage that helps to bring it back to me, and God answers my frequent prayers for gaining a blessing from my reading and study.

Recently, I read a precious story taken from the August 2006 issue of *Signs of the Times* by Leonora L. Warriner. It has a practical spiritual lesson for all of us who often have trouble retaining in our minds the things we read:

"A touching story is told of an aged Christian who had long grieved over her inability to remember what she read in the Bible. Day after day, as old age and infirmity drew on, she would read from the Book she loved, only to find that a few minutes after closing her Bible, she could not recall a word.

"One evening, after going through the same experience again, she lay down to sleep, tired and discouraged, telling herself it was useless to read what so soon passed from her mind.

"That night she had an impressive dream. She seemed to be standing, with a loosely woven basket in her hand, by the bank of a beautiful stream whose crystal waters flowed softly at her feet. By her side stood an angel in shining robes, who bade her stoop and fill her basket with living water. Again and again she tried to fill it, but the loose mesh would not retain the water and it flowed out again. Disappointed and disheartened, she turned weeping away, but the angel, bending tenderly over her, whispered, "Look inside your basket, dear one." Gazing with tear-dimmed eyes, the woman saw that the basket, which had once been soiled and dusty, was now white as the driven snow, sparkling in the sunlight.

"And so it is with the word of God. Even though we may often be unable to recall what we have but recently read, if we will constantly fill our minds and hearts with the word, it will exert its cleansing, life-giving power in our lives." ♥

Chapter 10

More than a Ride

Dan was traveling when he came across a hitchhiker who was looking for more than just a ride. After picking him up, Dan discovered the young man, Leo, was looking for answers to some troubling questions. "Is there a God? Is the Bible a book we can depend on? Why do good people suffer? Where is God during this injustice?"

Dan Pratt is a deep-thinker, a genuine and pleasant Christian. He is eager to help. No doubt he sought guidance from on High! Dan is a consecrated believer who has a desire to share his faith in such a winning, convincing way that people will continue to seek more spiritual information and grow in faith on their own.

Leo was unfamiliar with the Bible. When Dan offered to give him a preview of fulfilled prophecy and a history of mankind from an eagle-eye view—from Genesis to Revelation, Leo was all ears. The help Leo received as the car sped on its way was so valuable to him that he accepted Dan's offer to come home with him to continue their study. Leo's original travel plans became secondary to his eagerness to learn answers to his troubling questions.

I do not recall more details of what Leo asked or how Dan answered in the car or in the continued Bible study carried on in Dan's home. I can only imagine what Dan shared. One thing I am sure of, Dan followed the counsel given in the following texts: "Let your speech be always with grace, seasoned with salt, that ye may know how ye ought to answer every man" (Col. 4:6) and "But sanctify the Lord God in your hearts: and be ready always to give an answer to every man that asketh you a reason of the hope that is in you with meekness and fear" (1 Peter 3:15).

As I imagine what Dan covered as he endeavored to establish faith in

Leo's mind and assure him of the great truths of the Bible and the relevancy of these truths to all mankind throughout all time, I will write what I think Dan shared. In this way, Dan's adventure becomes mine.

Dan may have thought: "What could be more convincing of the accuracy of the Bible than to go to the book of Daniel?" After sharing the amazing story of the loyalty of the four young Hebrew youth to God during their captivity in Babylon, he probably told him how God used one of these young men, Daniel, to bring Him glory in the presence of the king of Babylon.

When Daniel was brought before the king, the king asked him: "Art thou able to make known unto me the dream which I have seen, and the interpretation thereof?" Daniel answered . . . "The secret which the king hath demanded cannot the wise men, the astrologers, the magicians, the soothsayers shew unto the king; But there is a God in heaven that revealeth secrets, and maketh known to the king Nebuchadnezzar what shall be in the latter days. The dream, and the visions of thy head upon thy bed, are these" (Dan. 2:26-28).

No one but a servant of God could interpret a dream that God had sent. The king had seen a great image. "This image's head was of find gold, his breast and his arms of silver, his belly and his thighs of brass, his legs of iron, his feet part of iron and part of clay. Thou saweth till that a stone was cut out without hands, which smote the image upon his feet that were of iron and clay, and brake them to pieces . . . and the stone that smote the image became the great mountain, and filled the whole earth" (verses 32-35).

The names of countries represented by different metals were not told to the king in the interpretation other than the head of gold represented his kingdom of Babylon.

Later, Daniel himself had a dream of different animals that represented the same kingdoms. The interpreter, the angel Gabriel, named two of the other kingdoms: Medo-Persia, followed by Grecia (Greece). The next kingdom was not named at this time, but the activities carried on by this kingdom point to Rome. To Daniel, the seriousness of this made him faint and he was sick for days (Dan. 8:20-27).

Following the iron kingdom of Rome, the mixture of part iron and part clay in the feet and toes of Nebuchadnezzar's dream told that the kingdom would be divided. The fulfillment came about in the division into the ten kingdoms of

More than a Ride

the Western Empire (Europe), ten kingdoms, no more, no less. They will never be united (Dan. 2:41-43).

These dreams—or visions—laid out the history of the world from Daniel's time through our time and even beyond to the end of time. The "stone cut out without hands" represented the second coming of Christ—when He will set up His kingdom and rule as King of Kings and Lord of Lords for eternity! Our own history books verify that every nation that came on the stage to rule was exactly as the dream was interpreted. Of course, the final, everlasting kingdom is yet to come. Our faith in that which is yet to come is fortified by that which has taken place. The prophecies of the Bible and their fulfillment, more perhaps than any other one thing, bear witness to its divine inspiration (Isa. 46:9, 10; Amos 3:7).

No doubt Dan and Leo read these fascinating prophecies from the Bible and talked in detail about their meaning. Through the Bible and prophecy, God has revealed Himself. This proves that not only does He exist but that the Bible can be trusted to be true. A confession would surely follow: "But there is a God in heaven that revealeth secrets" (Dan. 2:28; see also verse 47).

Prophecy is not meant merely to predict the future but to strengthen our faith when we discover it as unerring truth. Anyone seriously interested in the study of prophecy would do well to give thoughtful study to the book of Daniel. It is one of the most interesting, remarkable, and valuable books in the Bible. Another invaluable source of information is the book *Bible Readings for the Home*. In simple question-and-answer style, it covers every subject found in the Bible. Answers to questions are given from Bible texts. Other notes from well-known, accepted authors are added for explanation and clarity. This book is available at any Adventist Book Center at a very reasonable price.

No doubt the study by Dan and Leo must have continued with a brief *eagle-eye view* of the entire Scriptures. Before I continue Dan's adventure and make it mine, I have thoughts to share that are alluded to in various parts of the Bible—experiences that happened in heaven before the Genesis record was written. This will be the foundation to what I will further share in brevity of the entire sixty-six books of the Bible.

Millenniums ago an awesome Being, a triune God—Father, Son, and Holy Ghost (Spirit) (1 John 5:7)—who existed with no beginning or ending, lived in a matchless, beautiful place called heaven. Here they created beings called angels to enjoy it with them. The angels were given honorable tasks to perform. Lucifer was the highest of the angels. He was full of wisdom and perfect in his ways from the day of his creation. He made heaven glad with his music as leader of the heavenly choir.

All of God's created beings were given freedom of choice. They could love and serve their Creator, or not. But there was one who perverted the freedom that God had granted, and with his misused freedom, Lucifer presented the purposes of God in a false light and convinced one-third of the angels that God was not fair or just. "Thine heart was lifted up because of thy beauty, thou hast corrupted thy wisdom" (Eze. 28:17). He was filled with great pride and became jealous over Christ's position in the Godhead and as Creator (Col. 1:16). He was not content to accept that all his glory was from God; he wanted to receive the homage due alone to the Creator. "Thou hast said in thine heart . . . I will exalt my throne above the stars of God . . . I will be like the most High" (Isa. 14:13, 14).

Though we can picture an all-loving God, in this tragic scene, God was unable to change Lucifer's course of action and the other angels who were convinced by him. This made for a very disastrous event in heaven. It led to war in heaven and Lucifer, along with one-third of the angels, was cast to the earth. "How art thou fallen from heaven, O Lucifer, son of the morning!" (Isa. 14:12; see also Rev. 12:7-9). All of Revelation 12 tells of Lucifer and his activities on earth. A few of the other verses that mention his business on earth can be found in Genesis 3, throughout the book of Job, and Jude 9.

If God had considered earth's upcoming fate and the work of Lucifer, who became Satan, and decided to cancel His plans to create the earth, the rest of the unfallen angels and the entire universe would have thought Lucifer was right about God being unfair. There was nothing an honest and loving God could do but go ahead with plans to create the earth. The triune God went through with the creation of the world in six days as recorded in Genesis 1 and 2. At this time God made plans to redeem mankind (Gen. 3:15; Eph. 1:4, 5). "But where sin abounded, grace did much more abound" (Rom. 5:20).

Were it not for the Bible, sin and evil and its origin would remain unexplained. ♥

Chapter 11

Mining for Gold

When we hear the complaint that the Bible is hard to understand, I agree—even all great scholars agree. It is understandable when we realize that most of the ancient history of the human race was written in ancient languages by people with different personalities and qualifications. God chose forty men with a variety of skills and occupations to author sixty-six *little books* in the period of 1,500 years. Among these authors was an emancipator who started a new nation for God, kings, scholars, prophets, herdsmen, a tax collector, fishermen, a physician, and those of other walks of life.

What we must realize is that all were called of God. There are many differences in how we think and the words we use. Our modern day vocabulary is quite different than that of the Bible authors. We should realize too that our customs and culture are different. Sometimes things were written the way they happened, sometimes in a parable, allegory, discourse, mystery, or by symbols—as in prophecies or by using figures of speech and illustrations, which are not to be taken literally. Yet a deep lesson can be learned from all of the authors. For example, read Matthew 5:29, 30 and John 6:47-60. We may ask the Holy Spirit to reveal specific lessons. The Bible is described by some as the *divine puzzle*. Some say it's *a gold mine waiting to be excavated*. Whatever it may be called, it is our Creator God's *love-letter* to mankind.

The Scriptures begin with the creation of a perfect world. Then comes the fall of mankind into sin and the rest of the Bible is a record of God's never-ending efforts to bring the human race back to His original plan for them.

God's love is the focus of the Bible, which is seen particularly through Christ who came to this world, lived as a human being, and died on Calvary for the sins of mankind. This is the greatest truth of the universe.

The Bible gives us a complete message from Genesis to Revelation. The last chapter tells of a new beginning—a restoration—"Behold, I make all things new" (Rev. 21:5). From Paradise lost to Paradise gained—or from Eden to Eden!

As I read this divine book of ancient history, I am saddened over *God's dilemma*, having to deal with a *stiff-necked*, stubborn, and disobedient human race. Yet, I read it with joy and gladness as I contemplate God's great love and effort to save mankind. God has left nothing undone to win and save those He created.

The gift of free will—freedom of choice—was very costly for God and for the human race. We can choose to love and serve Him or choose otherwise. This choice involves life and death. *God's dilemma* will be changed to *God's satisfaction* for those who follow Him! Heaven will once again have fullness of joy, for the sacrifice of Christ's life was not in vain! He will rejoice with His followers (Isa. 53:11).

The thought of my s*hared adventure with Dan* inspires me to study to satisfy my own desire to be so firmly established in God's Word that nothing can shake me. I have chosen never to turn back or give up by God's keeping power. I also wish to "be ready always to give an answer to every man that asketh you a reason of the hope that is in you with meekness and fear" (1 Peter 3:15). For Dan, and for me, the Bible contains a lot more than necessary information; it contains an introduction to Jesus Christ and the heavenly family. True Christians desire to know Christ personally. They love, obey, and trust Him to keep His promises to save.

My own adventure in "Mining for Gold" will cover the following:

How and for what purpose the Scriptures were written

Scoffers' attempts to discredit the Word

Tools to use for digging for spiritual treasures

A few interesting "ties" between the Old and New Testaments

A brief introduction to the sixty-six books of the Bible followed by a poem "How Readest Thou?"

This *eagle-eye view* of the Scriptures is written not to take the place of reading the entire Bible, but to encourage and inspire readers to dig for themselves and enjoy the *mining*! By studying prayerfully, humbly, and sincerely, it is amazing how thrilling Bible reading becomes and spiritual growth is experienced.

An understanding of Bible truth doesn't depend as much on intellectual ability as on the intent, the earnest longing, to do right. If God's *greatness*, *majesty*, and *ways of operating* the universe could be fully understood by finite minds, He would cease to be BIG enough to run our world. He would be reduced to our level. The Bible bears the unmistakable credentials of a divine Sovereign. God made sure that His thoughts were transmitted to the human race in a way to be understandable, not in a superfluous way, but with searching and guidance of the Holy Spirit. Without the Spirit's help, we cannot understand. Notice 1 Corinthians 2:14: "But the natural man receiveth not the things of the Spirit of God: for they are foolishness unto him: neither can we know them, because they are spiritually discerned."

Many years ago, I felt that God guided the pen of the Bible writers, but I later found that this idea is not so. Instead, He inspired His chosen authors and guided their thinking by His Holy Spirit. When we read the Bible from cover to cover, we discover that God, the Creator of ideas, impressed different minds with the same thoughts. Each writer may have expressed a thought in a different way, but they did so without contradictions. Even the apostle Peter says there are things in the Scriptures that are "hard to be understood, which they that are unlearned and unstable wrest . . . unto their own destruction" (2 Peter 3:16).

How and for what purpose the Scriptures were written

"For the prophecy came not in old times by the will of man: but holy men of God spake as they were moved by the Holy Ghost" (2 Peter 1:21; see also verses 19 and 20)."God, who at sundry times and in divers manners spoke in time past unto the fathers by the prophets, hath in these last days spoken unto us by his Son, whom he hath appointed heir of all things, by whom also he made the worlds" (Heb. 1:1, 2).

"Surely the Lord GOD will do nothing, but he revealeth his secret unto his servants the prophets" (Amos 3:7).

The Bible is of divine origin. "All scripture is given by inspiration of God"

(2 Tim. 3:16). The Greek word for inspiration in this verse literally means God-breathed. The Scriptures originated from God. He enabled His messengers to grasp and then communicate that which He revealed to them in a trustworthy and authoritative fashion. What a privilege to think on these things.

Let me share some beautiful quotes, texts, and comments on the purpose and value of the written word:

> "Education is useless without the Bible, wrote Noah Webster regarding the value of the Bible."

> "Nothing like the Bible liberates our human kind. Nothing like the Bible elevates the human mind. Nothing like the Bible stimulates to nobler things. Nothing like the Bible cultivates the life on wings," declared Adlai Esteb.

> "The Bible was not given to increase knowledge but to change lives," wrote D. L. Moody.

> "All scripture is inspired by God and is profitable for teaching, for reproof, for correction, and for training in righteousness, that the man of God may be complete, equipped for every good work" (2 Tim. 3:16, 17, RSV).

> "Now these things happened to them as a warning, but they were written down for our instruction, upon whom the end of the ages has come" (1 Cor. 10:11, RSV).

> "For the word of God is quick, and powerful, and sharper than any two edged sword, piercing even to the dividing asunder of soul and spirit and of the joints and marrow, and is a discerner of the thoughts and intents of the heart" (Heb. 4:12).

> "The secret things belong unto the LORD our God: but those things which are revealed belong unto us and to our children for ever, that we may do all the words of this law" (Deut. 29:29).

> "That which is vital is clear and that which is not vital is not clear" (author unknown).

"Thy word have I hid in mine heart, that I might not sin against thee" (Ps. 119:11).

"For whatsoever things were written aforetime were written for our learning, that we through patience and comfort of the scriptures might have hope" (Rom. 15:4).

"Neither have I gone back from the commandment of his lips; I have esteemed the words of his mouth more than my necessary food" (Job 23:12).

"And beginning at Moses and all the prophets, he expounded unto them in all the scriptures the things concerning himself" (Luke 24:27).

"Sanctify them through thy truth: thy word is truth" (John 17:17).

"Thy word is a lamp unto my feet, and a light unto my path" (Ps. 119:105).

If we come to the Scriptures with humility and the desire to do His will, God will give us a life-changing faith that will permeate all we do. "Thy words were found, and I did eat them; and thy word was unto me the joy and rejoicing of mine heart: for I am called by thy name, O LORD God of hosts" (Jer. 15:16). What a beautiful testimony written by the weeping prophet (Jer. 9:1-3). He wept for the wickedness of Israel, but he rejoiced for God's gracious promise to the repentant.

The Bible does not give instructions on every problem known to humanity But it does give us wonderful principles that we can apply to our daily lives. Using these principles, along with sanctified common sense and guided by the Holy Spirit, we can learn to walk in the spirit. We will be sensitive to the leading of God. We will learn from Bible heroes to follow the guidelines of the Bible and our lives will be changed. God has shown us in His Word how to live.

I have often thought that as His followers we do not take God at His word as we should. My prayer is to fill my mind with God's *promises* and *marching orders* to be recalled for praise, thanksgiving, expressions of love, trust, repentance, times of discouragement or temptation, and healing. He is always there for us to give us victory over sin and healing of mind, soul, and body. Making God's Word the most important message for our lives brings peace and satisfaction amidst a troubled world.

Read the following promises from His Word and keep them in your mind so that God can guide you: Genesis 39:9; Exodus 20:3-17; Psalm 91; Psalm 141:3; Proverbs 3:6; Proverbs 15:1; Romans 8:28, 12:2; Philippians 4:8, 13. Add your own verses that speak to your heart and have them ready for your daily life experiences.

"In the Bible are found the only safe principles of action. It is a transcript of the will of God, and expression of divine wisdom. It opens to man's understanding the great problems of life, and to all who heed its precepts it will prove an unerring guide, keeping them from wasting their lives in misdirected effort" (*The Acts of the Apostles*, p. 506).

Scoffers' attempts to discredit the Word

Ever since the fall of man, there have been scoffers against God, His plans, and His Word. "The fool hath said in his heart, there is no God" (Ps. 53:1). "Knowing this first, that there shall come in the last days scoffers, walking after their own lusts, and saying, Where is the promise of his coming? for since the fathers fell asleep, all things continue as they were from the beginning of the creation" (2 Peter 3:3, 4; see also verses 5-7).

The infidel Voltaire boasted: "I am weary of hearing people repeat that twelve men established the Christian religion. I will prove that one man may suffice to overthrow it." More than a century has passed since his death. Other *scholars* have made predictions about the inevitable demise of the Bible and that it would soon fade into obscurity and be seen as nothing but an interesting historical relic of a bygone era.

"The grass withereth, the flower fadeth: but the word of our God shall stand for ever" (Isa. 40:8). "No weapon that is formed against thee shall prosper; and every tongue that shall rise against thee in judgment thou shalt condemn" (Isa. 54:17).

The International Bible Society reported in 2002 that the Scriptures are available in no less than 2,287 languages and dialects with complete or partial translations. More translations continue to be made.

The translation of Scripture hit a soft spot in the heart of my husband, Fred, and me. His parents, Eric and Myrna Beavon, were missionaries in Kenya, East Africa, in the 1920s. To evangelize, the primitive tribes called for earnest prayer on the part of Dad Beavon for the *gift of tongues* to more quickly and effectively reach them with the gospel. He had always found it very difficult to learn languages. His prayer was answered as he learned three languages in a remarkably short time. He learned so well that he was soon able to translate a hymn book and large portions of Scripture in Swahili.

When the attacks of scoffers seemed the strongest, archeologists began making startling discoveries, and bit by bit challenges against the Bible were being answered. It's exciting to know that archaeology has confirmed the Old Testament writings. One of the many findings that speaks well and builds our faith was the discovery in 1947 of the Dead Sea Scrolls. Also in existence is the Greek translation of the Old Testament known as the Septuagint. There are many more. Check the library yourself for a fascinating study.

The infallibility of the Old Testament is established in so many ways. Even the rocks testify to its truthfulness. Archeology confirms its accuracy. Satan, however, is diligently at work encouraging scoffers in their misinterpretations, so our faith must depend on God's promises and the word of our Savior rather than on rocks and inscriptions. "But he said, Yea rather, blessed are they that hear the word of God, and keep it" (Luke 11:28; see also Isa. 30:21).

Here's exciting news about the New Testament! There is incredible evidence for its reliability! There are many copies of New Testament manuscripts still in existence—many more than any other ancient manuscript. Furthermore, these manuscripts have survived in purest form.

God, through His Word and nature, gave us reason for our faith. Yet, there is always room for doubt. "God never asks us to believe, without giving sufficient evidence upon which to base our faith. His existence, His character, the truthfulness of His word, are all established by testimony that appeals to our reason and the testimony is abundant. Yet God has never removed the possibility of doubt" (*Steps to Christ,* p. 105). We must choose to live, study, and think in a way to feed our faith. Information God gave to mankind to establish faith in inspired history, such as the worldwide Flood, has been used by scoffers to create doubt by making the wrong use of the information. Even material advantages invented by human beings for our good have been turned, by some, into a curse. Thomas Edison had this concern and expressed it in his later years.

I share the sentiments of writer Jon Dybdahl when he wrote, "I continue to wonder about many things. I still wish some things weren't there and some explanations now absent could be present. I'm quite sure the mystery will continue. The main thing I have learned is to doubt my questions and doubts. . . . The question as to why I have certain questions has often helped me more than supposed answers to these questions. I invite you to think about such issues for yourselves and continue your search for the God who is much, much bigger than all of us" (*Old Testament Grace*).

Bible scholar and writer Roy Adams penned a statement that no doubt all Bible students feel: "No question, some of Jesus' sayings (as well as His actions) are hard to understand especially if taken in isolation. When, however, we view them in context, particularly with other corrective statements that balance them out, many of them become much easier to understand." This kind of study requires prayer for the guidance of the Holy Spirit and deep thought on our part. But the benefit will be spiritual understanding with common sense.

"We can understand as much of His purposes as it is for our good to know; and beyond this we must still trust the hand that is omnipotent, the heart that is full of love. The word of God, like the character of its divine Author, presents mysteries that can never be fully comprehended by finite beings. . . . Everywhere are wonders beyond our ken. Should we then be surprised to find that in the spiritual world also there are mysteries that we cannot fathom? . . . The difficulties of Scripture have been urged by skeptics as an argument against the Bible; but so far from this, they constitute a strong evidence of its divine inspiration. If it contained no account of God but that which we could easily comprehend; if His greatness and majesty could be grasped by finite minds, then the Bible would not bear the unmistakable credentials of divine authority" (*Steps to Christ,* pp. 106, 107; see also 1 Cor. 2:10, 11).

The Savior's promise to His followers was that "when he, the Spirit of truth, is come, he will guide you into all truth . . . for he shall receive of mine, and shall shew it unto you" (John 16:13, 14). By faith we may look to the

Mining for Gold

hereafter and rejoice that all which has perplexed us in the providences of God will then be made plain. "For now we see through a glass, darkly; but then face to face: now I know in part; but then shall I know even as also I am known" (1 Cor. 13:12).

Perhaps the greatest evidence for the authenticity of the Bible is the influence and impact for good it has had, and still continues to have, on the lives of those who apply its teachings to their lives.

I could say this over and over: I refuse to allow what I do not understand to rob me of the joy, beauty, peace, and security I receive from what I *do* understand.

Tools to use for digging spiritual treasures

"And when he had sent the multitudes away, he went up into a mountain apart to pray: and when the evening was come, he was there alone" (Matt. 14:23). If the Son of God found it necessary, while on earth, to communicate with His Father for guidance and fellowship, how much more should we be led into truth in our search of the Scriptures.

Pray for understanding and a willing heart that says, "Speak; for thy servant heareth" (1 Sam. 3:10). Ask God to speak to you and make His messages personal to you. Place your name into His promises and His commands. Underline special thoughts that speak to you, or keep a Bible journal. Thank Him for answering your prayer.

"But the Comforter, which is the Holy Ghost, whom the Father will send in my name, he shall teach you all things, and bring all things to your remembrance, whatsoever I have said unto you" (John 14:26; see also John 16:13).

"But the natural man receiveth not the things of the Spirit of God: for they are foolishness unto him: neither can he know them, because they are spiritually discerned" (1 Cor. 2:14).

A center reference in a Bible is helpful in allowing the Bible to interpret itself. This is especially true for understanding the prophetic books such as Ezekiel, Daniel, and Revelation.

A good Bible commentary along with a Bible dictionary is most helpful in explaining the meaning of puzzling passages. Some people lose faith in the Bible because of a lack of understanding. Each may encounter things in Scripture that are difficult to understand and there will be room for doubt to those who prefer to doubt.

A concordance is a must. It helps locate verses on given subjects and also helps you compare different authors' thoughts throughout the Bible. A good concordance may include Hebrew, Chaldee, and Greek dictionaries that help to shed light on the original meaning of words and intent.

Some of the most puzzling and misunderstood portions in Scripture have to do with wars, killings, and immorality. Also puzzling are activities that are foreign to our culture. We must recognize that our honest God covers nothing up. The fact that some pretty sordid facts are revealed should help develop our confidence in the Bible because God hides nothing and tells it like it was. At the same time, we are shown that in spite of great sin, there is the grace of forgiveness for the truly repentant sinner

Some additional tools for understanding the Scriptures are *thought* tools—asking ourselves some questions that will help us get acquainted with what has been written and to see the big picture. We need to ask ourselves: Who wrote the book? Who was it written to? What was written about? When did it take place? Why was it written? Where did it take place? What personal applications can I make for myself?

The Bible from first to last—Genesis to Revelation—is God's *big picture* of restoration—from Eden lost to Eden regained. Ephesians 1:17 and 18 gives us encouragement in our understanding of what the Bible is saying to us through different writers: "That the God of our Lord Jesus Christ, the Father of glory, may give unto you the spirit of wisdom and revelation in the knowledge of him: The eyes of your understanding being enlightened; that ye may know what is the hope of his calling, and what the riches of the glory of his inheritance in the saints."

Another *thought* and *decision* tool would be to choose reading and hearing material that is wholesome and prompts us to stay close to God and His Word. While reading my Bible through, I came across a set of tools that we are always carrying with us—parts of our body—which are mentioned many places throughout the Scriptures. For example, the following impressed me about the parable of the sower and the seed found in Matthew 13 and the

Mining for Gold

results of the sowing, which all have something to do with the magnificent set of tools known as our body. Verse 9 says, "Who hath *ears* to hear, let him hear." Unfortunately, many use their ears only to hear the wrong things to their own detriment. "For this people's heart is waxed gross, and their *ears* are dull of hearing, and their *eyes* they have closed; lest at any time they should see with their *eyes* and hear with their *ears,* and should understand with their *heart,* and should be converted, and I should hear them" (verse 15).

To the disciples and followers throughout the ages, Jesus said, "But blessed are your *eyes,* for they see: and your *ears,* for they hear. For verily I say unto you, that many prophets and righteous men have desired to see these things which ye see, and have not seen them; and to hear those things which ye *hear,* and have not heard them. *Hear* ye therefore the parable of the sower" (verses 16-18). "Who hath *ears* to hear, let him hear" (verse 43). Read the entire chapter; it can be a blessing to you through your EARS, your EYES, and your HEART.

The last book of the Bible—Revelation—beautifully tells of the culmination of long struggles, the great controversy between good and evil, and the restoration of God's original plan, and it also talks of this tool, the EAR. Revelation 2:7 says, "He that hath an *ear,* let him *hear* what the Spirit saith unto the churches; To him that overcometh will I give to eat of the tree of life, which is in the midst of the paradise of God." Revelation 3:20 also says, "Behold, I stand at the door, and knock: if any man *hear* my voice, and open the door, I will come in to him, and will sup [fellowship] with him, and he with me" (Rev. 3:20). Let's keep those ears, eyes, and hearts attune to God's voice.

King David wrote, "Open thou mine eyes, that I may behold wondrous things out of thy law" (Ps. 119:18).

The following scriptures also testify to our responsibility to learn from God's Word. "But he said, Yea rather, blessed are they that hear the word of God, and keep it" (Luke 11:28; see also Isa. 30:21).

"Search the scriptures; for in them ye think ye have eternal life: and they are they which testify of me" (John 5:39).

"And that from a child thou hast known the holy scriptures, which are able to make thee wise unto salvation through faith which is in Christ Jesus" (2 Tim. 3:15).

Think on These Things

"If any man will do his will, he shall know of the doctrine, whether it be of God, or whether I speak of myself" (John 7:17).

To test opinions on God's Word should never be based on who else believes this or how the teaching makes you feel. We should be testing everything based on this question: Where is this taught in the Word of God?

Another test is found in Isaiah 8:20: "To the law and to the testimony: if they speak not according to this word, it is because there is no light in them."

"Whom shall he teach knowledge? and whom shall he make to understand doctrine? them that are weaned from the milk, and drawn from the breasts [a serious student]. For precept must be upon precept, precept upon precept; line upon line, line upon line; here a little, and there a little" (Isa. 28:9, 10). I understand these verses to mean that we should check out all the Scriptures on a subject. Do not make a final decision on a verse until all verses on a given subject are checked out to find what the various writers say on that subject. By this method, the true meaning of any doctrine (teaching) will be made clear.

"But be ye doers of the word, and not hearers only, deceiving your own selves" (James 1:22; see also verse 25). It is crucial in the study of the Scriptures to maintain a teachable spirit and a heart open to the leading of the Holy Spirit. This type of searcher will be filled with a sense of peace and joy.

Nature can be a tool to show us in unwritten language the glory of God and His creative power: "The heavens declare the glory of God; and the firmament sheweth his handiwork. Day unto day uttereth speech, and night unto night sheweth knowledge" (Ps. 19:1, 2). "For the invisible things of him from the creation of the world are clearly seen, being understood by the things that are made, even his eternal power and Godhead; so that they are without excuse" (Rom. 1:20).

Nature speaks to us of its Creator and is often called God's *second book*. Nature was here before the written word. We sing about its message in the words of the song "How Great Thou Art." Yet, the written has superseded it in importance as referenced in John 5:39. Nature was perfect in every way after it was created. But Scripture reveals that sin has altered the natural world (Gen. 3:17, 18). Nature, marred by the curse of sin, bears an imperfect testimony about God. God's character cannot be revealed in its imperfection. Nevertheless, there is still great beauty and a great message that nature proclaims.

Mining for Gold

Though I am ever so grateful for my spiritual heritage, I realize my path to heaven is not by inheritance—it comes by my personal choices as I study God's Word: "Let every man be fully persuaded in his own mind" (Rom. 14:5). The decision to be a Christian is a very serious matter. It should not be taken lightly. It is for one who takes the responsibility of representing Christ and sharing Him with others.

As we share we should avoid argument but instead "reason together" kindly while praying for the Holy Spirit to guide us. When dealing with those who differ from us, we need to be especially tactful and avoid any hint of arrogance or unkindness. If we believe in God's grace, we will treat others gracefully. We should endeavor to emulate the methods of our Savior Jesus. Note the story found in Luke 9:49-56 for how Jesus related to people who were different than He and His disciples.

I have a great desire to become so well acquainted with the Scriptures that when I read or hear some spiritual thought expressed elsewhere I can readily detect whether or not it lines up with "thus sayeth the Lord." If not, I cannot accept it even if it sounds more desirous and popular than God's Word—the truth. I have also made a commitment to refuse to allow what I do not readily understand or what I might consider strange in Scripture to dampen my love, trust, and confidence in the Bible because I have already found enough evidence on which to establish my faith.

Listen and *silent* consist of the same letters and effect. They are both tools for meditation and thought. "Be still and know that I am God: . . . I will be exalted in the earth" (Ps. 46:10). Modern technological advances claim to save time, but in many instances we discover time is lost instead of saved. For instance, television, computers, and the newer hand-held electronic devices can become an addiction with trivia, externals, less worthwhile activities, and even the filth of pornography. In order to overcome these addictions, it may take getting control of or rid of these mind-boggling inventions. It is our choice—our decision—how we will live our lives, and with God's help, we can overcome the things that tempt us. "Abstain from all appearance of evil" (1 Thess. 5:22). "For all that is in the world, the lust of the flesh, and the lust of the eyes, and the pride of life, is not of the Father, but is of the world" (1 John 2:16; see also verses 15-17 and Ps. 97:10, 141:4).

Fortunately, many use the marvels of inventions as a blessing to themselves and others. There are positive resources at Web sites such as Bibleinfo.com, KidsBibleInfo.com, BibleUniverse.com, BibleSchools.com, 3abn.org, and ExploringTheWord.com.

We all need to spend more time being still and thinking of eternal values. Many would agree with me that there is great value in early morning study of a particular subject: a book of the Bible or a spiritual growth subject from the Bible. You may find it difficult to set an early morning date with God, but it is important to make a habit of setting aside a time that fits your schedule. We should never be too busy to offer a prayer of thanksgiving, a prayer for guidance, and an invitation for God's presence to be with us through the day.

A few interesting "ties" between the Old and New Testaments

As we begin to travel through God's Word, how better could I introduce it than to quote the inspiring words of this unknown author as well as the words of Samuel Chadwick and Ellen G. White:

> "The Bible contains the mind of God, the state of man, the way of salvation, the doom of sinners, and the happiness of believers. Its doctrines are holy, its precepts are binding, its histories are true, and its decisions are immutable. Read it to be wise, believe in it to be safe, and practice it to be holy. It contains light to direct you, food to support you, and comfort to cheer you. It is the traveler's map, the pilgrim's staff, the pilot's compass, the soldier's sword, and the Christian's charter. Here paradise is restored, heaven opened, and the gates of hell disclosed. Christ is its grand object; our good, its design; the glory of God, its end. It should fill the memory, rule the heart, and guide the feet. Read it slowly, frequently, and prayerfully. It is a mine of wealth, a paradise of glory, and a river of pleasure. It is given you in life, will be opened in the judgment, and be remembered forever. It involves the highest responsibility, will reward the greatest labor, and will condemn all who trifle with its sacred contents" (author unknown).

> "Pay no attention to people who discredit it, for I tell you that they speak without knowledge. It is the word of God itself. Study it according to its own direction. Live by its principles. Believe its message. Follow its precepts. No man is uneducated who knows the Bible and

> no one is wise who is ignorant of its teachings" (Samuel Chadwick).

> "The Bible is like a fountain. The more you look into it, the deeper it appears. The grand truths of sacred history possess amazing strength and beauty and are as far-reaching as eternity. No science is equal to the science that reveals the character of God" (*Mind, Character, and Personality,* vol. 1, p. 97).

While writing about the Bible, I will touch on major events in each book. There is such a temptation to go into detail and write in depth, but that would make it far too lengthy and time-consuming. My goal in sharing this material is to inspire you to do your own digging and find precious gems that will increase your trust in a loving God.

The sixty-six books of the Bible are divided into two great divisions called the Old Testament and the New Testament. The Old Testament was written before Jesus was born and consists of thirty-nine books. The New Testament was written after Jesus was crucified and contains twenty-seven books. As many as forty authors wrote the Bible over a period of more than 1,500 years. From 1500 BC to about AD 100, some thirty authors wrote the books of the Old Testament. The New Testament was written by eight men in a period of about fifty years.

The Old and New Testaments stand together as one work, and the unity of the two is remarkable. The New Testament contains numerous direct quotations from, and many references to, the Old Testament. The Old Testament prophecies of Jesus' birth, life, and death are referred to in the New Testament, especially in the Gospels. "Beginning at Moses and all the prophets, he expounded unto them in all the scriptures all things concerning himself. . . . And he said unto them, These are the words which I spake unto you, while I was yet with you, that all things must be fulfilled, which were written in the law of Moses, and in the prophets, and in the psalms, concerning me" (Luke 24:27, 44).

God's gift of the Scripture, preserved miraculously throughout the centuries, is a priceless heritage. It is the *universal Book*, and it belongs to everyone.

A brief introduction to the sixty-six books of the Bible

The books of the Bible are not arranged in their chronological order but are grouped according to the nature of their content. This material may be new to some readers while to others it will be a review.

The divisions of the Old Testament are as follows:

The first five books are called the **books of Moses**— Genesis, Exodus, Leviticus, Numbers, and Deuteronomy. They are also referred to as the **Pentateuch**. They provide a foundation for our biblical faith.

The next group is called the **books of history.** These books tell the story of the Hebrews from their settlement in Canaan to their restoration after the Babylonian captivity. These books include Joshua, Judges, Ruth, 1 Samuel, 2 Samuel, 1 Kings, 2 Kings, 1 Chronicles, 2 Chronicles, Ezra, Nehemiah, and Esther.

The books in the third group are **inspirational,** consisting mostly of poems and proverbs. The books in this category are Job, Psalms, Proverbs, Ecclesiastes, and the Song of Solomon.

The fourth group consists of seventeen books of **prophecy**. The first five are called **"the major prophets"** and the last twelve **"the minor prophets."** The minor prophets are not less important than the major prophets, but they are given that designation because they are shorter in length. The books in this group are as follows:

Major: Isaiah, Jeremiah, Lamentations, Ezekiel, and Daniel

Minor: Hosea, Joel, Amos, Obadiah, Jonah, Micah, Nahum, Habakkuk, Zephaniah, Haggai, Zechariah, and Malachi

God reveals Himself in the Old Testament and shows His plan of redemption. In doing so, He weaves natural events in the lives of the children of Israel with His own activities. The Old Testament therefore differs from secular literature and history. To properly understand it as it is read, we must recognize the supernatural and the natural. As we study the Old Testament, we can see the record of God's activities in the past. We can also read of His divine plan for the future of mankind. How wonderful that we can learn through its pages about God's plan for humanity.

The Old Testament, mainly the first five books, is the foundation of the

Bible. If we question the truth of Genesis, we also question the truth of the New Testament, which time and again refers to Genesis.

Books of Moses

Genesis, the first of the five books of Moses, contains the only authentic account of the creation of the world, the origin of man, God's original plan for man, the entrance of sin into the world, and the first promise to mankind that a Savior would come to redeem them (Gen. 3:15). Genesis is first and foremost a revelation of God, our Creator and Redeemer. Throughout the entire Bible, Creation is frequently, colorfully, and gloriously mentioned (see Ps. 19).

We often consider each day of Creation and think of the form of nature God made on that day. There are other gifts God gave to the human race during that period. The gift of *time* was given on the first day! "And the evening and the morning were the first day" (Gen. 1:5; see also verses 8, 13, 23, and 31). Mankind needed the space and limit of time. For God, time is eternal: "Before the mountains were brought forth, or ever thou hadst formed the earth and the world, even from everlasting to everlasting, thou art God. . . . For a thousand years in thy sight are but as yesterday when it is past, and as a watch in the night" (Ps. 90:2, 4).

The division of time for the week has no scientific reason for it as the day has. Funk & Wagnall's New Encyclopedia tells us: "It is of Hebrew origin." It "began as a celebration of the creation of the world in six days with the seventh day for rest."

"And God blessed the seventh day, and sanctified it" (Gen. 2:3). The gift of the "sanctified seventh-day" was first called "Sabbath" in Exodus 16:23, 25-29, and then in the fourth commandment in Exodus 20:8. Here God asked us to "remember it." We are given time to reflect on the very first Sabbath—a celebration of the completion of Creation. If all of mankind had always kept holy the day God set aside as sacred and celebrated it as a weekly anniversary of God's creative power, evolution and atheism would never have gained a foothold. Scripture tells us we will come to worship God in the "new heavens and the new earth . . . from one sabbath to another" (Isa. 66:22, 23). What a glorious thought! The Sabbath is mentioned throughout the Bible (see the gem in Eze. 20:20).

Responsibility and *work* were other gifts that were given during the creation week. God said to Adam and Eve, "Be fruitful, and multiply, and replenish the earth, and subdue it: and have dominion over . . . every living thing that moveth upon the earth" (Gen. 1:28). "And the LORD God took the man, and put him into the garden of Eden to dress it and to keep it" (Gen. 2:15). Was God telling Adam that responsible people do not litter but preserve natural beauty and leave behind only betterment and our footprints? Adam was also given the joyful privilege of naming the animals (Gen. 2:20).

A companion was also given to Adam, formed from his own rib. This was the gift of *marriage*. "This is now bone of my bones, and flesh of my flesh: she shall be called Woman, because she was taken out of Man" (Gen. 2:23). Creating Eve from a bone from Adam's side tells us she was not superior or inferior to Adam—she was his equal to stand by his side.

At the fall of mankind, purity died. Fear, guilt, and blame took the place of the joyful eagerness Adam and Eve found in the fellowship with God in the Garden (Gen. 2:7-24). But God already had a plan of rescue after the world's greatest tragedy, for the first promise of a Savior is found in Genesis 3:15. Though sin hurt and changed the beautiful marriage relation—the equality—God also had healing and beauty for this change. Paul put it this way: "Wives, submit yourselves unto your own husbands, as unto the Lord. For the husband is the head of the wife, even as Christ is the head of the church: and he is the saviour of the body. Therefore as the church is subject unto Christ, so let the wives be to their own husbands in every thing. Husbands, love your wives, even as Christ also loved the church, and gave himself for it" (Eph. 5:22-25; see also verses 26-28).

Notice the beauty in the fact that the wives are to submit to a loving godly husband who patterns his life after the life of Christ! Paul also likens the relationship to the closeness between God's followers (the church) with Himself. Christ is in the triangle of a good, happy home!

When special friends of ours were renewing their marriage in a simple service on Wild Horse Island, I wrote this poem for them as a prayer. It is really about marriage from the beginning to the end—all in God's hands:

Wedding Prayer

"Our Father in Heaven,
The One Supreme Being who
Wraps His human creation
In His love.
You created and planned marriage.
You performed the first ceremony ever
By taking a rib from near the heart
Of the first man.
From this rib You created woman
And commanded that the two should be one.
To enjoy each others companionship
And to be the visual image of Your
Own relationship with humanity.
You attended another wedding
In the form of Your Beloved Son.
Who performed His first miracle
As He showed love and concern for
The happiness of married people.

"Be with us today and forever to
Give us beauty in our lives,
All we who witness this meaningful service.
Grant us the continued desire and strength
To be pure and faithful to You and to each other.
Fit us now for the wedding
Of the Heavenly Bride and Groom.
May all of us be safe to be with You
In Your eternal Home.
This is our prayer in Jesus' Name. Amen."

When I consider the genuine *Big Bang*—God's creation when He spoke and it was—I think of the critics who say there isn't a God. But the Bible tells us that "the fool hath said in his heart, There is no God" (Ps. 53:1). However, we know that "in the beginning God created the heaven and the earth" (Gen. 1:1) "and on the seventh day God ended his work which he had made" (Gen. 2:2).

Genesis contains the first 2,500 years of human history, which is more than all the other sixty-five books combined. Transgression became so universal that 1,656 years after Creation, the Lord sadly destroyed the world by a worldwide

Flood. Only faithful Noah and his family were saved to repopulate the earth. Next, we are shown the confusion of man's primitive language at the tower of Babel because of unbelief in God's promises (Gen. 9:13-15).

Genesis tells about the life of Abraham—God's chosen who was called the "Friend of God" (James 2:23)—a descendant of Shem who, though he sinned and made mistakes, obeyed and trusted God. Abraham was called to establish a nation in Canaan to preserve the knowledge of the Creator and to share this truth to the heathen nations around them. Five times the promise was given that through this nation all the nations of the earth would be blessed through Christ (see Gen. 12:3, 18:18, 22:18, 26:4, 28:14).

I recall a wonderful book titled *Greatest Stories Ever Told* that referred to the stories in the Bible. These true stories tell of love and hate, obedience and disobedience, promises fulfilled and unfulfilled (on man's part). All are colorfully told in the lives of Abraham and his descendents—Isaac and Ishmael, Jacob, and his twelve sons.

The story of the life of Jacob's eleventh son, Joseph, is a remarkable story of God's guidance in the life of a young man who wanted, above all, to please and represent God as a faithful ambassador after being sold as a slave by his brothers and taken to Egypt (Gen. 39:7-23). He became, in time, next to Pharaoh in authority. This story, especially the last part, brings tears to my eyes though I've heard it from childhood.

Because of guidance given by God in a dream, Joseph instructed the Egyptians to store great quantities of grain during seven years of plenty so they would have ample to take them through seven years of famine that followed. During the famine, Joseph's brothers came to Egypt to buy food, not recognizing their brother whom they dealt with. The story, as it unfolds in Genesis 41-47, is very touching and well-worth reading often.

Exodus means *the going out,* and it documents the national history of Judaism. Here, Moses describes God's marvelous intervention on behalf of His chosen people in delivering them from slavery. This story is told and retold by the prophets, the psalmists, the apostles, and by the oppressed and downtrodden of every age. Not only through the miracle of *going out* but story after story is told in this journey of deliverance: the journey to Sinai, the

Mining for Gold

giving of the law, the description of the tabernacle, food that fell from heaven (manna), water from a rock, and a multitude of God's care and blessings to the children of Israel, who were often ungrateful and rebellious.

Exodus is one of the Bible's best sources for how God goes about solving problems. The first example was the delivery of a baby hid in a basket made of bulrushes and placed by the river's edge. Pharaoh's daughter, who found him, named him Moses "because I drew him out of the water" (Ex. 2:10). His training in Pharaoh's court prepared him to be the emancipator of his people from a country that had once saved their lives but now enslaved them. God was about to fulfill His plans for them that He had promised His friend Abraham. God showed them that He keeps His promises.

The Promised Land was finally reached and inhabited by God's chosen nation. This deliverance from Egypt pictures our redemption and the difficulties along the way as we travel that path.

While Genesis is a family history, Exodus is a national history. Both books need to be studied together to get a true understanding. Exodus takes up the story of Israel's bondage in Egypt by a Pharaoh who "knew not Joseph" (Ex. 1:8). It tells of their deliverance under the leadership of Moses after a long sojourn—450 years—as slaves in the land of the pharaohs. Moses describes God's marvelous intervention on behalf of His chosen people in delivering them from slavery.

The historical part of Exodus (chapters 1-18) deals with the above described incidents during their encampment at Mount Sinai. The rest of the book (chapters 19-40) tells of the Ten Commandments, the judicial ordinances, the old covenant and its ratification (formal approval of validity), the Lord's directions for the construction of the earthly sanctuary, which enabled God to dwell among them, and the establishment of the Aaronic priesthood.

The delivery of Israel from Egypt was the beginnings of God's purpose to have them witness for Him (see Ex. 19:5, 6). In the land of Canaan, for which they were bound, they were to share news of God's love and what the true God was like, that all nations might learn to know and follow Him during the centuries to come. But alas, sad to say, they were more often a great disappointment!

Moses is mentioned in thirty-two books of the Bible, and Exodus is quoted twenty-four times in twelve New Testament books!

Leviticus is considered by many Bible readers to be difficult to read and understand. Yet, the book of Leviticus is full of gospel truth and in it *some of the deep things of God are revealed* as it points us to the true *Lamb of God*. Actually, we should keep in mind that the ceremonial laws were designed to teach the plan of salvation through faith in Christ.

The word Leviticus means *Law of the Priests,* and it was referred to as the *handbook* of the priests. The word Leviticus comes from the name Levi—the father of the priests. Their duty was to teach the law, and they were in charge of worship, celebration of the various feasts, ceremonies, and rituals. All these were symbolic of "the true tabernacle, which the Lord pitched, and not man" (Heb. 8:2), the "greater and more perfect tabernacle, not made with hands" (Heb. 9:11), which pointed to the true Lamb of God—Jesus Christ—who is "minister of the sanctuary" in heaven (Heb. 8:2).

The great lesson taught by the Mosaic system of animal sacrifice was that the wages of sin is death and that "without shedding of blood is no remission [of sin]" (Heb. 9:22). Paul drew heavily from this book when he wrote Hebrews. He gave several specific references to Leviticus. The thought of the seriousness of sin in God's sight and the necessity of atonement for sin, as well as mediation between God and man, is the primary emphasis. To understand the wisdom and love of God in the Hebrew ritual, we must focus our minds on the incarnation and death of Christ and His high priestly ministry to which it refers.

Leviticus also gives an account of the clean and unclean meats to eat (chapter 11). Because our bodies are God's temple and what we do to them can bring Him glory, this law of Moses would be applicable for all time, would it not? (see 1 Cor. 3:16, 17; 10:31).

This book contains more of the very words of God than any other Bible book. Throughout most of it, He is the direct speaker. We would do well to study this book more diligently and find that it leads us to a "deeper appreciation of Christ as High Priest, Saviour, and Redeemer" (M. L. Andreasen, *The Sanctuary Service*, p. 8).

Numbers is a sequel to the book of Exodus. The name reminds us that this book tells of numbering the people—census taking. There were two censuses: one when the Israelites left Egypt and the other at the close of their forty years of wilderness wanderings.

The events recorded take place during the forty years of the Hebrews sojourn in the wilderness before entering the Promised Land. It gives the route, the principal encampments, and interesting accounts of their experiences of trials and deliverances, their rebellions and punishments. The book also depicts the justice, the longsuffering, the mercy, and the protection of our loving heavenly Father over His children.

Other instruction is provided on the giving of offerings. Among the stories told are the provision of great quantities of quails to eat when they complained about their food; Miriam becoming a leper; the twelve spies; Korah, Dathan, and Abiram; and Moses smiting the rock for water. This disobedience on the part of Moses caused him to lose out on going into the Promised Land. However, later something better happens to him (see Luke 9:28-36 and Jude 9).

Also in this book, we find one of the most beautiful prophecies of Christ's first advent in the story of Balaam and Balak: "there shall come a Star out of Jacob, and a Sceptre shall rise out of Israel" (Num. 24:17). The record of its fulfillment is found in Matthew 2:1 and 2.

The story of the Israelites being bitten by the fiery serpents because of sin and unbelief and the lifting up of the symbolic serpent for them to behold by faith and receive healing is found in chapter 21. In the conversation between Jesus and Nicodemus, this same experience, "lifting up the serpent in the wilderness," is mentioned with this added comment: "even so must the Son of man be lifted up: that whosoever believeth in him should not perish, but have eternal life" (John 3:14, 15). The brazen serpent, which represented sin, was a symbol of the crucified Christ, who became sin for us. In 2 Corinthians 5:21 we read, "For he [God] hath made him [Jesus] to be sin for us, who knew no sin; that we might be made the righteousness of God in him."

For many, Moses' books—Exodus, Leviticus, and Numbers—do not make for favorite Bible reading. Much of it is very repetitive and difficult to understand. The complicated requirements for bringing a new spiritual nation into existence are a little mind-boggling. Most theologians admit we can't understand everything we read in scripture. Jon Dybdahl has this to say regarding our inability to understand all we read in the Bible: "I believe there remains a sense of mystery. I don't know all the answers. Learning to live with questions may in the end be more fruitful than arriving at final answers. I won't ever know how to explain fully why God seems to have behaved as He did, but He's God, and I'm man. I don't think He minds my asking, but I do believe He may not expect my human mind to fathom it all." (*Old Testament Grace*).

Though a little puzzled and confused as I read, I am impressed with the exactness and order required of the Israelites. Careful rules were made to prevent epidemics and plagues as thousands camped in the wilderness. Strict rules were given for sanitation, cleanliness, neatness, and order (Lev. 13). There were also many rules regarding their welfare—honesty, generosity, and integrity (Lev. 19:1-18).

I was intrigued with the order the different tribes were to pitch their tents and to post their family banners in specific places around the tabernacle (Num. 2:1-34). Picture the beauty in color and order! Also picture the entire nation getting everything ready to leave one campsite for another. Everyone had a job to do and all was done with great precision. Picture the tribes with their banners as they marched along. The sacred articles of the tabernacle, and the tabernacle itself, were in their places wrapped with great care (Num. 4:1-49). It must have been a beautiful, impressive sight with the cloud of the Lord by day and the pillar of fire by night. How awesome!

Deuteronomy means *second law* or *law repeated*. All the people who had been delivered from Egypt forty years before, except Caleb and Joshua, had died in the wilderness. Moses was eager that those who were children at the time of deliverance, or born during the wilderness wanderings, become well-acquainted with the story of Israel's liberation from Egypt. He wanted them to know God's plan to make of them a great nation of witnesses to the nations around them of the only true God.

This book is essentially Moses' farewell address to the Israelites. Moses emphasized the need of faithful and loving obedience to God's commandments (Deut. 10:12, 13). His love for these people is very evident through his efforts to prepare them for going into the Promised Land and becoming the great nation God had planned for them to be.

We find the song of Moses in chapter 32, where in beautiful language he tells of God's love and watch-care over Israel. God calls them "the apple of His eye" (Deut. 32:10). The Ten Commandments are repeated in chapter 5, verses 7 through 21. Beside practical instruction, the book contains warnings to the disobedient and blessings for the obedient. In the last chapter of Deuteronomy, Moses' death and burial are recorded, possibly written by Joshua.

Jesus quoted Deuteronomy as a weapon during His temptation in the wilderness (see Matt. 4:1-11; Luke 4:1-13; Deut. 6:13, 16, 8:3, 10:20). Prophets, such as Isaiah, based much of their message on Deuteronomy's laws and ideals. Jesus also quoted from it when asked what was the greatest of God's commandments (see Matt. 22:37 and Deut. 6:5).

Books of History

These records of the history of mankind found in the Old Testament are not recorded for entertainment or to cause succeeding generations to hate those who "did evil in the sight of the Lord" (Judges 3:7) or to cause us to question God. We can readily see these words were written for all generations to examine ourselves (2 Cor. 13:5). We should read them with a hatred for sin, which separates people from God. We should read and see the awesome love of God who never lost His great love for us and who strives to win back His rebellious people (2 Peter 3:9). God's character is love, which never changes, even if the circumstances cause Him, in love, to chasten or punish for our best interest (Mal. 3:6). When people humbly repent, He offers mercy: "If that nation, against whom I have pronounced, turn from their evil, I will repent of the evil that I thought to do unto them" (Jer. 18:8). But some will choose to be lost. I'll repeat again and again: "What more could He do?"

Joshua—the first of the twelve books of history—continues after the death of Moses as the Lord commissioned Joshua to lead Israel into the Promised Land. Joshua 1:1 and 2 shows that Joshua faithfully began his work by encouraging the people to be strong, courageous, obedient, and faithful to

God.

The stories of the spies, the harlot Rahab, the miraculous crossing of the Jordan River, and the fall of Jericho are fascinating and reveal the marvelous care and support of God. Joshua led from victory to victory until the land was possessed and divided among the tribes.

When the day of Joshua's death drew near, he assembled the people and made his farewell address, asking them to renew their covenant relationship to God, as did Moses in his last speech. Joshua briefly rehearsed the history of their nation from the time of Abraham down to their day, and he appealed to them to remain true to God. He is remembered by his own testimony: "choose you this day whom ye will serve . . . but as for me and my house, we will serve the LORD" (Joshua 24:15).

It can be said of his leadership that "Israel served the LORD all the days of Joshua, and all the days of the elders that outlived Joshua, and which had known all the works of the LORD, that he had done for Israel" (verse 31).

The book of **Judges** takes its name from the activities of a number of judges of Israel. It is thought that Samuel wrote this book. The judges were chosen by God to be His deputies, since He was the King of Israel. Four of these judges are listed among the *heroes of faith* found in Hebrews 11:32. They are Gideon, Barak, Samson, and Jephthah. The book covers the history of the first 350 years in the Promised Land—or from the death of Joshua to the ascension of Saul to the throne as the first king of Israel.

Judges contains some of the Scriptures' ugliest stories—stories of murder, torture, arson, and rape. It's not pretty, but it is honest. It's an explicit account of just what went wrong with God's people during a critical period in their national history. The heathen neighbors, to whom they were to be God's ambassadors, were an evil influence on them.

The book emphasizes how God raised *men of the hour* to meet specifically each crucial issue. When the people cried out in despair, God called forth a "judge" to deliver them from their oppressors.

As I read many incidents recorded in Bible history, I often think to myself: "If I had been on the planning committee of what went into the Bible, I'd surely have skipped many of these horrible experiences." Then I begin to compare

Mining for Gold

the ancient history of many thousands of years with the short history of which I've been alive to see and hear about and realize it has not improved—in fact, it grows worse as time goes on. We hear on the news of activities that have taken place in countries such as Cambodia, Rwanda, Sudan, and many other countries that make the Bible horror stories pale in comparison.

The thought comes to mind: "The heart is deceitful above all things, and desperately wicked: who can know it?" (Jer. 17:9). Sometimes our minds have a roller-coaster experience. It is easy to develop a passionate hatred of the events that are taking place and of those who cause them. Then, as we realize that Christ died for them and if they come to Him with repentance He will forgive and save them, we turn our hatred to compassion and love. I am overwhelmed at the mercy, grace, forgiveness, and love of God for the human race. The troublesome phrase "the wrath of God" becomes understandable to me when I realize His wrath is aimed at sin, for it is sin that has *kidnapped* His creation to serve evil. I am willing to accept Bible history as it is recorded in God's Word when I realize the truth of this statement: "It is one of the best evidences of the authenticity of the Scriptures that the truth is not glossed over nor the sins of its chief characters suppressed" (*Testimonies for the Church*, vol. 4, p. 9).

When I was a child growing up, we had special charts laid out to guide us as we read through the Bible. The gross wickedness and immorality was not in our list of chapters to read. The news of today makes me shudder when I think of children who hear it. There is a sacred responsibility of parents and teachers to put today's events in their proper place.

The period of the judges is often called the *dark ages* of Hebrew history, which is the story of disobedience, corruption, and disaster. Yet, in this book can be seen God's long-suffering, mercy, and justice beautifully portrayed.

Ruth, according to Jewish tradition, was written by the prophet Samuel. It is a jewel of a story sandwiched between the many unpleasant tales of the judges and the saga of Samuel, Saul, and David in 1 Samuel. Ruth is a literary and spiritual masterpiece. It is a *threefold* love story that doesn't use the word *love*.

The book deals with the family of Elimelech, a man of Bethlehem, who was forced to take his wife, Naomi, and two sons to Moab during a severe famine. This story reveals how Ruth—a Moabitess and heathen woman—learned to know the true God through the faithfulness of a pious Hebrew mother-in-law. This is the *first* part of the threefold love story.

When Ruth's husband died, she was free to return to her own people, but she chose instead to cast her lot with God's people. She refused to return to her idolatrous kindred. After all of the men of the family had died, Ruth joined Naomi when she returned to her home in Bethlehem. Ruth expressed her choice to Naomi in these beautiful words: "Intreat me not to leave thee, or to return from following after thee: for whither thou goest, I will go; and where thou lodgest, I will lodge: thy people shall be my people, and thy God my God: Where thou diest, will I die, and there will I be buried: the LORD do so to me, and more also, if ought but death part thee and me" (Ruth 1:16, 17). This book gives a lovely picture of the manners and customs of ancient life.

The *second* part of the threefold love story features Ruth and Boaz. Ruth later married Boaz—a wealthy landowner of Bethlehem and near-kindred to Naomi. Ruth became the mother of Obed, the grandfather of David. Thus, she became one of the ancestors of Jesus, the Savior.

The *third* part of this love story focuses on Ruth's simple faith, hope, and love. It shows how God cares for those who put their trust in Him, and it proved that He loved the Gentiles and would have them obey and serve Him even as He did Israel. Ruth is a love story based on redemption.

1 and 2 Samuel appeared as one volume in all Hebrew manuscripts. When the Old Testament was translated into Greek in about the third century, it was divided into two books.

Samuel is the principle figure in the first part, beginning with his miraculous birth and childhood. For this reason his name was attached to the book. The name Samuel means "asked of God" (see 1 Samuel 1). Nathan, Gad, and others are mentioned as the authors most likely to have written this book. Included in the book of 1 Samuel are the stories of Samuel and Eli, David's anointing, David and Goliath, David and Jonathan, the death of Samuel, and Saul's attempts to kill David. This book covers the period from Judges to the united kingdoms of Israel, including the last judgeship—that of Samuel—to the first king—Saul.

Because of the unrest and turmoil of the nation, Samuel wanted to do away with the evils of the day, and he devoted his life to reformation. Among his accomplishments was the establishment of the schools of the prophets. Samuel was seer (prophet) and judge for more than twenty years. When he grew old and his sons proved to be unfaithful leaders, the people clamored for a government like that of the nations around them. God had been their King, and this request was very displeasing to Him and to Samuel. However, Saul—a handsome, tall man from the tribe of Benjamin—was chosen as their king. His modesty and good character soon turned to jealousy and rebellion. He was rash in his judgment and became very wicked.

The Lord had Samuel secretly anoint David, of the tribe of Judah, as the king. David became the hero of the nations' warriors. This made Saul jealous, and he relentlessly pursued and persecuted David. The book closes with Saul committing suicide when he was defeated in a battle with the Philistines.

2 Samuel begins with David's coronation as king of Israel at Hebron and extends to the anointing of his son Solomon forty years later. David's story is the longest biography in the Old Testament. He is mentioned in the Bible 860 times—more than any other Bible character—in twenty-nine different books of the Bible.

David reigned about forty years. He was responsible for great achievements as well as the gravest blunders and sins. His life was anything but perfect. But when he sinned and was reproved, he repented, confessed his guilt, and showed sincere repentance by a changed life.

It was after his honest confession of his disgraceful conduct with Bathsheba and his planned murder of her husband, Uriah, that he was called a man after God's own heart (Acts 13:22). This humility of spirit and sincere willingness to do right was what made him precious in the sight of God. Psalm 32 and 51 reveal his deep, heartfelt repentance. David was the greatest of the kings of Israel, and during his reign and that of his son, Solomon, the nation enjoyed its greatest glory and prosperity as an earthly kingdom.

1 and 2 Kings, in the original Hebrew language, formed one book. They are a sequel to 1 and 2 Samuel and should be read as a continuation of the history of the Hebrew nation. They record the events of the reign of the kings of Judah and Israel covering a period of 400 years. These books are probably two of the most important books of history in the world.

Because of David's great love for God, he had a strong desire to build a beautiful, magnificent temple to honor and worship Him. God forbade him from building the temple because he was a man of war and bloodshed; yet, he devotedly and zealously gathered much of the material needed for it. God asked David's son Solomon to build it during his reign. Knowing his son would prosper if he kept close to God, David's last charge to Solomon was for the new king to be strong and "shew thyself a man; and keep the charge of the LORD thy God, to walk in his ways, to keep his statutes" (1 Kings 2:2, 3).

Several of David's sons tried to get the throne even though God had already made the decision as to who the next king would be. This treason caused loss of life and much grief to David and the kingdom.

When God asked Solomon what he desired as a gift, he pleased God by humbly asking for wisdom to guide the nation righteously. This was a period of Israel's glory. Yet, it was not too long before there was division, decline, and failure. Solomon reigned for forty years as his father David had done. Sad to say, Solomon was not the humble man of his early reign. He put heavy burdens on the people, one of which was excessive taxation. When the people asked his son Rehoboam, who reigned after him, to reduce the tribute, he refused to do so. This resulted in a revolt. Only the tribes of Benjamin and Judah remained loyal to the house of David, while the other ten tribes made Jeroboam their king with headquarters in Samaria. The Hebrew nation became divided into two separate kingdoms—Judah with two tribes, and Israel with the other ten tribes.

The record of most of the kings of both kingdoms was that they did "that which was evil in the sight of the Lord." To read of a king who "did that which was right in the sight of the Lord" was a rare and beautiful report. The righteous kings made a diligent effort to put a stop to idol worship. Unfortunately, often their efforts for good did not last when a wicked king followed them. This was true in both Judah and Israel. Though the authors of many of the historical books are not known, it is believed these histories of the reign of the kings of Israel and Judah were compiled under the direction of Ezra.

Mining for Gold

1 Kings includes the well-known and stirring stories about the prophet Elijah—one of the most outstanding men among the prophets who was translated without seeing death. His successor, Elisha, continued the mighty religious reformation begun by Elijah.

A very interesting record in 1 Kings 13:21 tells of the only miracle in the Old Testament that was performed by a man after his death! Because of the wickedness of His own people, God allowed the Assyrian armies to destroy the kingdom of Israel and take the people into captivity. Later, after the destruction of the temple in Jerusalem, the kingdom of Judah was taken captive to Babylon.

The chronological genealogy lists found in the Bible may not be our favorite reading. Some names, for me, are unpronounceable, yet they are vital to a historical study. There is the beauty of grace in Jesus' chronology.

1 and 2 Chronicles, as with 1 and 2 Samuel and 1 and 2 Kings, was originally a single volume and was called *Things or Events of the Days*. These two books are, to a large extent, a repetition of the record found in 1 Samuel and 2 Kings. Reading the historical records, I wearied of the wars and wickedness of God's people when kings "did evil in the sight of God." Often after I prayed for a personal blessing, my eyes were opened to the mercy, forgiveness, and grace God shows all the way through.

2 Chronicles is principally a history of the reigns of the kings of Judah from Solomon to Zedekiah and the destruction of Jerusalem by the armies of Nebuchadnezzar. Here we also find a copy of the remarkable dedicatory prayer that Solomon offered to God at the time the temple was dedicated.

Solomon's fame became known extensively and many from distant lands came to learn of his wisdom. His wisdom was not of his origin but given to him by the Lord to bring Him glory and make His truth known in the earth.

We read a heartfelt invitation from God to His people in these dark days: "If my people, which are called by my name, shall humble themselves, and pray, and seek my face, and turn from their wicked ways; then will I hear from heaven, and will forgive their sin, and will heal their land" (2 Chron. 7:14).

I found a remarkable report of God's grace to a very wicked king who was so brazen in his wickedness that he built altars for heathen deities in the house

Think on These Things

of the Lord! Of him, it is written: "So Manasseh made Judah and the inhabitants of Jerusalem to err, and to do worse than the heathen, whom the LORD had destroyed before the children of Israel" (2 Chron. 33:9). Yet, when Manasseh "was in affliction, he besought the LORD his God, and humbled himself greatly before the God of his fathers" (verse 12). He prayed, was forgiven, and sought to rectify his wicked reign before he died. At my first reading of this report of forgiveness, I was angry that a king who was so responsible for the sins of his people will be saved and many of them lost. When I was reminded that each person has his own choice to follow evil or good, I found this experience of God's grace so awesome—and I shall always be in *wonder*!

The question of why God ordered so many wars to do away with heathen nations has always been a great perplexity to His followers. God doesn't need me to defend Him, but when I consider what could have been His reasoning, it gives me confidence that He does everything right. God was in the business of starting a new nation from Israel slaves who had been in bondage in the land of Egypt—an idol-worshipping nation—for 400 years. This plan of a new nation to represent Him in Satan's territory was part of God's promise to Abraham, Isaac, Jacob, and their families—who were called Hebrews, Jews, or Israelites.

The possibility of His *chosen* being influenced by the heathen nations to whom they were to be ambassadors was a great possibility. This, in fact, happened over and over, and like a rotten apple it caused all around it to become rotten. They apostatized repeatedly, including intermarriage with heathens, worship of idols, and immoral practices of the nations around them.

The only way to save the spirituality of Israel was to destroy these wicked nations, including men, women, and children. Though it sounds extremely cruel, I trust that God does things *right*. Those nations had fully rejected the God of heaven and filled their cup of wickedness. He will give justice to all, for He knows the hearts of all and takes into consideration where people were born (Ps. 87:4-6).

From the book *Old Testament Grace* by Jon Dybdahl, I gleaned some thoughts on the wars Israel was involved in: "War is terrible. How can it teach of God's grace? The answer is that the best of Israel's battles were the strangest fights you've ever heard about. The worst of Israel's battles sounded like regular battles, but these special battles—the times when God does the fighting—are different. Just how different they are becomes apparent as they are studied.

"Let's briefly review some of these special wars and corresponding Bible verses:

The Exodus: After the night when the first-born of Egypt died, Pharoah allowed his slave-laborers, the Israelites, to leave Egypt. On second thought, Pharoah thought of this loss, mustered his army, and pursued them almost catching up as they were encamped by the sea. Terrified, the people asked if it wouldn't have been better to die in Egypt! Moses responded: 'Do not be afraid. Stand firm and you will see the deliverance the Lord will bring you today. The Egyptians you see today you will never see again. The Lord will fight for you; you need only to be still.' Exodus 14:13, 14. When the Red Sea opened and the Israelites went over on dry ground, the Egyptians followed and were drowned when the sea closed over them. Moses and his sister, Miriam, then led the people in this song of praise: 'I will sing to the Lord, for He is highly exalted. The horse and its rider He has hurled into the sea. The Lord is my strength and my song; He has become my salvation. He is my God, and I will praise Him.' Exodus 15:1, 2.

"This is the way God wanted to operate for Israel. The closer they stayed to Him, the less actual fighting they did. When they wandered from the gracious Lord, the more they had to do of the actual fighting. The more dependence there was on God, the more sure the victory." These battles glorified God, not the generals or the army.

In Judges 6 and 7, we have recorded another battle in which God did the fighting. He chose Gideon from the weakest clan in the tribe of Manasseh and the least in a family to become a "mighty warrior" in a war with the Midianites. The army of 32,000 was reduced to 300 to show that God was the Deliverer. Their strange *weapons* were trumpets and empty jars with torches inside. Jon Dybdahl describes what happened next: "The 300 surrounded the enemy camp, sounded their trumpets, broke their jars, waved their torches, and shouted. The enemy troops in confusion began fleeing and killing each other. A huge mop-up operation followed the great victory" (*Old Testament Grace*). Time and again in the book of Judges God delivered the Israelites graciously and fully even though they strayed from Him numerous times. What a gracious God.

Another thrilling example of God gaining a victory for the Israelites is found in 2 Chronicles 20. King Jehoshaphat panicked when he heard about the Moabite *coalition* that was coming against his nation—the Israelites. He gathered all Judah to the temple and prayed for deliverance, confessing their lack of power and the contrasting power of God. A Levite prophesied: "Be not afraid nor dismayed by reason of this great multitude; for the battle is not yours, but God's. . . . Ye shall not need to fight in this battle: set yourselves, stand ye still, and see the salvation of the LORD with you, O Judah and Jerusalem: fear not, nor by dismayed; to morrow go out against them: for the LORD will be with you" (2 Chron. 20:15-17). Jehoshaphat bowed his face to the ground along with all the Israelites to worship God, and the choir praised God with a loud voice.

Early the next morning when Israel went to battle, the choir went first! They praised God for the splendor of His holiness as they sang: "Praise the LORD; for his mercy endureth for ever" (verse 21). The Lord set ambushes against the invading army, and the enemy fought among themselves. When the Israelites came over the hill and looked down, the Scripture says: "They looked unto the multitude, and, behold, they were dead bodies fallen to the earth, and none escaped!" (verse 24). The victory was God's.

One of the strangest Israelite wars had some most exciting experiences preceding it. Joshua, the leader who took Moses' place when he died, sent two spies to search out the city of Jericho. Rahab, a woman who lived in Jericho, saved their lives by hiding them under some flax on the roof of her house. Men from Jericho were looking for the spies. Rahab took this great risk because she knew that the God of the Israelites was the true God and that He had given their land to His people. After hearing of the history of God's guidance since the Israelites left Egypt, the hearts of people were fearful of them.

Due to Rahab's kindness, the spies promised protection for herself and all her relatives who were in her house during the coming battle. When the spies were let down from their hiding place by a scarlet cord from the roof of her house, they hid in the mountains until it was safe to go back and give a report of their findings. A scarlet cord was hung from the window of her house to let the Israelites warriors know what household to save.

The Israelites were sure of God's presence as they followed His instructions.

Mining for Gold

God performed a miracle as He opened up the Jordan River so the entire nation could cross on dry ground. When their enemies heard of their river march, their hearts melted in fear. God told Joshua to have twelve men bring stones from the middle of the dry river path and build an altar—a memorial. It was to remind them and future generations of the marvelous act of God on their behalf.

God's directed the army to march around the city with the Levite priests leading the way with the Ark of the Covenant and the warriors following. They were to march around the city and then repeat it for seven days. Other than the priests blowing horns, the warriors were to remain silent until they were ordered to shout. That order came on the seventh day of marching and the walls of Jericho came tumbling down. The warriors then stormed the city with victory, saving Rahab and those in her house with the scarlet cord. For more details, see Joshua 2 through 6.

I would like to add this thought: when one considers the grace God expressed for those living in wicked Sodom, through Abraham's pleas for ten righteous people living there, as well as the grace God showed repentant Nineveh, we should have no question about God's love and mercy for all people. He is merciful and just!

There will be one last great war God will sadly wage. It will be a war to end all wars. The final destruction of the wicked is described as "his [God's] strange act" (Isa. 28:21). "The Lord . . . is longsuffering to us-ward, not willing that any should perish, but that all should come to repentance" (2 Peter 3:9). "I have no pleasure in the death of the wicked" (Eze. 33:11). It is alien to God's character to inflict pain, suffering, and death upon His creatures. Yet, at the same time, He will "by no means clear the guilty" (Ex. 34:7). God created the earth with perfection. God has given His creatures *free will*. Both Lucifer, some of the angels, Adam, and Eve chose their own way, not God's, and brought sin and suffering upon the world. The way of obedience leads to life—a rich life. The other way leads eventually to a shallow existence ending in death. "He will make an utter end: affliction shall not rise up the second time" (Nahum 1:9). Disobedience and its outcome will never happen again. The final war is to cleanse the earth and prepare it for the new earth, which will be the home of the saved (Rev. 20:7-9).

Think on These Things

My discovery from the study of Scripture shows God's love, patience, mercy, grace, and justice. This gives me assurance that the wars in Old Testament history would not have had to be fought if Israel had been, at all times, the ambassadors they were sent out to be on their way from their bondage in Egypt to the Promised Land. The surrounding countries through which the Hebrews had to pass did have a period of grace as they witnessed what the true God was doing for His chosen along the way: a pillar of fire by night and a cloud for protection from the sun by day, manna from heaven for food, water from a gushing rock, and many other evidences of God's love, care, and power. The main problem was that all these people did not always choose to accept God's plan for them.

With the failure of man caught in the great controversy of pleasing God or doing Satan's bidding, God constantly had to alter His plans. Through the twists and turns of thousands of years, He will finally bring war to an end. Meanwhile, the wars were fought, and God did show His love and mercy to the heathen nations in such stories as before the destruction of Sodom (Gen. 18:23-33); the warning given through Jonah to Nineveh (Jonah 1:1, 2); His mercy to a repentant wicked nation (though their repentance did not last long); and His mercy for a prostitute in Jericho, Rahab, as she confessed her belief in the true God of the Hebrews. God saved her life and that of her family (Joshua 2). Time and again, we notice that God has never been a "respecter of persons." Yet He did have something to say about the Jewish nation: "Then what advantage has the Jew? Or what is the value of circumcision? Much in every way. To begin with, the Jews are entrusted with the oracles of God. What if some where unfaithful? Does their faithlessness nullify the faithfulness of God? By no means! Let God be true though every man be false" (Rom. 3:1-4, RSV; see also Deut. 7:6-9). With every privilege comes great responsibility! This could be said of Christ's followers in every age, especially the current one!

Consider the verse: "But thou, O Lord, art a God full of compassion, and gracious, long suffering, and plenteous in mercy and truth" (Ps. 86:15). What more can be said? I am convinced of God's fairness and love. One day, the whole universe will admit this fact! "That at the name of Jesus every knee should bow, of things in heaven, and things in earth, and things under the earth;

and that every tongue should confess that Jesus Christ is Lord, to the glory of God the Father" (Phil. 2:10, 11).

I can hardly wait to sing in heaven the "song of Moses the servant of God, and the song of the Lamb, saying, Great and marvelous are thy works, Lord God Almighty; just and true are thy ways, thou King of saints" (Rev. 15:3).

Both **Ezra** and **Nehemiah** were written by the men whose name they bear. In the original Hebrew manuscripts, they appear as one book. The history of these books covers the restoration of the Jews from their captivity of more than half a century of bondage in Babylon to the subsequent rebuilding of Jerusalem, its temple, and its walls.

Ezra was a learned priest and spiritual leader of the Jews who returned from the land of their captivity to Palestine and was one of the most important figures there. He taught in the schools of the prophets and is credited for compiling the books of Moses, the historical, poetical, and the prophetic books called "the writings," which constituted the Old Testament at that time. He was a godly man: "Ezra had prepared his heart to seek the law of the LORD, and to do it" (Ezra 7:10).

Nehemiah was born while in captivity. He was the cupbearer to the king and given a leave of absence by the king to oversee the work of rebuilding the walls of Jerusalem. He was a man of action and few words. The surrounding heathen nations gave the builders much trouble. At one time, when *urged to come down and talk business* with these people, Nehemiah answered that he, and his people, were doing such a great work they could not bother to come down to them!

The rebuilding of the temple walls and the very time the Jews were accomplishing it in was prophesied in Isaiah and Jeremiah. Also predicted were the kings that would authorize the Jews to go back to Palestine and would actually be involved with financing this great undertaking. Artaxerxes Longimanus, King of Persia, was one of them. It was also prophesied, long before the birth of Cyrus, calling him by name, that God had this mission for him to perform (Isa. 44:28). He issued the decree to rebuild Jerusalem in 457 BC.

Both Ezra and Nehemiah were passionate about their love and service for

God and their great responsibility to inspire God's people to reformation. The failure of the people to keep separate from the idol worshipers around them and inter-marrying with them was of great concern to them and their keen sense of right. So troubling was it for Ezra that he rent his garments, plucked off the hair of his head, and sat down appalled. Later, he fell on his knees and spread out his hands to God with a heartfelt prayer of forgiveness for his people (Ezra 9:3-6).

Nehemiah, acting as governor, had a different way to show his righteous anger over their sin: "I contended with them, and cursed them, and smote certain of them, and plucked off their hair" (Neh. 13:25). Nehemiah made God his source of strength and confidence. He was a man of prayer and a tireless worker. Ezra and Nehemiah illustrate, by a series of examples, how a few people can do great things for God when led by God-fearing, sincere, unselfish, and determined leaders.

Esther is the second and last book of the Bible that bears a woman's name. Her original name was Hadassah, but she probably came to be known as Esther about the time of her marriage to Ahasuerus, king of the Medo-Persian Empire. God is never mentioned in this book, but His overruling hand is discerned throughout the story.

The book of Esther is a dramatic story of how God used a courageous young woman of surpassing beauty to save her people at a time of crisis when extermination threatened them. The story gives a vivid picture of the Jews in exile, of the hostility of their non-Jewish enemies in Persia, and how Esther, later, risked her life to save her people from total destruction. It was said to Esther by her cousin, Mordecai, "Who knoweth whether thou art come to the kingdom for such a time as this?" (Esther 4:14).

She declared her willingness: "so will I go in unto the king, which is not according to the law: and if I perish, I perish" (verse 16). May I suggest you stop your reading of this brief description and right now read this short thrilling story!

Books of Poetry

The next five books— Job, Psalms, Proverbs, Ecclesiastes, and Song of Solomon—are called the books of poetry.

The book of **Job** is a worthy subject for a poem. It is believed to have been written by Moses about the same time of his writing Genesis while he was a shepherd in Midian. It is thought that Job was a contemporary of Isaac. He was a wealthy, God-fearing chieftain of Uz, located on the edge of the Arabian Desert.

Unbeknown to Job was the controversy over his love and loyalty to God. He was accused by Satan of serving God because everything about him was protected by God and going exceedingly well. Satan was given permission, by God, to test Job's sincerity. He lost children, property, suffered intense physical pain, and was misjudged by his friends. In addition, his wife tried to discourage his trust in God.

Down through the ages of time, Job's reaction to these terrible, unexplainable events has inspired many God-fearing people who have had to go through intense suffering. "Naked came I out of my mother's womb, and naked shall I return thither: the LORD gave, and the LORD hath taken away; blessed be the name of the LORD" (Job 1:21). "He knoweth the way that I take: when he hath tried me, I shall come forth as gold" (Job 23:10).

Other inspiring thoughts from Job at this time of great trial are: "Though he slay me, yet will I trust in him" (Job 13:15), and "For I know that my redeemer liveth, and that he shall stand at the latter day upon the earth: and though after my skin worms destroy this body, yet in my flesh shall I see God: whom I shall see for myself, and mine eyes shall behold, and not another; though my reins be consumed within me" (Job 19:25-27).

After all Job's chastening, God turned the tide, and his prosperity was given back to him double when he prayed for his friends. One of the grandest contributions of this book is its picture of God.

The book of **Psalms** is a collection of 150 sacred poems, which were sung as hymns by God's people. David, the sweet singer of Israel, composed 73 of them. There are eight names appearing as authors including Moses, David, Asaph, and Solomon. Psalms is a book of devotion. It is the longest book in the Bible and contains the longest chapter—Psalm 119—and also the shortest—Psalm 117. The book has been called a *treasury of prayer, praise, and adoration*—a Bible in miniature. Almost every aspect of man's relationship to God is depicted in this book. In it can be found words for the sick and suffering, poor and needy, prisoner and exiles, people in danger, people facing persecution, and sinners.

The psalms of David pass through the whole range of experiences, from the depths of conscious guilt and self-condemnation to the loftiest faith and most exalted communion with God. David's life record declares that God's love and mercy can reach to the deepest depths and faith will lift up the repenting soul to share the adoption of the sons of God (Ps. 51). "Of all the assurances which His word contains, it is one of the strongest testimonies to the faithfulness, the justice, and the covenant mercy of God" (*Patriarchs and Prophets,* p. 754).

Many of David's psalms start with the depths of despair and end in the heights of praise and adoration. He knew from experience that finding and expressing thanksgiving and praise to God lifted him from his present difficult experiences to the *throne on high* where his strength and courage came from.

The poems in Psalms abound with prophecies about the first and second advents of Jesus. They are quoted by Jesus or the apostles at least seventy times. Psalms 22 and 69 foretell various details of Christ's suffering and death and speak of His coming in glory to judge the world.

Some of the most quoted and most loved portions of Holy Scripture are in Psalms. *The shepherd psalm* has been committed to memory more than any other. Psalm 46 and 91 have been a comfort and help to God's children in times of great danger.

Psalm 104 celebrates creation. Many psalms repeat the history of the wanderings in the wilderness and the guidance God gave the children of promise.

It is difficult for me to limit my sharing, but Psalm 19 is one of my favorite psalms. As I look up at the heavens on a starry night, a mix of humbleness and awe flood my soul and the beauty of this psalm comes to my mind. I often say it aloud: "The heavens declare the glory of God; and the firmament sheweth his handywork. Day unto day uttereth speech, and night unto night sheweth knowledge" (Ps. 19:1, 2). The result of this creation meditation makes the last verse a humble prayer: "Let the words of my mouth, and the meditation of my heart, be acceptable in thy sight, O LORD, my strength, and my redeemer" (verse 14).

Proverbs means *wise sayings*. King Solomon contributed the largest number of them. There are two types of wisdom—the wisdom of the world and the wisdom that comes from God. Proverbs is a treasury of practical ethics and wisdom. Nearly every relationship in life is covered. It abounds with instruction and counsel for young and old, single and married, children, neighbors, kings and their subjects, employers and employees, businessmen, farmers, scholars, artisans—in a word, *everybody*!

Many people, including ourselves at times, may shy away from advice from others, even if it comes from a wise, experienced, loving person, or even if it comes from the Bible! If we read the book of Proverbs, we will be impressed at how many times it tells the reader to *listen up* and compliments those who do. One of my favorites is Proverbs 15:31-33: "He whose ear heeds wholesome admonition will abide among the wise: He who ignores instruction despises himself, but he who heeds admonition gains understanding. The fear of the Lord is instruction in wisdom and humility goes before honor" (RSV).

George H. Taggart, in his book *Happiness Is*, could add this thought to the above: "A true friend will point out your defects and offer suggestions on how you can overcome them. If you accept these suggestions in the right spirit, you will keep your friends and improve your character. Thus, true friendship is one of the best ways to achieve self-development and growth" (p. 31). Check out another favorite found in Proverbs 4:23: "Above all else, guard your affections, for they influence everything else in your life" (TLB).

These inspired maxims contain principles of holy living and high endeavor needed by men and women in every walk of life. The secret of true wisdom is revealed in these words: "The fear of the LORD is the beginning of wisdom" (Prov. 1:7). The promise is as follows: "Incline thine ear unto wisdom, and apply thine heart to understanding; Yea, if thou criest after knowledge, and liftest up thy voice for understanding; If thou seekest her as silver, and searchest for her as for hid treasures; Then shalt thou understand the fear of the LORD, and find the knowledge of God" (Prov. 2:2-5). Proverbs supplies its *own directions for its use*!

Reading the forgoing verses has put in my mind and heart a beautiful, positive, sacred definition to the phrase "fear of the Lord" instead of a *shaking in your boots* type of fear of God. I've noticed that wherever I've read this phrase in the Bible it is always a positive experience. Here's what it says to me: the fear of the Lord is to maintain an attitude of such deep, awesome reverence and respect for my Maker, more than anything else in my life—and more than life itself—that I want to obey and please Him. It would trouble me to no end to disappoint Him by wrong actions. In response to the unbounded love, mercy, and grace of an Omnipotent and Omnipresent being for such a beloved sinner, my *fear of the Lord* turns into a joyful, sacred *hallelujah!*

Ecclesiastes means *the preacher*. What a sermon Solomon felt compelled to deliver during the last years of his life. When realizing his mistakes, he repented and turned back to God. Chastened in spirit and enfeebled in body, he turned, wearied and thirsty, from the world's broken cisterns to drink again at the sacred foundation of divine truth.

Though Solomon was preeminent among Hebrew kings, both in wisdom and in temporal prosperity, he relates how all of these advantages failed to provide truth and lasting happiness. This book has been called the greatest collection of pessimism and skepticism in literature. Yet, there are scattered chapters and verses that are very beautiful and give wise counsel. Among my favorites is Ecclesiastes 3:11, 14: "He has made everything beautiful in its time, also He has put eternity into man's mind; so that he cannot find out what God has done from the beginning to the end. . . . I know that whatever God does endures forever, nothing can be added to it, nor anything taken from it. God has made it so in order that man should fear before Him" (RSV; see also James 1:17).

Solomon knew he had turned from the wisdom God had given him; yet he also had confidence in God that He would do everything just right. I especially treasure the thought that God has put eternity in our hearts! No doubt that was an invitation that turned Solomon's heart back to God.

In the end, Solomon sets forth practical suggestions of how to have a sound philosophy of life, the purpose of man's existence, and His duty to God and man. In his closing words of Ecclesiastes, Solomon says to the youth: "Remember now thy Creator in the days of thy youth, while the evil days come not, nor the years draw nigh, when thou shalt say, I have no pleasure in them." (Eccl. 12:1). He was eager to spare others these bitter experiences in life. His final words are no doubt the wisest he ever wrote: "Let us hear the conclusion of the whole matter: Fear God, and keep his commandments: for this is the whole duty of man. For God shall bring every work into judgment, with every secret thing, whether it be good, or whether it be evil" (verses 13 and 14).

Song of Solomon was written by Solomon and is an Oriental love poem glorifying wedded love. It is a dialogue or song that describes the physical joys of love in graphic detail. This is the only book in the Bible with love as its sole theme. Some experts say Song of Solomon is nothing more than a collection of love songs. Yet, the Jews interpreted it as picturing the love of God for His people, and many theologians agree.

The book abounds in metaphors and portrays the love existing between Christ and His church under the figures of a lover and his beloved. To understand this book, we must consider the Redeemer as the loving bridegroom and the church as His bride. Paul presents the church as a chaste virgin espoused to Christ (2 Cor. 11:2; Eph. 5:22-27). His beloved church is presented as one "fair as the moon, clear as the sun, and terrible as an army with banners" (S. of Sol. 6:10). Over it is unfurled God's banner of love (S. of Sol. 2:4).

King Solomon was well-acquainted with the plan of redemption and the privileges of the Christian life. He speaks of the coming King as the "beloved," the one who is "altogether lovely," "the rose of Sharon," and "the lily of the valley," the "chiefest among ten thousand," and the "well of living water" (S. of Sol. 2:8; 5:16; 2:1; 5:10; 4:15). Incidentally, Solomon's description of spring in chapter 2, verses 11 through 13, is unsurpassed in literature.

Books of Major Prophets

The prophets, chosen of God, have always been among my favorite Bible characters even though some of their messages proved painful (see Heb. 4:12). However, painful reproof can be a blessing if heeded.

The prophets were very unpopular servants of God. Most of them died because of their loyalty to God. Each of them was aware of the fate of other prophets before them. Is it any wonder that some made excuses? Moses couldn't speak well enough (Ex. 4:10-12). Jeremiah was just a child (Jer. 1:6). But their love for God won out and caused them to obey.

I greatly admire the willingness of some like Samuel who said, "Speak LORD; for thy servant heareth" (1 Sam. 3:9). And Isaiah, who when called of God, and asked, "Whom shall I send, and who will go for us?" responded and said, "Here am I; send me" (Isa. 6:8). Much later in time, Mary surrendered willingly to fit into God's plan for the birth of the Savior: "Behold the handmaid of the Lord; be it unto me according to thy word" (Luke 1:38). God gives good advice in defense of His humble servants, the prophets: "Despise not prophesyings. Prove all things; hold fast that which is good" (1 Thess. 5:20, 21).

Isaiah wrote the book bearing his name. As a young man, he was given a glorious vision of the Lord of hosts whom the seraphims (angels) described as they cried, "Holy, holy, holy is the LORD of hosts: the whole earth is full of his glory" (Isa. 6:3). This experience gave Isaiah his direction in life and he said: "Woe is me! For I am undone" (verse 5). And when the Lord called him, he quickly responded positively: "Here am I, send me" (verse 8). This was his call to prophetic ministry. Then God said: "Go, and tell this people" (verse 9). The prophecy of Isaiah is one of the world's greatest masterpieces.

When Isaiah answered God, "Here am I, send me," he didn't even know his assignment! He did not respond because he had confidence in his own skills. He responded because he knew he was unworthy but God is worthy. Isaiah knew he was powerless but God is all powerful to do a mission Isaiah may not have chosen. He was willing to do it because God chose it, and likewise, if we are willing, God will make us able.

For sixty years he served as a prophet of God under the reign of five kings. How joyfully he served as "the gospel prophet!" He spoke often about Christ and His love for man. This book is filled with beautiful portrayals of the person and mission of Christ and of God's glorious purpose for His church.

Isaiah lived in a troubled world. For both Judah and Israel, it was an era of peril and crises. The people of God had fallen deeply into ways of sin. It was during Isaiah's time that the northern kingdom of Israel fell to Assyria. Isaiah spent his life trying to get Judah to become acquainted with God. The last few chapters of Isaiah prophesy of God's spiritual salvation and are among the most beloved and often quoted in the Bible. The book means "salvation of Jehovah" and is filled with messages of detailed prophecies of the coming of Christ as the Messiah, His kingdom on this earth, the coming destruction of Jerusalem, and the new heavens and new earth to come.

The prophecies of Isaiah often have a dual application, referring not only to the immediate future but to time far ahead. Some of his prophecies of a Savior are applicable to both Christ's first and second coming.

There are present-day Jews who do not believe in Christ as the Messiah for they say He did not fulfill the prophecies they expected and wanted Him to fulfill. The prophecies of Christ's coming are an example. The main chapter that describes in detail Jesus' first coming (Isa. 53) is not accepted by the orthodox Jew. It is hated and unread by them. "He came unto His own and His own received Him not" (John 1:11; see also Isa. 53:2). This chapter in Isaiah gives a tragic description of the treatment of our Savior at His first advent, but we also find woven in this chapter, along with verses in Isaiah 65:17-25, glorious details of Christ's second coming, descriptions of the new heavens and new earth. Even our joyful activities in the peaceful place are described.

George Frederick Handel must have been captivated by the awesome beauty of these prophecies in Isaiah and other Old Testament verses. He shut himself away with a holy ambition and worked day and night to compose the lofty strains of *The Messiah*. It was, without doubt, inspired of God, and is a deeply moving mental picture, in words and music, of the life of Christ.

The reverence felt by the audience at its first London performance inspired a standing ovation led by King George II and has continued to inspire audiences with spiritual uplifting. The melody and message gave to this work of sacred art the reputation of being the finest oratorios in the English language. That's quite a testimony for not only the great musician and composer but for the awesome prophecies found in God's Word.

According to ancient tradition, Isaiah died a martyr's death, being sawed in pieces at the hands of the wicked King Manasseh. In 1947 the entire book of Isaiah, with the exception of two small breaks, was discovered in a cave northwest of the Dead Sea. Since then, some seventy more transcripts have been discovered. Isaiah is quoted more in the New Testament than any other prophet. He is quoted fifty times in eleven books.

Through Isaiah the Lord made gracious and loving appeals to His disobedient people (which include His followers of all time) to repent and return to Him. Best known is this invitation: "Come now, and let us reason together, saith the LORD: though your sins be as scarlet, they shall be as white as snow; though they be red like crimson, they shall be as wool" (Isa. 1:18). Read the entire book for a moving spiritual feast!

Jeremiah and the book he wrote bearing his name hold a very special place in my heart. He was born into the tribe of Levi. He was only between 15 and 20 years old when God called him to serve as a prophet. The Lord said to him: "Before I formed thee in the belly I knew thee; and before thou camest forth out of the womb I sanctified thee, and I ordained thee a prophet unto the nations. Then said I, Ah, Lord GOD! behold, I cannot speak: for I am a child" (Jer. 1:5, 6). Check out God's reply to Jeremiah and how He prepared the young man to prophesy to a nation in crisis for forty turbulent years (Jer. 1:4-10.)

Jeremiah's outspoken demands for morality and his unflinching declaration of God's message to the kingdom of Judah to surrender to Babylon and thus save Jerusalem from destruction by fire brought him the scorn of other prophets who where proclaiming peace and safety. The false prophets were more popular than the true prophet.

The suggestion of a death decree for Jeremiah ended up with him being imprisoned in a miserable dungeon where the prophet sunk in the mire. He was rescued by an Ethiopian who let down cords into the dungeon to draw the prophet out. At another time, his written messages were destroyed by the king in the fire of his hearth. Later, God asked him to have another copy made of his words (Jer. 36:1-32).

Jeremiah's ministry continued until after the destruction of Jerusalem (588 BC). He remained in Palestine and prophesied there for a time. Later, he was taken to Egypt by a band of rebellious countrymen, and there he also prophesied (Jer. 43). He presented messages from the Lord to many different nations in addition to his own.

Jeremiah has been called *the weeping prophet* because of the tears he shed for his wayward people: "Oh that my head were waters, and mine eyes a fountain of tears, that I might weep day and night for the slain of the daughters of my people" (Jer. 9:1). His was the grievous task of prophesying against Judah in the final days of the kingdom before its destruction. He bore messages of reform and revival to five different kings.

Scattered in with the many warnings God gave to His people through Jeremiah are many beautiful words of entreaty, comfort, and love to the wayward, begging them to repent. The books of prophecy are more valuable to me when I understand the loyalty of God's men in spite of being persecuted. What role models they are for God's followers!

Jeremiah wrote **Lamentations** to meet the needs of the people of Judah. The nation was no more and Jerusalem lay in ruins. Its leaders were in chains; its people dead or demoralized. Jeremiah wrote in anguish and sorrow of heart. Yet, he knew the people of Judah thoroughly deserved what had happened to them. They had refused to listen to God's warnings.

At the heart of this sorrowful book, the weeping prophet gives a message of hope: "As I grieve over my loss, yet I still dare to hope when I remember this: The faithful love of the Lord never ends! His mercies never cease. Great is His faithfulness; His mercies begin afresh each morning. I say to myself, 'The Lord is my inheritance; therefore, I will hope in Him!' The Lord is good to those who depend on Him, to those who search for Him. So it is good to wait quietly for salvation from the Lord. And it is good for people to submit at an early age to the yoke of His discipline" (Lam. 3:20-27, NLT). The fact that God was too good to allow Judah's sins to go unpunished, means He's too good not to forgive them. If Judah would repent, they could still have been restored (Lam. 3:25, 26).

Returning from an early morning walk, my son Eric called and shared these verses with me. "It is of the LORD's mercies that we are not consumed, because his compassions fail not. They are new every morning: great is thy faithfulness" (verses 22 and 23). Continue to read Jeremiah's testimony further to verse 26. If you mark your Bible, this verse certainly deserves underlining.

The book of **Ezekiel** bears the name of its author. Ezekiel was a contemporary of Jeremiah, and both were members of the tribe of Levi. He was a youth of seventeen years of age when taken as a captive to Babylon by King Nebuchadnezzar. He was among the second group of captives in 597 BC, while Daniel and his three friends were in the first group in 605 BC.

Ezekiel wrote the prophecies while in captivity. These messages, written over a period of twenty-two years, were given by God to encourage His people to change their ways. Ezekiel was instructed to foretell by means of a variety of solemn messages and symbols (some of them strange—but very descriptive) of the siege and utter destruction of Jerusalem. No doubt the way Ezekiel delivered his messages got the attention and thoughts of the people. There is deep meaning in the messages of this book. Because of the imagery of Ezekiel 28:12-18 in regards to the king of Tyrus, many theologians feel the history of Lucifer (who became Satan) is revealed. Other references to Lucifer and his fate are recorded in Isaiah 14:12-16 and Revelation 12:7-9.

"The word of the Lord came unto me" appears forty-nine times in this book. God called Ezekiel "son of man" more than ninety times during his visions. The best known parts of the book are chapters 1 and 37 in which the prophet saw the wheels and a valley of dry bones.

Ezekiel explained to his people the justice of God in His dealing with both Israel and Judah, and he made it clear that the hand of the Lord had control over the affairs of the world. He foretold that after the captivity a reunited kingdom was to comprise remnants of both Israel and Judah.

The book of Ezekiel is probably one of the most neglected parts of sacred scriptures. Though the book speaks of judgment and destruction, it also portrays the forgiving mercy of God and breathes an atmosphere of hope and renewal for a repentant people. "For I have no pleasure in the death of him that dieth, saith the Lord GOD: wherefore turn yourselves, and live ye" (Eze. 18:32). God has always voted for life—eternal life! In vision, Ezekiel sees the glory of God re-entering a new temple and rebuilt city of Jerusalem. He sees God coming back to dwell among His people.

Though much, or all, of Ezekiel requires deep thinking and study (some of it is beyond my present understanding) many gems nestle in its forty-eight chapters. It is clear that the book describes the longing in God's heart for His chosen people—Israel—and His great disappointment in their rebellion and sins. A special chapter that comes through loud and clear with this message is in chapter 16. I had tears in my eyes as I read that section. Another gem of God's care is recorded in chapter 34. You can no doubt find more.

Another vital truth I found is in Ezekiel 44:23: "And they shall teach my people the difference between the holy and the profane, and cause them to discern between the unclean and the clean." The priests should have been teaching the people about the sin of priests Nadab and Abihu who offered "strange fire" and the result (Lev. 10:1-3). Another example is the death of Uzzah who made an effort to protect the ark of the covenant from falling (1 Chron. 13:1-14). The priests, who knew better, had disregarded the proper way to transport the sacred ark (see Ex. 37:1-5 and 1 Chron. 15:15). There is a lesson for all God's people for all time.

Another vital truth is repeated in two chapters: Ezekiel 18:21-32 and 33:1-19. The message is repeated more than once in chapter 33. The truth is taught that our salvation depends on the outcome of our choices at the end of our lives. Being faithful to the end brings a crown of life (see Rev. 2:10). If an evil person repents and chooses to do God's will to the end, he will be saved. If a righteous person turns from God for the rest of his life, his good deeds will not be remembered—he will be lost.

God's eager plea is this: "Say unto them, as I live, saith the Lord GOD, I have no pleasure in the death of the wicked; but that the wicked turn from his way and live: turn ye, turn ye from your evil ways; for why will ye die, O house of Israel?" (Eze. 33:11). This message is for all—to the end of time. Ezekiel brings out the fact that it is how mankind is at the *finish line* that determines his destiny.

Daniel is the next book, authored by the Hebrew prince Daniel whom the Babylonians took captive. With him were his associates: Shadrach, Meshach, and Abednego. After three years of study in Babylon, these youth entered the service of King Nebuchadnezzar (see Dan. 1). Daniel served that kingdom

Think on These Things

until its last king—Belshazzar—was slain in 528 BC. He also served as prime minister for King Darius who set up a new world government under a Medo-Persian regime. He was still alive in the third year of Cyrus (Dan. 10:1). Each of these kings was much aware of the importance that Daniel placed on serving his God. Daniel wrote his book while in captivity.

The book of Daniel is one of the most readable books of the Bible and has some of the most vivid and exciting stories about Daniel and his three friends. The miraculous escape from the fiery furnace and Daniel in the lion's den have inspired people of all ages for centuries.

Daniel has been called the prophet of dreams. The rise and fall of the earthly kingdoms to the end of time are prophesied in both Daniel and Nebuchadnezzar's dreams, including pinpointing the exact year Jesus would appear as Messiah.

Daniel was very troubled over some of his visions and dreams. He was unable to understand them. In the last chapter of the book, an angel brought Daniel this message: "But thou, O Daniel, shut up the words, and seal the book, even to the time of the end: many shall run to and fro, and knowledge shall be increased" (Dan. 12:4). The increase of knowledge refers to spiritual knowledge as well as material wisdom and inventions.

The book of Daniel is referred to as a handbook of history and prophecy. Its prophecies are closely related to those of the book of Revelation and one helps us to understand the other. How important these prophecies are to God's people in end times. Reading Daniel's prayer (Dan. 9) and witnessing his great concern for his people as well as his consistent loyalty to God helps us to understand why he was called "greatly beloved" by God. "O man greatly beloved, fear not: peace be unto thee, be strong, yea, be strong. And when he had spoken unto me, I was strengthened, and said, Let my lord speak; for thou hast strengthened me" (Dan. 10:19).

Our hero, Daniel, is described in the meaningful youth song "Standing by a Purpose True." Daniel purposed in his heart not to defile or pollute himself. He did not excuse himself due to a different culture. He was very much aware that he was facing tests that were a battle for his mind. I think of his many brave decisions when I sing the refrain: "Dare to be a Daniel, dare to stand alone; Dare to have a purpose firm, dare to make it known." Daniel, dearly beloved by God, knew that *standing alone* was not really standing alone, for God was standing with him!

The Twelve Minor Prophetic Books

As mentioned before, "minor" refers merely to the shorter length of the respective compositions and not to any distinction in the prophetic office.

Hosea has been called the prophet of *divine love*, but little is known about him. He was called to be God's spokesman during the darkest period of the kingdom of Israel, just before the nation was taken captive by Assyria, though he doesn't make mention of the event. This was a time when men were totally devoted to idolatry, dishonest, mutual distrust, and deception toward God. King after king was assassinated to make way for others ambitious to rule. For two centuries and more, the rulers of the ten tribes had been doing what they wanted to: "For they have sown the wind, and they shall reap the whirlwind" (Hosea 8:7).

The story of Hosea has some deep lessons to teach us. His situation is remarkable. His wife runs away and has children with other men. God calls Hosea to take her back and fully show his love to her again. This story is a real happening in Hosea's life—yet, it is meant as a parable about Israel and God. The Israelites had left God and were going after other gods, but God still loved them and wanted to show His love to them.

The dominant theme of his book represents the love of God for all His erring children, and He pleads with them to repent and avail themselves of this divine compassion and love by saying: "O Israel, return unto the LORD thy God; for thou hast fallen by thine iniquity. Take with you words, and turn to the LORD: say unto him, Take away all iniquity, and receive us graciously" (Hosea 14:1, 2). The Lord said: "I will heal their backslidings, I will love them freely" (verse 4). Amazing!

The book of **Joel** has only three chapters. Nothing is known about Joel other than what he reveals in his book. He must have been a native of Judah since his prophesies concerned only Judah and Jerusalem. Joel wrote at a time when the judgments of God were about to fall upon the Hebrew people, particularly in the form of war by enemies from outside the nation.

Through this prophet the Lord called upon the people to repent of their evil ways and thus avert impending wrath. He pleaded with them saying: "Turn ye even to me with all your heart, and with fasting, and with weeping, and with mourning: and rend your heart, and not your garments, and turn unto the LORD your God: for he is gracious and merciful, slow to anger, and of great kindness, and repenteth him of the evil. Who knoweth if he will return and repent, and leave a blessing behind him" (Joel 2:12-14).

The "day of the Lord" is used five times in this short book. It refers to a time when God would punish the unfaithful, and also a time when He would vindicate the faithful. Joel speaks of the promise of the early and latter rain (verses 23-29). He also prophesied about signs in the sky with the sun, moon, and stars (Joel 3:15).

My favorite thought from Joel declares God's great love and care for His wayward people: "And ye shall know that I am in the midst of Israel, and that I am the LORD your God, and none else: and my people shall never be ashamed" (Joel 2:27). This is followed by a caring promise and prophecy: "And it shall come to pass afterward, that I will pour out my spirit upon all flesh; and your sons and your daughters shall prophesy, your old men shall dream dreams, your young men shall see visions: and also upon the servants and upon the handmaids in those days will I pour out my spirit" (verses 28 and 29; see also Acts 2:17, 18). Joel also spoke of the last days regarding the triumph of God's people when the great day of the Lord shall come (Joel 3).

There is wisdom for us when we consider the rebukes, reproofs, and admonishments as loving, caring instruments from a God who treasures us. "As many as I love, I rebuke and chasten: be zealous therefore, and repent" (Rev. 3:19). When I consider the many messages of warning, entreaty, invitation, and blessings promised for repentance, I say in awesome amazement: "What MORE could He say? What more could He DO?" in word and action than to give His Son to come and live among us. Unfortunately, the prophets often lifted their voices in vain.

"They hate him that rebuketh in the gate, and they abhor him that speaketh uprightly. . . . They afflict the just, they take a bribe, and they turn aside the poor in the gate from their right" (Amos 5:10, 12).

Amos is probably the first prophetical book to have been written. It was penned by Amos, a herdsman of Judah whose name means "burden bearer." He is noted for the statement: "Surely the Lord GOD will do nothing, but he revealeth his secrets unto his servants the prophets" (Amos 3:7). His chief purpose was to call the attention of God's people to their sins and to repentance. The future greatness of the people was not to be secured by power and wealth, but through justice and judgment.

His messages were so unpopular that he had to flee for his life. In spite of his treatment, he regarded the prophetic office as a sacred privilege. Amos foretold that a remnant of faithful ones would be saved to possess the earth as God's everlasting kingdom (Amos 9:11-15).

The prophecy of **Obadiah** has only twenty-one verses. It is the shortest book in the Old Testament. It was written 500 years before the birth of Christ. It carries a reproof to the people of Edom for having aided the Babylonians in destroying the Hebrew nation. The Edomites were kinsmen of the Jews, being descendants of Esau, the twin brother of Jacob from whom the Israelites had descended. The prophecy has been fulfilled as far as Edom is concerned, for that nation has disappeared from the face of the earth and her people are known no more.

The message of Obadiah states that the victory of the heathen over Israel was not permanent. Ultimately, salvation and victory would come to the faithful remnant among the professed people of the Lord.

Jonah is author of the book that bears his name. It is the only prophetic book written as a story of an obstinate prophet who said *no* to God. When commissioned by God to warn the wicked city of Nineveh of its speedy destruction, Jonah tried to turn his back on God's request.

Jonah did not wish to go to Nineveh, and he attempted to flee by ship to a place called Tarshish. In order to spare the vessel and its crew from destruction by a storm, Jonah asked to be tossed overboard into the sea. The storm then stopped.

Once, when my husband came home from one of his many trips, our child Eric jumped up into his arms and said, "Daddy, I wish you didn't have to be gone so much. I really miss you!"

Fred replied, "I wish, too, I didn't have to be gone so much, but Daddy has to go and preach."

At which Eric responded, "Yes, Daddy, you'd better go and preach or a big fish will come and swallow you up and spit you out—then you'd obey!" This was the *reality* for Jonah.

The repentant prophet preached the message of warning, and the king and his people sincerely repented in sackcloth and ashes! In God's mercy, He delayed the coming of the fate foretold for that great Gentile city. Jonah, who felt that now he looked like a false prophet, became angry with God. He had a lesson to learn regarding God's gracious dealings with the human race. Some have regarded this book as a symbolic story, but Jesus testified of it as a historical narrative (see Matt. 12:38-41, 16:4; Luke 11:29-32).

Micah, who wrote the sixth book of the minor prophets, was preaching at the same time as Isaiah in Jerusalem and Hosea in Israel. The books of Micah and Isaiah are much alike, showing threats and promises, both judgment and mercy. God's promises were, of course, conditional upon the response of the people.

Micah laid the responsibility for the idolatry prevalent among God's people, principally upon the leaders, charging them with corruption, injustice, oppression, and robbery. The Lord, through Micah, urged the people to repent and return to Him and promised to pardon them, purge them of their iniquities, and "cast all their sins into the depths of the sea" (Micah 7:19).

One of my favorite texts revealing what God requires of us is found in Micah 6:8: "He hath shewed thee, O man, what is good: and what doth the Lord require of thee, but to do justly, and to love mercy, and to walk humbly with thy God?"

Nahum means *consolation* or *comfort*. Little is known of him except that he was a Jew. The theme of his prophecy is the coming fate of Nineveh, and it was written about 150 years after Jonah warned the city, resulting in

Mining for Gold

their repentance. Unfortunately, this repentance didn't last. "The Lord bears long with men, and with cities, mercifully giving warnings to save them from divine wrath; but a time will come when pleadings for mercy will no longer be heard, and the rebellious element that continues to reject the light of truth will be blotted out, in mercy to themselves and to those who would otherwise be influenced by their example" (*Prophets and Kings,* p. 276).

Nineveh is a type of any nation who turns their back on God. Much of what this prophet wrote concerning Nineveh applies also to society in the last days, and some of his predictions of impending wrath refer to our time, to the coming of the Lord to execute judgment upon all: "He will make an utter end: affliction shall not rise up the second time" (Nahum 1:9). That's wonderful news!

The prophet **Habakkuk**, a Levitical chorister, wrote the book bearing his name. As with most of the books of prophecies, Habakkuk was written during a time of deep apostasy. It was written mainly to answer Habakkuk's question: "Why does God permit sinners to flourish while He seems indifferent to their wicked acts?" God's answer assures him that when the time is ripe, He will act! He lets him know that He—God—is still in control of the affairs of earth. One thing we learn from this book is that we can ask God questions. He will listen to our complaints, but we need to listen to His answers.

Of the many special thoughts in this book, here are some that are my favorites: "But the just shall live by his faith" (Hab. 2:4); "For the earth shall be filled with the knowledge of the glory of the LORD, as the waters cover the sea" (verse 14); and "But the LORD is in His holy temple: let all the earth keep silence before him" (verse 20).

Habakkuk wrote a beautiful hymn/poem to close his book. It shows that he is satisfied with God's answers to his questions and feels secure in Him. He tells of complete material collapse. "Although the fig tree shall not blossom, neither shall fruit be in the vines; the labour of the olive shall fail, and the fields shall yield no meat; the flock shall be cut off from the fold, and there shall be no herd in the stalls: Yet I will rejoice in the LORD, I will joy in the God of my salvation" (Hab. 3:17, 18). What compares, in life, with this testimony of the peace in the heart of God's followers?

Zephaniah was a prince of royal blood, descended from Hezekiah, king of

Judah. He prophesied shortly before Jeremiah began his ministry. He denounced the apostasy of Judah and foretold the judgments that would come upon the kingdom.

Always with God's warnings and judgments, even as he is speaking of the *last days*, he always offers glorious hope for His repentant people. "The great day of the LORD is near, it is near, and hasteth greatly" (Zeph. 1:140 "Seek ye the LORD, all ye meek of the earth, which have wrought his judgment; seek righteousness, seek meekness: it may be ye shall be hid in the day of the LORD's anger" (Zeph. 2:3). Woven in this book are prophecies that will be fulfilled when Christ comes the second time to reign in power and glory.

This verse is, to me, Zephaniah's jewel: "The LORD thy God in the midst of thee is mighty; he will save, he will rejoice over thee with joy; he will rest in his love, he will joy over thee with singing" (Zeph. 3:17). We are spiritually serenaded by God Himself!

Haggai was a contemporary of Zechariah and had a prominent part in the movement for the restoration of the Hebrew captives to their homeland after the Babylonian captivity. Some believe he was advanced in years when he delivered the prophecies of his book, given during one year.

Ezra names Haggai as one of the seers who prophesied during the second year of Darius, king of Persia (Hag. 1:1; see also Ezra 5:1). To better understand the book of Haggai, read the book of Ezra.

Haggai was raised up to reprove but also encourage the people. The Jews, after being in their homeland for sixteen years, had made little progress beyond the laying of the foundation of the temple. They made their personal interests first—their own houses—and neglected the Lord's work. Their work was made difficult by their enemies, but the people and their leaders responded to Haggai's call, and the temple was built.

Through Haggai it was promised that Christ, "the desire of all nations," would visit that temple and thereby honor it above the one Solomon had built (Hag. 2:7, 9). Haggai was one of the most successful prophets in the Bible, for we read that the Jews listened to what the Lord their God had said (Hag. 1:12). In contrast, most of the prophets were utterly and openly spurned, ignored, or cast out.

Zechariah was a contemporary of Haggai who God raised up to urge the people to carry out the command to rise and rebuild the temple. Ezra tells us that Zechariah had a part in helping to rebuild the city and temple. He sent words of encouragement to Zerubbabel, governor of Judah, in charge of reconstruction, and to Joshua, the high priest.

Through Zachariah God's people were given assurance that the Lord's protecting care was over His work and that it would succeed despite great obstacles that lay in the way.

Several interesting visions of a symbolic nature are recorded in this book. He foretells the coming of the Savior and His work more than any other prophet except for Isaiah. There are prophecies relating to both the first and second advents of Christ. The prediction concerning the triumphal entry of Jesus into Jerusalem as he rode on a donkey is quoted by the Gospel writers (see Zech. 9:9 and Matt. 21:4, 5).

Other encouraging prophecies in this book speak of the fountain that shall be opened for all sin and uncleanness (Zech. 13:1). Christ is the only One who can cleanse us from sin (1 John 1:7-9). Christ is also spoken of as the Branch who shall build the temple of the Lord, which is His church (see Zech. 6:12 and Eph. 2:19-22).

The final restoration of all things is foretold as taking place when "the LORD shall be king over all the earth" (Zech. 14:9). He was a prophet of restoration and glory. His book is one of the future—a book of *revelation* of the Old Testament. Zechariah accomplished mighty things for God in the three years he was a prophet.

Malachi was the last of the Old Testament prophets to write a book of the Bible. This book is a bridge between the Old and New Testaments. There were 400 years between this book and the voice of John the Baptist preparing for the coming of Christ as recorded in Matthew.

Malachi's name means "my messenger." His message dates nearly 100 years after the return of God's people from captivity. Special reproof is given to the priests for their bad example. Their high calling is set forth in these words: "For the priest's lips should keep knowledge, and they should seek the law at his mouth: for he is the messenger of the LORD of hosts" (Mal. 2:7).

The themes that are predominant in this book are the sin and apostasy of His people and their coming judgment. The book ends with the assurance that God will keep them in the Day of Judgment. Malachi's writing style differs from the other prophets' messages. He has a way of encouraging while he rebukes, and he shows God's love even while pointing out sin.

Here are verses that are especially meaningful to me: "Return unto me, and I will return unto you. . . . Will a man rob God? Yet ye have robbed me . . . in tithes and offerings. Ye are cursed with a curse: for ye have robbed me, even this whole nation. Bring ye all the tithes into the storehouse, that there may be meat in mine house, and prove me now herewith, saith the LORD of hosts, if I will not open you the windows of heaven, and pour you out a blessing, that there shall not be room enough to receive it" (Mal. 3:7-10). "Then they that feared the LORD spake often one to another: and the LORD hearkened, and heard it, and a book of remembrance was written before him for them that feared the LORD, and that thought upon his name. And they shall be mine, saith the LORD of hosts, in that day when I make up my jewels; and I will spare them, as a man spareth his own son that serveth him" (verses 16 and 17). I want to be a part of this group, don't you? Divine blessing is proceeded by human obedience and produced by divine love in our hearts.

Between the Old and New Testaments

Though some Christians define the difference between the Old Testament and the New Testament as the difference between *law* in the Old, and *grace* in the New, I have found both law and grace flowing side by side through the entire Scripture. If sin is the transgression of the law and sin started with the rebellion of a heavenly being, Lucifer, there had to be an unwritten law in the hearts of all those who lived in heaven. I like to think of these principles as a result of such a law: faith, truth, reverence, obedience, respect, love, purity, honesty, truthfulness, and contentment. Since the law needs grace, grace existed even in heaven where sin began. Grace is part of God's character, which has existed from time eternal.

The plan to rescue the human race after the fall was discussed before the foundation of the world. It was the covenant of grace that gave us the promise of a Savior (see Gen. 3:15 and Eph. 1:4-7). Though the word *grace* may not

Mining for Gold

have been used, there were many evidences of it in Old Testament times. The first is Genesis 3:15. In this verse, grace was personified in Jesus' victory over Satan.

Some say that people were saved by keeping the law in Old Testament times. They also say that the law was done away with in New Testament times and people were saved by grace. Because law and grace flow through the entire Bible, we all need and are saved in the same way—a free gift bought by Jesus' life, death, and resurrection. In Him only are we saved: "Neither is there salvation in any other: for there is none other name under heaven given among men, whereby we must be saved" (Acts 4:12).

In the Old Testament this *plan* was illustrated by the offering of animals—the giving of life's blood. In the New Testament, Jesus gave Himself and His own blood as the sacrifice. Type (Jesus) met antitype (the animal sacrifices) so that illustration was no longer necessary. God made that very clear when the curtain between the *holy* and the *Most Holy* was ripped from top to bottom, indicating the end of the ceremonial system (Matt. 27:51).

The law is like a mirror—it lets us know there is sin in our lives and that we need a Savior. If there were no law, there would be no sin for "sin is the transgression of the law" (1 John 3:4; see also Rom. 4:15). The following testimony is from the Lutheran Church from *The Creeds of Christendom*: "Although they who truly believe in Christ, and are sincerely converted to God, and though Christ set free from the curse and constraint of the law, they are not, nevertheless, on that account without Law, inasmuch as the Son of God redeemed them for the very reason that they might meditate on the Law of God day and night, and continually exercise themselves in the keeping thereof" (vol. 3, p. 131).

"We teach that this law was not given to men, that we should be justified by keeping it; but that, by the knowledge thereof, we might rather acknowledge our infirmity, sin, and condemnation, and so despairing of our strength, might turn unto Christ by faith" (*A Testimony of the Reformed Church*, p. 855).

In the 1942 edition of *Bible Readings for the Home,* the following list appears on page 396 detailing the same types of testimonies for the law from most Protestant creeds.

The Moral and Ceremonial Laws Contrasted

The Moral Law	The Ceremonial Law
Is called the "royal law" (James 2:8)	Is called "the law . . . contained in ordinances" (Ephesians 2:15)
Was spoken by God (Deuteronomy 4:12, 13)	Was spoken by Moses (Leviticus 1:1-3)
Was written by God on tables of stone (Exodus 24:12)	Was "the handwriting of ordinances" (Colossians 2:14)
Was written "with the finger of God" (Exodus 3:18)	Was written by Moses in a book (2 Chronicles 35:12)
Was placed in the ark (Exodus 40:20; 1 Kings 8:9; Hebrews 9:4)	Was placed in the side of the ark (Deuteronomy 31:24-26)
Is "perfect" (Psalm 19:7)	Made nothing perfect (Hebrews 7:19)
Is to "stand fast forever and ever" (Psalm 111:7, 8)	Was nailed to the cross (Colossians 2:14)
Was not destroyed by Christ (Matthew 5:17)	Was abolished by Christ (Ephesians 2:15)
Was to be magnified by Christ (Isaiah 42:21)	Was taken out of the way by Christ (Colossians 2:14)
Gives "knowledge of sin" (Romans 3:20, 7:7)	Was instituted in consequence of sin (Leviticus 3-7)

Loving God with a desire to obey Him goes hand in hand in both Old and New Testament times. "I will put my law in their inward parts, and write it in their hearts" (Jer. 31:33; see also Heb. 10:16). There are many Old Testament characters who obviously had God's law written in their hearts. Two of them, Enoch and Elijah, were translated without seeing death. Many others are listed in God's who's who in Hebrews 11—the *faith scroll*. They too were saved by grace, the only way mankind can be saved (Acts 4:12, 15:11; Eph. 2:8). Their worthy works were a by-product of a love relationship with God and testified as to whose side they had chosen. They had also chosen to accept God's free gift of salvation!

In speaking of the *old and new covenants*, no time frame was involved. The difference in the covenants was a *state of the heart*. There were people in the Old Testament times, such as Enoch, Abraham, and many others who, though no Bible had been written in their time, had their own personal loving relationship with God. They understood the symbols of the sacrifices that pointed forward to Christ. They came under the new covenant. It was written in their hearts (Eze. 11:19, 20 in the Old Testament; 2 Cor. 3:3 in the New Testament). Their love for the heavenly family was supreme.

There were *men of the cloth* in New Testament times who knew the commandments inside and out and added more rules to the ten. They were a law unto themselves. Their hearts were far from the heavenly Father. They did not accept Christ. The law was not written in their hearts, only on tables of stone. They were legalistic. Of course, there were others who did have God's law in their hearts and their lives testified that they were gladly willing to live and die in service and obedience to Christ.

Some Christians claim they are New Testament Christians rather than Old Testament Christians. No doubt Christians who make this claim have in mind their pleasure of reading the New Testament more than the Old Testament. The history of God's chosen people tells us they were often rebellious and worshipped false gods. "My people have forgotten to do right" (Amos 3:10, NLT). These actions called forth from their Creator God rebukes and threats to those He loved. God loves more than the human mind can fathom. Deep love can produce deep hatred for sin because sin separates. All of God's reproofs and punishments were for redemptive purposes. God relented from His plan to destroy when prophets or the people confessed and asked forgiveness. God was eager to see His followers live lives of justice and right living.

Atheists and non-believers don't get beyond the righteous anger and threats recorded about God against sin. They see a picture of God as a wrathful being. Yet, the Christian who has experienced God's unchanging character of forgiveness, mercy, grace, and guidance finds God's love in these books.

The only scriptures written before Christ's time on earth were the Old Testament books. It is impossible to be a Christian from only one testament since the two flow together from Genesis to Revelation. The Old Testament is the foundation for the New Testament. Paul quotes more than forty times directly from the Old Testament. From Isaiah, he quoted twenty-five times! Peter also quotes from the Old Testament. All of the Epistles have a strong foundation in Old Testament scriptures. Jesus often quoted the prophecies of the Old Testament about Himself.

My favorite of these quotes has to do with a day of discouragement when some of the disciples were perplexed at the meaning of the crucifixion weekend—not having seen the risen Christ. Their hearts were heavy when Jesus caught up to them on their way to Emmaus and He entered their conversation. They didn't recognize Him, but they explained to Him what they were conversing about.

Jesus then responded: "And beginning at Moses and all the prophets, he expounded unto them in all the scriptures the things concerning himself" (Luke 24:27). When Jesus accepted a meal and lodging invitation from them, they recognized Him when He gave thanks and broke the bread. When He vanished from their sight, they exclaimed: "Did not our hearts burn within us, while he talked with us by the way, and while he opened to us the scriptures?" (verse 32). The entire account is documented in Luke 24:13-53. When I read this account, my heart also burns within me.

There are about sixty Old Testament prophecies regarding the coming Messiah. Following is a short sample of Old Testament prophesies and the New Testament fulfillment about Jesus. Check them out:

Old Testament	**New Testament**
Isaiah 7:14	Matthew 1:23
Micah 5:2	Luke 2:4-7
Daniel 9:25	Luke 3:1-23
Hosea 11:1	Matthew 2:14

Here are more prophecies, the fulfillment of which we hear about on the news and see with our own eyes:

Increase of knowledge	Daniel 12:4
False messiahs	Matthew 24:4, 5
Wars and rumors of wars	Matthew 24:6, 7a
Famine	Matthew 24:7b
Earthquakes	Matthew 24:7b
Preaching of the gospel	Matthew 24:14
Signs and wonders	Luke 21:11

People living in fear	Luke 21:26
Social problems, capital & labor problems	2 Timothy 3:1-5; James 5:1-5
Increase of skepticism	2 Peter 3:3, 4

The Ancient Book, including both Old and New Testaments, is as relevant and up to date as tomorrow's news.

New Testament

The New Testament is divided as follows:
- The first four books are called the Gospels and tell of the life of Christ on this earth: Matthew, Mark, Luke, and John.
- The Acts of the Apostles is a historical book and reports the growth of the early church.
- The next fourteen books are Epistles, or letters, of Paul: Romans, 1 and 2 Corinthians, Galatians, Ephesians, Philippians, Colossians, 1 and 2 Thessalonians, 1 and 2 Timothy, Titus, Philemon, and Hebrews; 1 and 2 Timothy and Titus are called pastoral Epistles—a handbook for all Christian pastors.
- The next seven books are Epistles, or letters, of other followers of Christ: James, 1 and 2 Peter, 1, 2, and 3 John, and Jude.
- The last book of the New Testament is a book of **prophecy**: Revelation.

Dramatic world events occurred during the 400 years of silence between the Old and New Testaments. The seat of government passed from Asia to Europe, and Palestine experienced six different systems of rule. This was the longest period in Israel's history without a prophetic witness.

"But when the fulness of the time was come, God sent forth his Son . . . to redeem them that were under the law, that we might receive the adoption of sons" (Gal. 4:4, 5). Along with this thought are these beautiful words: "From the days of Enoch the promise was repeated through patriarchs and prophets, keeping alive the hope of His appearing, and yet He came not. . . . But like the stars in the vast circuit of their appointed path, God's purposes know no haste and no delay. . . . When the great clock of time pointed to that hour, Jesus was born in Bethlehem" (*The Desire of Ages*, p. 32). The hopeful thought came to my mind: He will come again the second time as King of Kings and Lord of Lords "when the fulness of time has come."

Matthew, Mark, and Luke are known as the *Synoptic Gospels*, meaning *collective view* of Christ's life. Gospel means *good news*. John, the other writer, portrays Christ's life more in a meditative form. None of the Gospel writers give an account of the eighteen years of Jesus' life between the ages of twelve to thirty.

Levi-**Matthew**, a wealthy tax collector and disciple of Jesus, wrote the book bearing his name prior to the destruction of Jerusalem (AD 70). He wrote primarily to tell the story of Jesus to the Christian Jews. He was an eye-witness of the events that occurred during the last half of Jesus' ministry.

Matthew begins his Gospel by tracing Jesus' genealogy back to Abraham whom God had said would be a forbearer of the promised seed—the Messiah (Gal. 3:16). In this genealogy are mentioned four women: Tamar, Rahab, Ruth, and Bathsheba. Some of these women have stories in their lives of rape, the offspring of rape, infidelity, and murder! Jesus became "sin for us, who knew no sin; that we might be made the righteousness of God in him" (2 Cor.5:21). From adoration in heaven to this sinful human genealogy, what condescension, what love!

Matthew alone tells of the visit of the wise men and the flight of Joseph, Mary, and Jesus to Egypt. He gives us the most notable of the discourses of Jesus—the Sermon on the Mount. He also reported many of Jesus' other sermons and parables and miracles. His theme was the moral and doctrinal teaching of Jesus. Jesus was emphasized as King. The narrative extends from the *birth of Christ* to *His ascension*, and it closes with the *gospel commission* (see Matt. 28:19, 20). No doubt the disciples drew great comfort in the last words of this commission: "and, lo, I am with you always, even unto the end of the world."

The complete picture of the gospel story can be understood when the four accounts of the Gospels are properly blended together into one unified, chronological narrative. Each makes its own special contribution to the gospel story, and by studying each of their characteristics, you receive a blessed understanding and appreciation of the gospel narrative as a whole. This is called *harmony of the Gospels*.

Mark was the son of a pious woman living in Jerusalem who was the sister of Barnabas. Mark was the first of the Gospels written, and the shortest. His purpose was to report what Jesus did, rather than what He said. His Gospel was to the Romans, the Gentiles.

It is generally believed that Mark narrates from what he heard from the apostle Peter, for it is thought he was a convert of Peter since Peter speaks of him as "my son" (1 Peter 5:13). Mark was probably not an eye-witness to all the events he describes; yet it is believed that he was personally acquainted with Jesus and that he was the young man referred to in chapter 14, verses 51 and 52, for he is the only Bible writer to mention the incident.

He emphasized Jesus' life as a "servant." His theme was salvation through a suffering servant, and that the righteous, too, must suffer. He also presents Christ as the mighty *miracle-worker*. Mark is the only Gospel writer to preserve the beautiful story of mothers bringing their children to Jesus when He took them up in His arms and blessed them.

Luke was written by a Greek physician known as "the beloved physician." He is the only New Testament writer who was a Gentile. His Gospel was written to a person whom he calls "most excellent Theophilus"—a Christian convert (Luke 1:3). Luke is referred to as the first church historian because of his attention to important details such as the name and year of the Roman emperor who was reigning when John the Baptist began to preach (Luke 3:1-3). His book was probably written after Matthew and Mark had penned theirs for he mentions that others had already written accounts of the life of Christ. He starts out with the birth of John the Baptist and ends with the Savior's ascension to heaven. As a medical man would do, he gives special attention to details relating to the births of John and Jesus that no other Bible writer mentions. He gives the longest account of Jesus, and the only account of His childhood, including His visit to the temple at the age of twelve. Luke's genealogy of Jesus starts in Luke 3:23-38. It goes back to Adam, "which was the son of God" (verse 38).

Luke is the only Gospel writer to recount the stories of the angel Gabriel's announcement to Mary that God had chosen her to be the mother of the Messiah; the miraculous conception of Elizabeth, mother of John the Baptist; the visit of the shepherds at Jesus' birth; the angels ministering to Him in the Garden of Gethsemane; His prayer on the cross; and the very human account of the walk to Emmaus.

He emphasizes the discipleship of women, even naming them. Luke's writings are noteworthy for the many descriptions of the Master's sympathetic interest in the sick and the outcasts. In fact, his Gospel seems to be for the outcast: the story of the Good Samaritan; the Publican; the prodigal son; and Zacchaeus. He alone tells of the healing of Malchus' ear; about Jesus beholding the city of Jerusalem and weeping over it; of His bloody sweat in Gethsemane; and His showing mercy to the dying thief.

The author of the book of **John** was the brother of James, one of the sons of Thunder, and the "beloved disciple." Jesus called him from his trade as a lowly fisherman to be a disciple. No other apostle was so close to Jesus as John, and none lived so long. He outlived Peter and Paul by a whole generation.

The book of John was written at least thirty years after the other Gospels and at least two generations after Jesus died on the cross. John doubtless understood the mind and heart of Jesus better than any other person of his time. John's gospel gives a portrait of Jesus that is more personal than the other Gospels. It tells of the most intimate conversations with His closest friends. John is the only Gospel writer to share the experience of the death and resurrection of Lazarus and His close friendship with the family—Mary, Martha, and Lazarus.

John is not so much a reporter of sermons like Matthew, or a biographer like Mark, or a historian like Luke, but he is pre-eminently a theologian whose inspired insights led him to reveal Jesus Christ as the incarnate Son of God.

Although John omits the birth of Jesus, his book begins similarly to the book of Genesis by portraying Jesus as God, before all things and Creator of all. In the first chapter of this book, John the Baptist is introduced, not as Christ, but as a "voice of one crying in the wilderness, make straight the way of the Lord" (John 1:23). He revealed John the Baptist's declaration that he was the forerunner of Christ and quoted his statement found in John 1:32-36. Testifying about Christ, he said: "I saw the spirit descending from heaven like a dove, and it abode upon him. . . . And I saw, and bare record that this is the Son of God" (verses 32-34).

Following this confirmation given after Jesus' baptism (Matt. 3:13-17), Jesus was inaugurated to His earthly mission. His disciples gathered about Him for the mission of miracles and messages from Jesus' life. All of this profound information and inspiration is found in John's first chapter!

John's central purpose in writing his book is expressed in John 20:31: "But these are written, that ye might believe that Jesus is the Christ, the Son of God; and that believing ye might have life through his name." The word "believe" or its equivalent appears in this book more than 100 times! It occurs less than forty times in the three Synoptic Gospels. The quotations of Jesus where He used the metaphor "I am" appear only in John's Gospel. As you read this most-prized book of the Bible, you may wish to take special note of each "I am"—you should find seven.

John 3:16 is probably the most favored and memorized verse in Scripture and one that tells much about the kind of God we have: "For God so loved the world, that he gave his only begotten Son, that whosoever believeth in him should not perish, but have everlasting life." This verse has been translated into more languages than any other portion of the Bible. The following verse adds more to the reason Jesus was sent into this world: "For God sent not his Son into the world to condemn the world; but that the world through him might be saved."

John 3:16	**God's Love**
For God	the greatest Being
so loved	the greatest motive
the world	the greatest number
that He gave	the greatest act
His only begotten Son	the greatest gift
that whosoever	the greatest invitation
believeth in Him	the greatest requirement
should not perish	the greatest fear
but have everlasting life	the greatest hope

John was eager to share with his readers his great love for Christ. He quotes

Jesus: "Ye are my friends, if ye do whatsoever I command you. Henceforth I called you not servants; for the servant knoweth not what his lord doeth: but I have called you friends; for all things that I have heard of my Father I have made known unto you" (John 15:14, 15).

John describes what it means to serve Him: "If any man serve me, let him follow me, and where I am, there shall also my servant be: if any man serve me, him will my Father honor" (John 12:26). Reading these verses makes me think of Jesus' followers who felt honored to be His servant. Paul did (see Rom. 1:1). Over and over the beautiful thought of servanthood is encouraged. Jesus was an example of true servanthood. This was His mission to this world. "Even as the Son of man came not to be ministered unto, but to minister, and to give his life a ransom for many" (Matt. 20:28). "In calling His followers "friends," Jesus was combining the two thoughts of the blessedness of "service" and the special privilege of receiving secrets of His Father as a "friend." In Jesus' description, there is no greater honor than being His *servant-friend*.

A thoughtful reader of the Gospels will be impressed by Jesus' compassion, mercy, love, and forgiveness expressed to the sinner who knows his needy condition and desires to come to Him. What a contrast to Jesus' disappointing, revolting knowledge of what was in the minds and hearts of the religious leaders who saw no need, had no desire, and rejected the only help mankind needs. They not only rejected Him but executed Him!

While some consider the Synoptic Gospels written with certain cultures in mind, truly the Gospel of John was written for the *world*! John was so full of desire to share Jesus that the last verse in his book expressed the hopelessness of sharing it all: "And there are also many other things which Jesus did, the which, if they should be written every one, I suppose that even the world itself could not contain the books that should be written. Amen" (John 21:25).

The four Gospels are not really biographies of Christ's life. It should be noted that at least one-third to one-half of their space is devoted to the last events of Christ's life and summaries of the significance of Jesus' death. Jesus was born to die. The cross is the pivotal message of the Bible from Genesis to Revelation. "For the preaching of the cross is to them that perish foolishness; but unto us which are saved it is the power of God" (1 Cor. 1:18).

"Jesus the author and finisher of our faith; who for the joy that was set

Mining for Gold

before him endured the cross, despising the shame, and is set down at the right hand of the throne of God" (Heb. 12:2). He has conquered! "Wherefore God also hath highly exalted him, and given him a name which is above every name: That at the name of Jesus every knee should bow, of things in heaven, and things in earth, and things under the earth; and that every tongue should confess that Jesus Christ is Lord, to the glory of God the Father" (Phil. 2:9-11).

People may ask, "Why several Gospel writers—why not one with the entire story?" It is because the minds of the writers differed—not all comprehended events in the same way. Some scriptural truths appear more strongly to some minds than others. Actually, the whole truth is presented more clearly by several writers than by one. Though the Gospels differ, the records blend into one harmonious whole.

The book of **Acts** is a history of the foundation of the early church and the story of the spread of Christianity from Jerusalem into the Gentile world. It records exciting accounts and adventures of the early church and its founders. Luke, "the beloved physician," is the author of this narrative. He was the first historian of Christianity.

I was recently given a list of the *one-hundred best adventure stories* ever written. Some are done so well the reader feels they are actually experiencing the adventure. When I read the book of **Acts**, I feel that it could well be added to the *best of the best* books of adventure.

Acts continues on where the Gospels leave off. It covers a period of approximately thirty years. It begins with the ascension of Jesus forty days after His resurrection. We have the account of the outpouring of the Holy Ghost upon the believers at Jerusalem on the day of Pentecost preparing them to fulfill the gospel commission given by Jesus. "Go ye therefore, and teach all nations, baptizing them in the name of the Father, and of the Son, and of the Holy Ghost: Teaching them to observe all things whatsoever I have commanded you: and, lo, I am with you always, even unto the end of the world. Amen" (Matt. 28:19, 20).

More were converted by one sermon on the day of Pentecost than were converted during all the years of Christ's ministry! Jesus predicted it as quoted in the book of John 14:12: "Verily, verily, I say unto you, He that believeth on me, the works that I do shall he do also; and greater works than these shall he do; because I go unto my Father." Jesus continued: "But the Comforter, which is the Holy Ghost, whom the Father will send in my name, he shall teach you all things, and bring all things to your remembrance, whatsoever I have said unto you" (verse 26). The name "Acts of the Apostles" shows the working of the Holy Spirit through Peter, Paul, and their many companions. Those who were part of the early church were united in love and ministry to each other's needs (Acts 2:42-47).

The early church was organized. Evidence of its organization was made obvious. When a question came up that caused a dispute, the leaders involved went to the *headquarters* in Jerusalem and sought the advice of the leader, James, as to the solution for the controversy (Acts 15).

The stoning of Stephen and the persecution of the church by the unbelieving Jews in AD 34 scattered the believers to lands afar, where they proclaimed the gospel. This opened up the way for the gospel to go to the Gentile world. The purpose of *God's chosen people* was now about to be realized in a remarkable way, and it gets more so as time goes on.

Saul, the feared persecutor of Jesus' followers, was converted and became Paul the *chosen vessel* to bear the message of Jesus to the Gentiles, kings, and the children of Israel. See the thrilling story in Acts 9. Paul never tired of telling the thrilling story of his conversion, for he was not "ashamed of the gospel of Christ" (Rom. 1:16). A fire burned within his soul to preach the *good news*.

The same church leaders that crucified Jesus also sought to kill Paul for his testimony. He was held prisoner in Caesarea. Wearing his prison chains, Paul stood before King Agrippa telling the thrilling story of his conversion to Jesus. Paul's spiritual enthusiasm prompted him to ask, with passion: "King Agrippa, believest thou the prophets? I know that thou believest" (Acts 26:27).

Then, Agrippa said to Paul, "Almost thou persuadest me to be a Christian" (verse 28).

Paul replied, "I would to God, that not only thou, but also all that hear me this day, were both almost and altogether such as I am, except these bonds [chains]" (verse 29). Paul was deeply disappointed over the lack of results from his earnest plea. Finding nothing worthy of death, Agrippa could have set

Paul free if he had not appealed to Caesar in Rome (Acts 26:30-32).

I'm sure Paul's personal experiences led him to write: "All things work together for good to them that love God, to them who are the called according to his purpose" (Rom. 8:28). Paul had been very eager to go to Rome and no doubt planned a visit as a missionary journey, but now going to Rome instead as a prisoner proved advantageous for his witnessing. Paul, a Roman citizen, traveling as a prisoner, was allowed to be accompanied by a slave and a personal physician. The "we" in Acts 27 referred to these men—Aristarchus and Luke—who were with Paul. They found themselves treated kindly by government officials. Quoting Acts 28:30-31, we are told: "And Paul dwelt two whole years in his own hired house, and received all that came in unto him, preaching the kingdom of God, and teaching those things which concern the Lord Jesus Christ, with all confidence, no man forbidding him." Paul was a prisoner for nearly five years, which gave him the opportunity to witness to governors, kings, and to Nero himself.

The book of Acts closes very abruptly. It's the only unfinished book in the Bible, for the sharing of the gospel of Christ goes on. As Christ's followers, we are still living the "Acts," now being recorded in the *book of life* in heaven!

The Epistle of Paul to the **Romans,** which follows the recording of the founding of churches among the Jews and Gentiles in the book of Acts, is the first of the Epistles or letters to believers. Paul, the author of Romans, prayed unceasingly for his Roman readers, and he longed to fellowship with them again. He had deep compassion, love, and concern for the members of the newly established churches. His letters urged loyalty to the true gospel, purity of lifestyle, unity and love between believers, submission to God's Word, and respect for church authority. He gave guidance for every area of the Christian life.

Paul solicited funds from the Gentile believers for the needs of the poor in Jerusalem. He felt this gesture would help to unify and develop love between Christian Jews and Gentiles. Paul's deep desire for the new followers was prompted by his conviction that the message of God's power would change and keep all lives committed to Him. Paul's testimony was: "I am not ashamed of the gospel of Christ: for it is the power of God unto salvation to every one that believeth; to the Jew first, and also to the Greeks" (Rom. 1:16).

This Epistle is the longest of Paul's letters. It was addressed to Christians in the world's greatest metropolis. Heresy and division were already creeping into the Roman church (Rom. 16:17, 18). The letter was written to confound the unbelieving Jew, to convert the idolatrous Gentile, and at the same time to confirm those who were converted. The theme of this Epistle is the universal sinfulness of man and the universal grace of God. The letter sets forth so clearly the doctrine of justification by faith (Rom. 1:17). It gave the Great Reformation of the sixteenth century the keynote of its message.

He makes many attempts in his letters to stress, in the minds of his readers, the balance of grace, faith, and law for the salvation of the human race. Law-keeping is not the focus of salvation; yet Paul emphasized the fact that faith and grace do not annul God's law and thus give mankind license to continue in sin. "Do we then make void the law through faith? God forbid: yea, we establish the law" (Rom. 3:31). Obedience is the fruit of love. Jesus said: "If ye love me, keep my commandments" (John 14:15). Obedience brings us closer to God. The final word about obedience is proclaimed in reference to the second advent of Jesus: "Blessed are they that do his commandments, that they may have right to the tree of life, and may enter in through the gates into the city" (Rev. 22:14).

Paul's dedicated devotion to the subject of salvation often causes problems when we don't understand it. Peter described it this way: "even as our beloved brother Paul also according to the wisdom given unto him hath written unto you; as also in all his Epistles, speaking in them of these things; in which are some things hard to understand, which they that are unlearned and unstable wrest, as they do also the other scriptures, unto their own destruction" (2 Peter 3:15, 16).

Perhaps we can simply summarize the book of Romans by saying: The first part of the book is what God did for us. The last part is what we may do for Him.

1 Corinthians was written to the church in Corinth. Corinth was a great commercial center of the Roman Empire and was also *sin city*. Paul had spent more than eighteen months in Corinth where he established a church under

Mining for Gold

considerable opposition. He was about fifty years of age when he went to Corinth.

Later, during the latter part of Paul's labor at Ephesus, he received a letter telling of the serious condition in the church at Corinth (1 Cor. 1:10, 11). This led him to write 1 Corinthians about AD 58. His message is two-fold: first, it is a reproof for backsliding, and second, it offers instruction and explanation of points of belief and practice the believers didn't understand. The Bible is the greatest handbook for behavior given to the human race!

In this Epistle Paul deals with matters such as: His authority as an apostle; divisions based on leadership; lawsuits between brethren; marriage relations; food dedicated to idols; the Lord's Supper; the resurrection of the dead; lessons from the history of Israel; behavior in church services; and the proper exercise of spiritual gifts. He follows by saying: "Let all things be done decently and in order" (1 Cor. 14:40). God's house is a sacred place where mankind meets their Creator in worship.

The Epistle abounds with both doctrinal and practical instruction mingled with gentle reproof and earnest exhortation. He writes in his letter of the significance of the new life in Christ and its demonstration of love as can be seen in the masterly exposition of chapter 13. Would that the theme of this beautiful chapter be emulated by all of us. Take time to read it now!

Paul compares the Christian's life to a race run in the Olympia Games. But in the race for eternal life, every faithful participant can win the crown of eternal life—a prize that does not fade away as did the olive-leaf wreath given to just one contestant in the games of long ago. This book has been described as *one of the richest, most instructive, most powerful* of all of Paul's letters.

2 Corinthians details Paul's continued instruction to the church in Corinth. No doubt Paul's prayers for the members in Corinth increased after his first letter to them! Titus had been sent to visit this church, and shortly after, he joined Paul on another missionary journey. It was the encouraging report from Titus that prompted Paul to write his second letter to the Corinthians. The first nine chapters, written to the majority who accepted Paul's counsel and reproof, are characterized by gratitude, appreciation, and rejoicing over the desired effects of his first letter.

Paul speaks of the Christian worker as an ambassador for Christ (2 Cor. 5:19-21). He mentions the trials and sufferings that the messengers of the truth must pass through and recounts many of those he himself had endured. He learned, by experience, that God's grace was sufficient for him (2 Cor. 12:7-10). The love of God for man and the manifestation of it through Christ—as our Savior—are ever the theme of the apostle's letters. Many Bible scholars consider that this Epistle gives the clearest and most complete picture of Paul's nature, personality, and disposition.

The Epistle to the **Galatians** was written to the Christian believers scattered among the idolatrous people of the region of Galatia. There were numerous churches in that area (1 Cor. 16:1). The message of this letter was so important to Paul that he wrote it by his own hand instead of using a secretary. His letter was stern.

The gospel had been preached to Galatia by Paul and his fellow workers, but when they were absent, *Judaizers* (false teachers) crept in to teach these Gentile converts to observe the rite of circumcision and to keep the Mosaic ordinances in order to become heirs of the blessings God had promised to Abraham. This was part of the Mosaic law that was "nailed to the cross" and no longer required. When circumcision was practiced before the cross, it was used to *set apart* those who were God's followers.

Paul had this encouraging thought to say to the Gentiles in Galatians 3:29: "And if ye be Christ's, then are ye Abraham's seed, and heirs according to the promise." Paul put it all together in these words found in Romans 2:28, 29 and 3:1, 2: "For he is not a Jew, which is one outwardly; neither is that circumcision, which is outward in the flesh. But he is a Jew, which is one inwardly; and circumcision is that of the heart, in the spirit, and not in the letter; whose praise is not of men, but of God. What advantage then hath the Jew? or what profit is there of circumcision? Much every way: chiefly, because that unto them were committed the oracles of God." They were assigned the sacred office of being God's ambassadors, to which God now called all Christians. As Christians we are considered *spiritual Jews—Abraham's seed.*

The major theme of this Epistle is righteousness attained by faith in Jesus Christ. It exalts what God has done through Christ for man's salvation and dismisses the idea that man can be justified by his own merits. The book of Galatians, being the strongest declaration of the doctrine of justification by faith, was Martin Luther's favorite Epistle. It has been called the *Magna Carta of the early church* and was the masthead of the Reformation, although one could say the same of the book of Romans.

Paul marveled in his great disappointment—that the believers in Galatia could be led astray so quickly to accept a gospel not of Christ. This book ends with an appeal not to abuse the newfound liberty of the gospel, but to live a holy life and be known for good works. He reminds his readers though that good works are not a substitute for faith in the saving merits of Christ.

Paul's letter accomplished good results. In later years, Peter addressed two Epistles to the Christians in Galatia, which shows that they did not succumb to the *Judaizing* apostasy (1 Peter 1:1; 2 Peter 3:1).

Ephesians was written at Rome while the apostle was imprisoned there, awaiting a hearing from Nero, the Roman Emperor at that time. To the believers at Ephesus, the chief city of the Roman province in Asia Minor, Paul addressed this Epistle.

I treasure Paul's beautiful attitude, although he is in prison. No doubt it was prompted by these thoughts: "For I reckon that the sufferings of this present time are not worthy to be compared with the glory which shall be revealed in us" (Rom. 8:18). Paul wrote other letters while in prison, including Philippians, Colossians, and Philemon.

The church in Ephesus had been raised up years before by the labors of Paul and his associates in the midst of much opposition and persecution. Paul had stayed longer here than any other place, and the people there heard more Bible teaching from Paul than did any other church. Paul loved the church at Ephesus.

This Epistle is one of the richest and noblest of the Pauline Epistles. Modern writers call it the *jewel case of the Bible*. One of these gems is surely recorded in Ephesians 1:4-6. It has made an indelible impression on my heart from my first absorption: "According as he hath chosen us in him before the foundation of the world, that we should be holy and without blame before him in love: Having predestinated us unto the adoption of children by Jesus Christ to himself, according to the good pleasure of his will, to the praise of the glory of his grace, wherein he hath made us accepted in the beloved."

The apostle's theme is "the love of Christ, which passeth knowledge" (Eph. 3:19). His burden was to establish the believers in that love. He spoke of the church as *the body of Christ* with a focus on her relationship to God. He is writing to a church consisting of Jews, Gentiles, Asiatics, Europeans, slave, and freemen, all restored to love and unity in Christ. He exhorts them to be a cleansed church, ready for Christ's coming (Eph. 5:25-27).

The Christian is urged to "put on the whole armour of God" that he "may be able to stand against the wiles of the devil. For we wrestle not against flesh and blood, but . . . against spiritual wickedness in high places" (Eph. 6:11, 12). "Stand therefore, having your loins girt about with truth, and having on the breastplate of righteousness; and your feet shod with the preparation of the gospel of peace; above all, taking the shield of faith, wherewith ye shall be able to quench all the fiery darts of the wicked. And take the helmet of salvation, and the sword of the Spirit, which is the word of God: Praying always with all prayer and supplication in the Spirit, and watching thereunto with all perseverance and supplication for all saints" (verses 14-18).

Paul is masterful at balancing deep spiritual thoughts of God's love with practical matters such as the duties of home relationships (see Eph. 5:21, 6:6). He exhorts the church to be pure, holy, and to love one another. The phrase "in Christ" is used 167 times in the Bible—it is found thirty-six times in Ephesians and fourteen times in the first chapter!

Philippians was written to the first church established in Europe (Acts 16:6-40), which was more Gentile than all the other churches. Another *imprisonment* letter from Paul, it was written the same time as Ephesians—about AD 62. Timothy was with Paul and Paul promised to send him to them shortly.

Philippi was the chief city of Macedonia. Paul was called to Philippi by a vision and the words: "Come over into Macedonia, and help us" (Acts 16:9). This Epistle was written ten years after he first preached the gospel there.

The Epistle has been labeled *the secret of joy* even though it was written in prison; it is considered the sweetest of all Paul's letters. The word *joy* or *rejoice* occurs sixteen times. The more I study the Bible, the more favorite books I have! Among them is Philippians. My favorite list of *mind healers* is in chapter 4, verse 8. In fact, the title of my book comes from this verse: "Think on these things."

In Paul's fervent love for Christ, he mentions *Savior* forty times, and some of the most wonderful things concerning Christ and the Christian life are included in this Epistle. Tears come to my eyes when I consider Paul's beautiful attitude when suffering imprisonment, and it causes me shame at my own occasional negative attitude, though no doubt *suffering for Christ's sake* would be different than suffering from *overload*!

In the church Paul attended, the women occupied a prominent place—first of all, a prayer meeting of women met "out of the city by a river side" (Acts 16:13). Outstanding among those present was Lydia, "a seller of purple, of the city of Thyatira" (verse 14). She and her family readily received the apostle's message and were converted and baptized.

It was at Philippi that Paul and Silas were beaten and imprisoned. Then came an earthquake at midnight, followed by the conversion of the jailer and his family. The Philippi church was formed with its charter members being Lydia and her husband, the jailer and his household, along with others. Even in his *bonds*, Paul's witness for Christ in Rome was not in vain for members of the emperor's household accepted the Savior.

Although suffering in confinement, Paul was not discouraged. He was confident that God would work out everything to His honor and glory. He rejoiced in the Lord and admonished his readers to do the same (Phil. 4:4). He was resigned to whatever fate God should think best for him (Phil. 1:20). What a wonderful mentor! Let us join Paul as he looked to Christ and exhorted: "Let this mind be in you, which was also in Christ Jesus" (Phil. 2:5). As for himself he said: "This one thing I do, forgetting those things which were behind, and reaching forth unto those things which are before, I press toward the mark for the prize of the high calling of God in Christ Jesus" (Phil. 3:13, 14). He could forget because he remembered the way the Lord had led him in the past.

Colossians was written to the people of Colosse, an ancient Greek city that stood about 100 miles east of Ephesus in Asia Minor and consisted of Gentile

Christians. Three of Paul's *imprisonment* letters, Ephesians, Philippians, and Colossians, were written about the same time (AD 62), during the time of his first imprisonment. Paul had never been to Colosse before he wrote this letter. Yet, he wrote to them as though they were his own. That's a true *church-family* feeling! Paul intended to visit them when released from prison. The Colossians may have first heard the gospel during Paul's ministry in Ephesus (see Acts 19:10). His coworker, Epophras, ministered to the Colosse church.

Though the letter was dictated to a secretary, Paul wrote the salutation himself: "Paul, an apostle of Jesus Christ by the will of God, and Timotheus our brother, to the saints and faithful brethren in Christ which are at Colosse: Grace be unto you, and peace, from God our Father and the Lord Jesus Christ. We give thanks to God and the Father of our Lord Jesus Christ, praying always for you, since we heard of your faith in Christ Jesus, and of the love which you have to all the saints" (Col. 1:1-4).

A friend, George Boundey, paraphrased Colossians 1:9-14. I have been blessed by this prayer, and I hope you will be too:

> "My loving heavenly Father,
>
> "Today, I pray that You will fill me with the knowledge of Your will, give me all the wisdom and spiritual understanding I need, so that in every decision of life that I meet today, I will be able to follow clearly the path You have laid out for me.
>
> "Lord, please do a work in my life today that will enable me to walk worthy of Your high calling, that I may fully please You in everything I do, and that I will be fruitful in every good work. And Lord, I pray that I will know you better when this day ends than I do now.
>
> "Please strengthen me with Your glorious power so that I may have the patience and longsuffering to endure any trials or discouragements that might come to me today, without compromising principle or losing any of the divine joy You have given me.
>
> "And as I come to You in confession and repentance, Lord, I pray that You would remind me that You have delivered me from Satan's power and I don't need to be his slave today, for You have already made me a citizen of heaven.
>
> "Thank You for giving me such a marvelous hope for the future, the promise of wisdom and strength for today, and the joy of knowing that I am a dearly loved child of Yours every moment.
>
> "In Jesus' name, Amen."

In the Epistle to the Colossians, Paul expressed himself strongly against the heresy prevalent in the church. The purpose of this letter is to set forth the majesty and glory of God's person and character. Paul makes it clear that Jesus was not simply just a good man, but rather was actually God in the flesh. He declares that Christ exclusively is Creator and Mediator (Col. 1:16, 20) and has wrought out our redemption. He is the head of both material and spiritual things—He is over all and sustains all.

Practical duties of wives, husbands, children, and servants are beautifully given in the third chapter, especially verses 18-23. The entire chapter speaks of character traits to develop so that the "peace of God [may] rule in your hearts" (Col. 3:15). He also states the need to be dead to a sinful life: "Set your affections on things above, not on things on the earth" (Col. 3:2).

Paul wrote to combat the heresy that the ritual law was still in effect (Col. 2:14). Paul wanted to make it very clear that the ritual law (the ceremonial law) was nailed to the cross—done away with, no longer necessary. Paul warned of heresy creeping into the church. He urged the members to study and stay faithful to what they were taught.

This message was also to warn against judging others. Exhortations were given to holiness and steadfastness. Both Ephesians and Colossians contain great doctrines of the gospel and were to be read aloud in the churches.

1 Thessalonians, the earliest of the Pauline letters, was written at Corinth about AD 51 when the apostle visited this Greek city while on his second missionary journey (see Acts 18). It is possibly the first book of the New Testament to be written, with the exception of the Epistle of James. Since the four Gospels were written after Paul's letters (some of them as much as thirty years later), if we want to know what the Christians were thinking and teaching in the very first decades of the church's existence, our best guide is in the letters of Paul.

Thessalonica was the chief city of Macedonia and very important to the Roman Empire. It was 100 miles west of Philippi, and about fifty miles north of Athens. Paul's first contact with Thessalonica was on his second missionary journey just after his departure from Philippi (Acts 16:40-17:1). Paul was able to spend only three weeks in Thessalonica before a riot drove him away (Acts 17). It is amazing that in those few weeks he was able to establish a church! His letters were a source of continued guidance for their thinking on many great doctrines of the church. The glorious advent of the Lord is the most prominent doctrine presented. A radiant glow of ardent love permeates this book—the theme is practical godliness in view of Christ's return. Other doctrines mentioned are the death and resurrection of Christ as well as the future resurrection of the righteous dead. They were to "comfort one another with these words" (1 Thess. 4:18). He also wrote about future rewards and punishments; the personal existence and active working of Satan; and the doctrine of redemption, including election and sanctification.

Paul tells us how these Christians worried about complex issues such as the relationship between faith and works and the exact status of those who had died in Christ. That is why Paul talks so much in this letter about hope: *hope* in forgiveness, *hope* in holiness, and *hope* that Jesus will come again, reuniting us with our loved ones and enabling us to live both with them and with Him forever. Could anything but Christianity offer this *hope*?

2 Thessalonians was written by Paul at Corinth soon after he had sent the first letter. This was the shortest of the letters that he addressed to the churches, but it contains important doctrinal matter. Some who had read the first epistle erroneously deduced from the letter that Paul said that some of the brethren then living would not die but would live to see Jesus come (1 Thess. 4:16, 17). These words, which were meant to "give comfort," gave to some confusion! To correct this misunderstanding, Paul wrote this second letter.

Earlier in the letter the apostle said: "Let no man deceive you by any means: for the day shall not come, except there come a falling away first, and that man of sin be revealed, the son of perdition; who opposeth and exalteth himself above all that is called God, or that is worshipped; so that he as God sitteth in the temple of God, shewing himself that he is God. Remember ye not, that, when I was yet with you, I told you these things" (2 Thess. 2:3-5). According to this prophecy, there will come a great apostasy in the Christian church before the Lord shall come, and it will result in the elevation of a man in the church to the degree that he will claim to occupy the place of God in it. Furthermore, he will be a "man of sin," and the Bible defines sin as follows: "Sin is the transgression of the law" (1 John 3:4). Hence, this personage will be a notorious violator of God's law.

This book shows that even while the apostles were alive apostasy had already begun (2 Thess. 2:7) and will continue to plague God's true believers. It points us to the need to be well grounded in truth as is presented in Jesus and His Word.

1 Timothy was written by Paul soon after he had been released from prison at his first trial before Nero in AD 63. Paul visited Lystra, Timothy's home, when he was a boy. Among Paul's most enthusiastic converts were Eunice, Timothy's mother, and Lois, his grandmother. Paul calls Timothy "his beloved son," and he trained him in the service of Christ.

Later when Paul was on his second missionary journey, he took Timothy with him as his companion. This Epistle was written to Timothy while he was pastor of the Ephesus church and is composed primarily of instructions addressed to him as a leader of the church. It is classed as a *Pastoral Epistle*, a handbook for all Christian pastors.

Paul admonished him to give himself fully to the work of the ministry and to beware lest he become ensnared by errors that were becoming rampant. A special warning is given against the deceptions of spiritualism (1 Tim. 4:1-3). How timeless these warnings are! With the current interest growing in witchcraft, using enchantments, and dealing with familiar spirits and wizards, we need desperately to keep our thoughts on our Creator God. Why should humanity turn to the works of Satan instead of to God? The shelves in libraries are filled with books promoting Satan's lies. A very popular set of books for children featuring the character Harry Potter promotes good character traits mixed with wizardry. Our good conscience should put up a red flag to *beware*!

Paul instructs how to direct public worship and choose church officers, giving the requirements for both bishops and deacons (1 Tim. 3:1-11). He gives a beautiful description of the church and speaks of the conduct of men and women professing the faith of Jesus. He exhorts the reader to remain faithful in the Christian warfare, as one expecting the return of his Master to whom he must give account of himself.

Although the letter appears to have been written hurriedly, it is still packed full of concise and practical instructions for both ministers and laypeople.

Instructions are given regarding behavior and dress that will bring respect and glory to God in the "church of the living God, the pillar and ground of truth" (1 Tim. 3:15). This Epistle exhorts those who "professing godliness" (1 Tim. 2:10) should "walk the talk" and let their actions match what they profess to believe.

2 Timothy, the second Epistle to Timothy, was written in AD 65, the year after Rome was burned by Nero and after Paul had been released from his first imprisonment. He left Rome at Nice to work for a closer unity between the Greek and Eastern churches. In the meantime, the burning of Rome was charged to the Christians, and they were barbarously persecuted for it. Thousands perished as martyrs in Rome and elsewhere.

While Paul was laboring in Troas, he was suddenly arrested and taken back to Rome where he was put in a Roman dungeon. The instigator of his arrest was Alexander the coppersmith (2 Tim. 4:13, 14). Few of Paul's friends stood by him. Only Luke remained to comfort and care for him.

Paul wrote this last letter to his "beloved spiritual son," Timothy, and generally to the church. This Epistle has been called the last will and testament of the great apostle to the Gentiles. He felt the need of strengthening his younger coworker's faith while warning him and all Christian believers against heresies that were to enter the church after his time, that all might hold firm to the inspired Word and remain faithful to their Lord until His *second coming*. The heart of the Pastoral Epistle is found in this solemn charge: "That good thing which was committed unto thee keep by the Holy Ghost which dwelleth in us" (2 Tim. 1:14).

In this letter Paul urged Timothy, who was still in Ephesus, to come at once and bring the things Paul had left behind in Troas and try to reach Rome before winter (2 Tim. 4:11-21). There is a note of sadness here not detected in his other Epistles. Paul's farewell statement is touching: "I am now ready to be offered, and the time of my departure is at hand. I have fought a good fight, I have finished my course, I have kept the faith: henceforth there is laid up for me a crown of righteousness, which the Lord, the righteous judge, shall give me at that day: and not to me only, but unto all them also that love his appearing" (2 Tim. 4:6-8).

Titus, like 1 and 2 Timothy, this small book is another handbook for pastors and is the last of the *Pastoral Epistles*. Titus is not mentioned in Acts, yet his career can be put together from Paul's other letters. He was a Gentile, thought to be a convert during Paul's early ministry. Seventeen years after Paul's conversion, Titus accompanied him and Barnabas to Jerusalem.

Titus seems to be very mature and of strong personality: "This is why I left you in Crete, that you might amend what was defective" (Titus 1:5, RSV). His mission of service included guiding the church officers and ministering to the aged, the youth, and the slaves on how to live a Christian life.

The Epistle was addressed to Titus at a time when he was working in ministry at Crete—a very hard post. Earlier, Paul had given him the difficult task of settling differences at Corinth. In Paul's second letter to the Corinthians, we see how successful he was in this mission (2 Cor. 7:13-16).

It is very obvious and gratifying to note that Paul had great concern that God's church is to be a consecrated body of believers that would maintain sacred respect for order in every category of its actions and work, thus bringing glory to God in worship, making religious exercises "holy, acceptable unto God" (Rom. 12:1) and bringing satisfaction and peace to the worshippers. Worship is a response to God's presence. Martin Luther said that this little Epistle "is composed in such a masterly manner, that it contains all that is needful for Christian knowledge and life."

In Titus 2:13 Paul looks forward to the blessed "hope, and the glorious appearing of the great God and our Saviour Jesus Christ." Paul and all God's true followers have this hope burning in their hearts. At the climax of his letter, Paul reminds Titus, and the Cretans, and Christians of all ages, that God's kindness to man is not won by good deeds but is the gift of His mercy and grace.

Philemon is another of Paul's letters written while in prison in Rome about AD 63. It is his shortest epistle. Philemon was a well-to-do believer of the church at Colosse. The Epistle was written concerning a runaway slave, Onesimus, who belonged to Philemon. After having stolen money from his master, Onesimus fled to Rome and here came in contact with Paul. The apostle's heart went out in pity to the guilty servant, and he won the wretched man to Christ. Paul then counseled the converted fugitive to return to his master and live for God in the future.

This little gem of Christian love and tact is unique in Scripture because it is a purely personal letter regarding the relationship between a Christian master and a runaway, yet repentant, slave. This letter was sent at the same time of Onesimus' return, and he himself was the bearer of the letter to his master.

Whatever the slave had stolen, Paul promised to repay to Philemon. The servant had nothing with which to make restitution, and so how fitting an illustration of the love of Christ to the repentant sinner.

Hebrews has no salutation as the other letters have, but the tenor throughout the Epistle is that of Paul who doubtless wrote it to the church at Jerusalem when he was a prisoner in Rome the first time. Hebrews was written more like a sermon than a letter, and it has sometimes been called the *fifth Gospel*. The four Gospels describe Christ's ministry on earth; this one describes His ministry in heaven. It was written to Hebrew Christians to show that the sacrifices of the Old Testament were types of the greater sacrifices of the New Testament. The central point of the book of Hebrews is Christ's perfect sacrifice for the sins of the world.

Hebrews portrays a multi-purpose God: the Son of God was made the Son of man, taking upon Himself human flesh as the *Promised Seed* of Abraham; heir of salvation; giving assurance of salvation; acting as Mediator; and serving as eternal High Priest after the order of Melchizedek. I challenge you, dear reader, to watch for other *purposes* and think about what they mean to you.

The book of Hebrews rings with some of the most confident words of Christian assurance and acceptance in the Bible: "Therefore he is able to save completely those who come to God through him, because he always lives to intercede for them" (Heb. 7:25, NIV). But the book also contains terrible warnings of doom for the despisers of God's grace (see Heb. 6:4-6; 10:26-31; 12:15-17). Paul admonishes believers: "Let us hold fast the profession of our faith without wavering; (for he is faithful that promised;) and let us consider one another to provoke unto love and to good works: not forsaking the assembling of ourselves together, as the manner of some is; but exhorting one another: and so much the more, as ye see the day approaching" (Heb. 10:23-25). Simply put, it's important to worship in church with fellow believers, of which Jesus

Mining for Gold

was a good example (see Luke 4:16).

Hebrews 11 is known as *God's Hall of Fame*. Note the kind of people mentioned: we see repentant, converted former drunks, harlots, failures, and second-rate individuals, all who learned "to live by faith." Two of these individuals are Rahab (verse 31) and Samson (verse 32). Rahab, the harlot, was one of the first women to be singled out in the genealogy of Jesus (Matt. 1:5). This chapter shows that we are not a bigger sinner than God is a Savior—Rahab and Samson attest to that. It also shows that man cannot judge *who* will be in *God's hall of fame*.

God's hall of fame does bear names we would expect to find there. There are spiritual heroes such as Joseph, Daniel, and a multitude of other faithful servants of God. They realized their need of God and depended on Him. It is thrilling to note that no matter what the record has been in the past, the final score is what counts in the end (see Eze. 18:26-28). Remember, "be thou faithful unto death, and I will give thee a crown of life" (Rev. 2:10). God is just! He is so just and so wise that the whole human race, with the exception of Enoch and Elijah who were translated, will receive their reward at the same time. (Heb. 11:39, 40) Now that's something great to think about!

Our names are not recorded in Hebrews, but by our choice of love and God's grace, we can have our names "written in heaven" (Heb. 12:23) in the "book of remembrance" (Mal. 3:16) and the "book of life" (Rev. 20:12). What an awesome privilege! I want to answer *yes* to the question asked in this song: "Is your name written there on the page white and fair? In the book of Thy kingdom, is my name written there?"

The Epistle of James is known as one of the general Epistles of the New Testament and the authorship is identified with James, a brother of Jesus who was the leader of the church in Jerusalem. It is addressed "to the twelve tribes which are scattered abroad" (James 1:1), which seems to indicate that it was written primarily for the Hebrew Christians of the early church, and to the "universal" church as a whole. Many biblical scholars think that James was the first New Testament book, dating back to AD 45-50, and some say about AD 60. They believe this was the James slain by the Jews in AD 62.

James emphasizes that justification by faith is demonstrated by works. He speaks of the fruit of faith (James 3:17), pointing out that while works do not save us they are an evidence of our relationship with God (James 2:5). Because of its practical guide to Christian living and conduct, James has often been referred to as the *Proverbs of the New Testament.*

James' letter is one of general exhortation on many matters. He emphasizes the fact that faith must be accompanied by works or else that faith is dead. He censures favoring the rich against the poor, calls for guarded speech and the avoidance of envy and dissension, and recommends special prayer for the sick, anointing with oil by the elders of the church.

In this short Epistle, we find one of the most important Bible prophecies foretelling distressing social conditions in the world in the last days. Chapter 5 contains a notable forecast of the mighty struggle between capital and labor that has been troubling the nations in our own times. "In the annals of human history the growth of nations, the rise and fall of empires, appear as dependent on the will and prowess of man. The shaping of events seems, to a great degree, to be determined by his power, ambition, and caprice. But in the word of God the curtain is drawn aside, and we behold, behind, above, and through all the play and counterplay of human interests and power and passions, the agencies of the all-merciful One, silently, patiently working out the counsels of His own will" (*Education,* p. 173).

God's counsel to the oppressed in these days is that they do not become unduly alarmed: "Be ye also patient; stablish your hearts: for the coming of the Lord draweth nigh. Grudge not one against another, brethren, lest ye be condemned: behold, the judge standeth before the door" (James 5:8, 9).

1 Peter was written by Simon Peter, one of the apostles of Christ, around AD 64. It was written in the last years of Peter's ministry, which he was permitted to close in Rome. The message is addressed to believers scattered in the Roman provinces of Asia Minor. These believers had undergone great sufferings already, and soon—when the burning of Rome by Nero would be charged against them—the whole church would pass through a terrible period of persecution.

The readers are reminded of Christ's suffering and death when unjustly charged. Peter, himself, knew from his own experience what trials and suffering

Mining for Gold

meant, but he gives a formula for happiness in a world that is wretched and evil. "Casting all your care upon him; for he careth for you. Be sober, be vigilant; because your adversary the devil, as a roaring lion, walketh about, seeking whom he may devour: . . . but the God of all grace, who hath called us unto his eternal glory by Christ Jesus, after that ye have suffered a while, make you perfect, stablish, strengthen, settle you. To him be glory and dominion for ever and ever. Amen" (1 Peter 5:7-11).

Peter was the preacher at Pentecost, but before that he had denied knowing Jesus. His life was transformed by the power of the gospel from impetuous to patient, from boastful to loving, and from aggressive to courageous. Peter has been called the apostle *of hope*, Paul *of faith*, and John *of love*. Peter speaks of *hope* four times in his first book and mentions *joy* and *glory* twenty-six different times in the five chapters.

2 Peter was a general epistle written shortly after the first one and a short while before Peter's martyrdom. This letter is not addressed to any particular group, so it is presumed to have been written to the churches in general.

Whenever I read 2 Peter 1:3-10, pleasant memories come to me of early morning walks when, from notes I carried, these verses filled my mind as I attempted to put them to memory. I find beauty in the promised gifts whereby all can be "partakers of the divine nature, having escaped the corruption that is in the world" (verse 4). The list of *add-ons* in verses 5 through 7 makes me eager to do just what these admonitions from God suggest.

Peter says that the apostles did "not [follow] cunningly devised fables" in preaching the gospel of Jesus Christ, but proved everything by the "sure word of prophecy" (2 Peter 1:16-21). He sets forth sacred prophecy as something that we must heed, while warning the church against the false prophets who would arise in the years to come to plague the church with heresy. Looking with prophetic vision down the centuries, he foretold conditions that will prevail in the world just before the *second coming* of the Savior to the ushering in of "a new earth, wherein dwelleth righteousness" (2 Peter 3:13).

Peter and Paul give their last written message before their death in 2 Peter and 2 Timothy, respectively. Both warn of the coming apostasy and heresy. Both anchor the church on the Scriptures as their only defense against the coming storm. Peter also focuses on the matter of the apparent delay of Christ's return and warns that we not fall from our own steadfastness: "Wherefore, beloved, seeing that ye look for such things, be diligent that ye may be found of him in peace, without spot, and blameless" (2 Peter 3:14).

Peter, by his own request, was crucified upside down, considering himself unworthy to resemble, in any way, his Master's death. Jesus prophesied in John 21:18 and 19 the death Peter would suffer.

1 John was one of three Epistles written by the beloved disciple, John, during the last years of his life. He first wrote his Gospel, then the letters, and finally the book of Revelation. The Epistles were written about AD 90 from Ephesus.

John is best known as the apostle of love, and it is said he wrote with a pen dipped in love. He wrote so eloquently about God's love for us: "Behold, what manner of love the Father hath bestowed upon us, that we should be called the sons of God . . . and every man that hath this hope in him purifieth himself, even as he is pure" (1 John 3:1-3).

John urges God's followers to have brotherly and Christian love and have it dominate their lives. Love is catching: "We love him, because he first loved us" (1 John 4:19). Another of my favorite verses from 1 John is found in chapter 1, verse 9: "If we confess our sins, he is faithful and just to forgive us our sins, and to cleanse us from all unrighteousness."

This apostle of love was also a stern man and intolerant of heresy. He was an intense person. The times were full of peril for the early church—satanic delusions existed everywhere. How it must have filled the apostles' hearts with sadness as they warned of great errors creeping into the church. If this could be said of the days of the apostles, think of what could be said of the church today when Satan knows his time is short and is going about "seeking whom he may devour [and lead astray]" (1 Peter 5:8). The warnings are ever needful, but the solutions are always the same: "Brethren, I write no new commandment unto you, but an old commandment which ye had from the beginning. The old commandment is the word which ye have heard from the beginning" (1 John 2:7). (This sounds like the "everlasting gospel" of Revelation 14:6.) "Beloved, believe not every spirit, but try the spirits whether they are of God: because many false prophets are gone out into the world" (1 John 4:1).

2 John is written, like Philemon, as a personal letter to those whom the apostle John calls "the elect lady and her children" (2 John 1:1). This godly woman was a worker for Christ and a person of high repute in the early church. This letter, the shortest book in the Bible (thirteen verses) commends this mother for having taught her children to walk in truth.

The letter echoes much of 1 John, warning against giving hospitality to false teachers lest one become a sharer in their wicked work (see verses 7-11). The true charity of hospitality is too pure to cover an unconfessed sin. We are to make no compromise with evil.

The word *truth* is found five times in the thirteen verses of this book, and *love* four times. The two are inseparable, and John points out that the test of our love is whether we keep the truth of God and His commandments. Truth without love can be cruel. Love without truth can be deceptive.

3 John, almost as brief as the second, was penned about the same time as were John's other two letters. This is also a personal letter written to a friend named Gaius, who was noted for his hospitality. He greets his friend warmly: "Beloved, I wish above all things that thou mayest prosper and be in health, even as thy soul prospereth" (3 John 1:2). He adds these encouraging words, spoken in love: "I have no greater joy than to hear that my children [spiritual converts] walk in truth" (3 John 1:4).

In this letter John urges Gaius to continue his hospitality in spite of bitter opposition by Diotrephes, an elder in the church who had been led astray by false teachers and who, through malicious words, tried to hinder the cause (verse 10).

The letter ends on a positive note—the good example of another Christian brother, Demetrius, who represented Christ and the truth. In 2 John, John says the truth is worth *standing* for; in 3 John, he says it is worth *working* for.

The short book of **Jude** was written by Jude, the brother of James and a half-brother of Jesus. It is thought that this book was written between AD 66-69. It is a general or universal Epistle in which believers everywhere were urged to "earnestly contend for the faith which was once delivered unto the saints" (Jude 3).

The letter contains a clear call to the church to be on guard against the inroads of the heresy of Gnosticism, a philosophy that distinguished sharply between matter as being evil and spirit as being good. According to them, Christ's body was only apparent, not real, for if it was real, it would have been evil. As to its effect on Christian ethics, Gnosticism prompted two different results: the belief that one is not under obligation to obey the moral law, and the other belief led to a form of abuse of the body to promote spirituality. The Bible teaches no such doctrines. Jude also calls the attention of believers to the lessons learned by Israel when they let themselves be seduced into pagan error by Balaam, a time when thousands of Jews perished.

The theme of the book is *assurance in days of apostasy.* The closing two verses say, "Now unto him that is able to keep you from falling, and to present you faultless before the presence of his glory with exceeding joy, To the only wise God our Saviour, be glory and majesty, dominion and power, both now and ever. Amen" (Jude 24).

I'm counting on this *completion* for me!

Revelation, also known as "the Revelation of Jesus Christ," is the book written by John in about AD 95 when he was an old man. As a young man he had been a close companion to Jesus, following Him during the three-and-a-half years of His ministry. Jesus had given John to be a son to His mother, Mary, upon His death. John had watched Jesus die and had seen Him after His resurrection. At the time of his writing Revelation, it had been fifty or maybe sixty years since Jesus had shared His promise to return.

John wrote this book while he was on the isle of Patmos (Rev. 1:9). This rocky islet, located in the Aegean Sea, was a place to which the Roman government banished notorious criminals. The pagan emperor Domitian, determined to put a stop to the preaching of the gospel by this remaining survivor of Christ's apostles, had ordered John exiled to Patmos. Jesus appeared to John on the Island of Patmos to let him know that He would keep His promise—that He would be with him to the end and would come again to rescue His followers.

Revelation is the only book of *prophecy* in the New Testament, compared to seventeen in the Old Testament. The books of Revelation and Daniel go

Mining for Gold

hand in hand. While Daniel was given the following instruction, "shut up the words, and seal the book, even to the time of the end" (Dan. 12:4), Revelation is what the name implies—it *reveals* great secrets and truths. It is a book that promises a special blessing to the reader "for the time is at hand" (Rev. 1:3).

The book is a series of visions expressed in approximately 300 symbols, each having a definite meaning. Also, the number seven, considered a perfect number, is frequently used throughout the book.

There are approximately 500 references in Revelation to Old Testament passages. There are at least ten great subjects of prophecy that find their fulfillment in Revelation. The prophecies in this book point to events that are to take place in this world before Jesus comes again. The book of Revelation is more than just a book about the future; it is a book that tells us how we should live until the future comes to pass: "be thou faithful until death, and I will give thee a crown of life" (Rev. 2:10). Included in this book are the three angels' messages, the mark of the beast, the seven last plagues, the marriage of the Lamb, the first and second resurrections, the destruction of the wicked, and the reward of the righteous.

Most importantly, this book truly is the "Revelation of Jesus Christ" (Rev. 1:1). We find Him as both the Lamb who was slain and the Lion of Judah, both the Suffering Servant and the Conquering King, the Sacrifice and the Priest, the Advocate and the Judge, the forgiving Savior and avenging Warrior. In short, He is King of Kings and Lord of Lords, and He will come again, not as a homeless stranger, but with power and great glory!

My favorite part of Revelation is the detailed description of the new earth (Rev. 21 and 22) that should make us determined to be a citizen there! "He that overcometh shall inherit all things; and I will be his God, and he shall be my son" (Rev. 21:7). What a glorious book to climax the great controversy between Christ and Satan, which began at the fall of humanity (Gen. 3), that is recorded through the rest of the Bible revealing tragic choices against God as well as of those who chose to serve Him.

An older gentleman who was reading the book of Revelation was asked by a young seminary student if he understood what he was reading. He answered, "The last two chapters wrap it up with victory for God; He is justified, and His followers will share this victory with Him." The simplest word to define this book is *victory*.

"Blessed are they that do his commandments, that they may have right to the tree of life, and may enter in through the gates into the city" (Rev. 22:14). "Even so, come, Lord Jesus" (verse 20). ♥

How Readest Thou?
Author Unknown.
from *Bible Readings for the Home* (1942)

It is one thing to read the Bible through
Another thing to read to learn and do.
Some read it with design to learn to read,
But to the subject pay but little heed.
Some read it as their duty once a week,
But no instruction from the Bible seek;
While others read it with but little care,
With no regard to how they read, nor where.
Some read to bring themselves into repute,
By showing others how they can dispute;
While others read because their neighbors do,
To see how long 'twill take to read it through.
Some read it for the wonders that are there,—
How David killed a lion and a bear;
While others read it with uncommon care,
Hoping to find some contradictions there.
Some read as if it did not speak to them,
But to the people at Jerusalem.
One reads, with father's specs upon his head,
And sees the thing just as his father said.
Some read to prove a pre-adopted creed,
Hence understanding but little that they read;
For every passage in the book they bend
To make it suit that all-important end.
Some people read, as I have often thought,
To teach the book instead of being taught;
And some there are who read it out of spite,
I fear there are but few who read it right.
But read it prayerfully, and you will see,
Although men contradict, God's Words agree;
For what the early Bible prophets wrote,
We find that Christ and His apostles quote.
So trust no creed that trembles to recall
What has been penned by one and verified by all.

Chapter 12

Take Time to Remember

Throughout the entire Scripture, God has made it known that He wants to be uppermost in the minds of His followers. "Dear children, keep away from anything that might take God's place in your hearts, Amen" (1 John 5:21, TLB). "If your aim is to enjoy the evil pleasures of the unsaved world, you cannot also be a friend of God" (James 4:4, TLB). He asked men of old to establish memorials to bring back to their minds the marvelous works He had orchestrated in the lives of His followers that prompted their desire for fellowship. These memorials would also be beneficial to parents when asked by their children the reason for the memorial (see Ex. 12:26, 13:14).

We find in the Old Testament that the first memorial God established was a "day"—a time set aside as a memorial of Creation (Gen. 2:2, 3). He asks us to remember this first memorial (Ex. 20:8; Isa. 66:23).

Before sin entered the world, two institutions were given to man. The one I just mentioned was the Sabbath; the other was marriage (see Gen. 2:23-25). These two memorials have been called the *twin sisters of Paradise*.

God asked Israelite parents to diligently teach their children God's requirements by talking about them often and putting them on their houses and gates (see Deut. 6:3-12). This was meant to be a visible reminder of the promises God had made and kept with them and their forbearers. It would bring courage and trust in the fulfillment of promises for the future. Often, the *talking* God wants from His followers is not always audible but is seen and felt in their lives. There are other times when audible conversation is needed, especially that of thanksgiving, praise, and love.

In the ancient Near East and in other parts of the world, it was customary to write important sayings in conspicuous places or dwellings. We often see the same today. The history lessons in Scripture are for God's followers through all generations and should be taught positively to all children. For us, putting God's requirements on the "house and gates" is symbolic of living as He requires in and out of the home. This is making Bible history personal in our lives and those of our family. God wants us to make service to Him a joyful, happy experience—as it truly is. Some parents may wish they had done a better job of this in the past; they may wish to take back unkind or misunderstood words spoken to their children. Parents may regret a bad example they left. But it is impossible to erase the past, much as it may be desired. Thank God for His mercy, understanding, and forgiveness. How healing and comforting to all if forgiveness is given by those affected by these regrets. Words and acts of remorse should teach lessons that prevent a repetition of them by God's grace!

A beautiful ladder dream brought courage to the fugitive Jacob while on his way to find a wife among God's people. The rocks he used for a pillow became a memorial of God's promises. Jacob's gratitude offering was his tithe (see Gen. 28:10-22).

Another memorial came in the form of a song of deliverance sung by Moses and the children of Israel when they safely crossed the Red Sea. God made that very sea the burial place of the pursuing Egyptian army (see Ex. 14 and 15). If the Israelites had sung their memorial song as their theme song through their years of travel, it would have quieted their murmuring with trusting memory! It's a great lesson for all generations, including ours! This song of Moses and the Lamb will be repeated when Jesus comes again as a memorial of the deliverance from sin (Rev. 15:3).

The obstacles the Israelites encountered on their journey from Egypt to the *Promised Land* caused them to constantly complain to God, Moses, and Aaron. One would think the miracles along the way would have given them courage, but it didn't. During one of these discouraging times, they complained about not having bread and water and protested their dreadful dislike of manna. As a punishment God sent fiery serpents among the people, and many died. Recognizing their terrible sin, the people ran to Moses and asked him to intercede on their behalf that God would take the snakes away.

Instead, God asked Moses to make a replica of the poisonous serpent and attach it to a pole. All who were bitten were instructed to simply look at it and they would live. This was in no way an act of worship. The *looking and living* was to remind the people of their sin. The serpent was to direct their thoughts to Christ—the Savior—who would deliver and save them. It seems dreadful that a serpent, which represents sin, should represent Christ! But we must remember that "he hath made him to be sin for us, who knew no sin; that we might be made the righteousness of God in him" (2 Cor. 5:21). Jesus said of this occasion: "And I, if I be lifted up from the earth, will draw all men unto me. This he said, signifying what death he should die" (John 12:32, 33). It was truly a remarkable memorial that generates deep thoughts of gratitude for what Christ has done for us.

Picture another awesome scene when the entire nation of Israel crossed the Jordan River on dry ground! This miracle is described in Joshua 3:1-4:24. In this chapter on memorials, I want to focus on the altar God asked Joshua to build after they crossed the river. Twelve men, representing the twelve tribes of Israel, were asked to bring stones for this altar from the middle of the Jordan's dry riverbed. The priests bearing the ark were still standing there. The altar was to be built where the people were going to camp, which was on the other side of the river. As soon as the priests' feet left the riverbed, the imprisoned water rushed down, resuming the natural river. Coming generations were able to witness the memorial of this great miracle: "That all the people of the earth might know the hand of the LORD, that it is mighty: that ye might fear the LORD your God for ever" (Joshua 4:24).

Today, we could well ask ourselves: "What are my Jordan stones?" With each of our experiences with Christ, we have a message to share with others.

In the New Testament Paul calls our attention to how God wants His followers to regard the death, burial, and resurrection of Christ through the rite of baptism by immersion. It is interesting to note that the word *baptism* is mentioned ninety-seven times in the New Testament. It is another very important memorial: "Therefore we are buried with him by baptism into death: that like as Christ was raised up from the dead by the glory of the Father, even so we also should walk in newness of life. For if we have been planted together in the likeness of his death, we shall be also in the likeness of his resurrection" (Rom. 6:4, 5).

The Lord's Supper service, including the foot washing, is a minibaptism and is also a memorial of the Lord's death and resurrection. It is to refresh our thoughts of this sacred event that we celebrate the communion service. "This do in remembrance of me" (Luke 22:19). "For as often as ye eat this bread, and drink this cup, ye do shew the Lord's death till he come" (1 Cor. 11:26). What else could have brought Christ's gift of salvation to our mind in a more effective way? People have their ideas for remembering Jesus' resurrection, but God does everything just right!

Another memorial, in my way of thinking, is our body. "What? know ye not that your body is the temple of the Holy Ghost which is in you, which ye have of God, and ye are not your own? For ye are bought with a price: therefore glorify God in your body, and in your spirit, which are God's" (1 Cor. 6:19, 20; see also 1 Cor. 3:16, 17). When we look at our reflection in the mirror, let us say to ourselves, "Whether therefore ye eat, or drink, or whatsoever ye do, do all to the glory of God" (1 Cor. 10:31). The Bible contains many texts teaching us how to live, eat, and drink to God's glory (see Gen. 1:29; Lev. 11; Prov. 20:1, 23:31-33; and Rom. 12:2). We have greatly benefited by following the program of Weimar Institute in Weimar, California, an organization promoting healthful living by natural methods. They use an acrostic as a name for their program: it's called *NEW START*. The letters stand for:

Nutrition	**S**unlight
Exercise	**T**emperance
Water	**A**ir
	Rest
	Trust in God

God will be with His followers to the end of the world and will continue to give us memorials, physically seen or unseen, to constantly bring His blessings to our mind. "We have nothing to fear for the future except as we shall forget the way the Lord has led us, and His teaching in our past history" (*Testimonies to Ministers and Gospel Workers,* p. 31). In many of our Christian homes we see pictures of nature scenes or spiritual plaques on the walls or wholesome reading material and other items that reveal a focus on God. Hopefully there is also a desire to "*walk* the talk." Spirituality should be a lifestyle (see Col. 1:10 and 2:6).

I know that all over the world stand monuments of one kind or another to let us know that *God's hands* are at work and still working for His glory! Let me share briefly an amazing story of one such memorial: "In 1874, Methodists in Swan Quarter, North Carolina, found the ideal site—high ground in the heart of town—for the church they planned to build. The owner, Sam Sadler, did not want to *waste* his prime real estate on a church. Soon after his refusal, the Methodists accepted a gift of land on some low-lying property, and the members cheerfully built a modest, sturdy structure resting on brick piers.

"On September 17, 1876, right after they dedicated the small church, a powerful hurricane struck. Rain poured down until the rising water lifted the little church from its foundation. The floating church seemed to have a mind of its own and eventually settled in the very center of the property that the congregation had originally requested for their house of worship! After seeing the mighty work of Providence, Mr. Sadler, with trembling hands, deeded the land to the church. When the church was dedicated, it was named *Providence*. Today, a sign stands in front of the Providence church reminding visitors that this was the church '*moved by the Hand of God*'" (*Amazing Facts*).

Families have memories and memorials that bring to their mind pleasant or unpleasant occasions—times when God brought them through great difficulties, taught them lessons, and gave them peace. You may want to check the word "memorial" in a concordance for additional study. What memorials do you have for the celebration of your relationship with God? ♥

Chapter 13

We Can All Be Winners

Jon Dybdahl writes, "Both the Old and New Testaments speak clearly about God's justice and judgment, yet the subject of judgment is among the most unpopular today. Western Christians, in particular, want to hear about love, but cringe at the mention of judgment. While we want to avoid portraying God as a deity who delights in destroying people, we must be faithful to the part of Scripture that indicates that God will call every work into judgment. (See Ecclesiastes 12:14.)

"The same Paul who talked so eloquently about love in 1 Corinthians 13, also says that *"all must appear before the judgment seat of Christ"* (2 Corinthians 5:10). That message must be clearly proclaimed so people can be warned. It's part of our basic honesty" (*Old Testament Grace*).

My understanding of God's grace in the Old Testament is heightened whenever I read articles or books by the above-noted author. Though a well-known scholar of the Old Testament, his thoughts on grace—even when writing about wars or the sacrificial system—speak loudly for a God we can love and trust.

Forty-nine of the sixty-six books of the Bible mention the subject of judgment. There are a total of 292 references to the word *judgment* and more than 1,000 references on the subject. Jesus spoke of this subject often. In God's mercy and love, He never surprises mankind. "Surely the Lord GOD will do nothing, but he revealeth his secret unto his servants the prophets" (Amos 3:7). The last message to be given on this earth is found in Revelation 14:6 and 7. Here John the Revelator tells of a message of judgment.

A time prophecy in Daniel 7:9, 10, and 13 predicts a judgment that will occur in heaven before Jesus' *second advent*. (Study prayerfully and diligently, Dan. 2, 7, 8, 9 and Rev. 13 and 14) It was also foretold by Paul that God has set a day when He will judge the world with justice by the Man He has appointed—Jesus Christ (Acts 17:31). This judgment will settle our destiny for "he that is unjust, let him be unjust still: . . . and he that is righteous, let him be righteous still" (Rev. 22:11). When Jesus comes again, He will say, "my reward is with me, to give every man according as his work shall be" (verse 12).

How often we lament when we see the unjust world and the suffering taking place and wonder what Christ is doing about it. When will this pain be replaced by a home for the saved wherein is righteousness with *no more pain, sorrow, or death*? The pronouncement of the last message of this earth's history—"Fear God, and give glory to him; for the hour of his judgment is come" (Rev. 14:7)—is part of the everlasting gospel, the good news.

We, His followers, can actually look forward to this time—the end of this time. We will feel like David when he begged God: "Judge me, O LORD my God, according to thy righteousness" (Ps. 35:24; see also the beauty in Ps. 98:8, 9). During this time there is no fear for His followers, for abiding trust in God accepts His interceding as our Advocate. Jesus is the only sin-bearer and sin-offering. Salvation is within our reach because of Jesus (see Rom. 8:1; 1 John 2:1).

Jesus saves to the uttermost all who come to Him in faith. His glorious appearing is our blessed hope. He is not only our Advocate but also our righteous Judge (Heb. 7:25, 26). He will finish His good work, which He has begun in us (Phil. 1:6). He will make us safe to live with the holy beings in His new creation forever and ever!

The message of judgment is given to appeal to us to listen to God's Word, accept His love and grace, and help us be prepared for the final day of reckoning. God's true followers have no fear for the judgment. The apostle John wrote: "So we will not be afraid on the day of judgment, but can face Him with confidence because we live like Jesus here in this world" (1 John 4:17, NLT; see also Rom. 8:1).

Throughout the ages God has called for a message and a messenger for every critical time of spiritual need, starting with Noah and the Flood and continuing through history to the end-time crisis and the need for the presentation of the *three angels'* messages. The last day messengers are not superior to others, but they do have more responsibility to get the message out!

The earmarks for the final remnant messengers are found in Revelation 12:17: "And the dragon [Satan] was wroth with the woman [the church], and went to make war with the remnant of her seed, which keep the commandments of God, and have the testimony of Jesus Christ." There are several explanations or definitions concerning the meaning of "the testimony of Jesus Christ." One is the self-revelation of Jesus—His own testimony found many times in the Gospels. Another is the part His followers have by witnessing for Christ (see Matt. 28:19, 20). The definition from the Scriptures is that "the testimony of Jesus is the spirit of prophecy" (Rev. 19:10). This is the only time this phrase is used in Scripture.

There are many times in Scripture where the remnant is mentioned. They were always in the minority and often unpopular. A cloth remnant is thought of as the last piece on the bolt of fabric. In reality, the last piece is also the first of what was put on the bolt! To me, the last, being also the first, recalls the term "the everlasting gospel." It was taught in the beginning. The promise found in Genesis 3:15 was the beginning of the everlasting gospel. Paul has this to say about the timing of this gospel: "According as he hath chosen us in him before the foundation of the world, that we should be holy and without blame before him in love" (Eph. 1:4).

God has called into existence a church prophetically foreseen and chosen for a very specific purpose—to proclaim the third angel's message to a lost and dying world. Those of the end-time remnant have been called to protect and restore truth that has been neglected or rejected through the years. They are to call the world back to Jesus and the apostles' teachings. There are God's remnant people in all persuasions who love God supremely and seek to do His will. This is a special message to them: "And I heard another voice from heaven saying, Come out of her [false doctrines], my people, that ye be not partakers of her sins, and that you receive not of her plagues" (Rev. 18:4). Those who obey this invitation will be the greater part of the end-time remnant.

Salvation is not guaranteed by any church membership, nor does it accord its members an exclusive status with God any more than being a Hebrew (the chosen) in ancient Israel did. It's a sacred privilege and a great responsibility because we have a sacred calling. Receiving salvation is an individual matter.

Meanwhile, I've heard it stated well as follows: We need a religion that commits us to a lifetime of making the world a better place while at the same time longing for deliverance from the world. We need a religion that watches the signs of the times while resisting the urge to create signs from events that don't deserve to be invested with significance. We need a religion that remembers that prophecy is not merely to foretell what is coming but to confirm our faith when we recognize the predictions fulfilled.

Deeper study shows that God's judgments are a product of His love for humanity. God's "strange act"—the destruction of the devil, his angels, and those who choose to cling to sin in spite of His loving pleas—is a necessity in order to have a new earth "wherein dwelleth righteousness" (2 Peter 3:13). Rightfully understood, the truth of the Bible about judgment leads us to love Christ! He is always fair and always right.

The best thing about the judgment is the vindication of God! I am looking forward to the time when the entire universe, the saved and the unsaved, will admit their satisfaction with God's balance and justice! "Even so, Lord God Almighty, true and righteous are thy judgments" (Rev. 16:7; see also Phil. 2:11).

Next to the satisfaction of God's vindication is the vindication of His followers: "Blessed are they that do his commandments, that they may have right to the tree of life, and may enter in through the gates into the city" (Rev. 22:14; see also verses 12 and 13). This is possible because His followers have been faithful unto death! (Rev. 2:10). Also responsible for the salvation of Christ's followers is their willingness to exchange their filthy garments for the garments of Christ's righteousness (see Zech. 3:1-8; Mal. 3:16).

Consider this thought: "My people are destroyed for lack of knowledge" (Hosea 4:6). I must know what I believe and find it to match in every way the standard of truth—the Bible. I must line up verses from both the Old and New Testaments that define the meanings of God's teachings so that they support one other, are balanced, and complete.

The Holy Spirit also inspired 1 Corinthians 13:13: "And now abideth faith, hope, charity [love], these three; but the greatest of these is charity [love]." Here's a thought to ponder: *Truth without love destroys. Love without truth deceives.*

Truth is not, and never has been, established by a majority. Truth has nothing to fear from examination. It is always possible that a fresh pair of eyes may see something that others have overlooked. Our spiritual forefathers fasted, prayed, and sought to be in one accord with their deep study. Are we as serious and dedicated in our search for truth as they were?

We must never feel that a Christian, regardless of his degree of growth, is superior or inferior to another Christian. God knows the heart and takes a lot more into consideration than any human being does. The more a person knows, or has the privilege of knowing, the more responsible he is to *walk the talk*. The understanding that God knows the heart removes all desire to judge another individual. Instead, we'll spend our energy and time discovering what the Lord requires of us.

I choose to *drink of pure streams* of what I've studied as truth with the Bible as my guide and standard. I choose to be in harmony with God's Word by meditating and studying that which will strengthen my faith and feed my soul. I want to think positively about my beliefs. Just as the expert on discovering counterfeit money will study primarily the genuine bills—not the fakes—I, too, want to concentrate on the genuine. *The light of truth grows brighter with consecrated study—but the test is: What am I doing with the truth I already have?*

God has let us know what He would have us think on: "Set your affection on things above, not on things on the earth" (Col. 3:2). "When Christ is the center of our lives, our daily existence becomes a beautiful balance—a wonderful symmetry," wrote Stephen Chavez. We can turn sadness to joy by contemplating Christ's willingness to step down from His beautiful home in heaven—where He was adored—to come to earth and die for our sins! "He shall see of the travail of his soul, and shall be satisfied: by his knowledge shall my righteous servant justify many; for he shall bear their iniquities" (Isa. 53:11). He wants to see you and I as part of His *satisfaction*! Christ's second coming is the hope of all ages, for the entire universe, since sin entered the earth. Our sin-cursed earth will be Eden restored—*a new earth*.

What an awesome thrilling time to be among the vast multitude of saved from every distant time until now and from every nation under the sun! These are people who responded to God's love for them. They loved God with all their hearts and chose to obey and serve Him according to all they were able to know.

Trusting God's love, justice, mercy, and grace, I believe there will be people saved who, because of where and when they were born, had never had the opportunity to read or hear of Jesus, but God saw their hearts and minds were in tune with the divine (see Ps. 87:6). I can just picture them with rivers of joyful tears on their faces as they fall prostrate at Jesus' feet at being introduced to the only One who can save. "Neither is there salvation in any other: for there is none other name under heaven given among men, whereby we must be saved" (Acts 4:12). Augustus Toplady's classic hymn "Rock of Ages" expresses it well: "Nothing in my hand I bring, Simply to the cross I cling." What an inheritance! I plan to make it mine. It's an awesome, joyful scene! Let's *all be winners* at this homecoming.

The followers of God will be so happy in heaven. Humanity will continue to have free choice, so the saved must be *safe to save*, for "he will make an utter end: affliction [and sin] shall not rise up the second time" (Nahum 1:9). There will never be another heavenly sinner such as Lucifer!

There are not words to describe this glorious time of renewal! "What no eyes have seen, nor ear heard, nor the heart of man conceived, what God has prepared for those who love Him" (1 Cor. 2:9, RSV). The glories of heaven and life there, with no sin, sickness, crying, death, or parting are described in Isaiah 35, Isaiah 66:22-23, and Revelation 21 and 22. Best of all, we will be with our Creator, Sustainer, Savior, King of Kings, and Lord of Lords! Now that's a thought worth thinking about! ❤

Chapter 14

A Revolutionary Challenge

After the storming of Rome, Italian revolutionary leader Guiseppe Garibaldi made this proclamation to his soldiers: "Soldiers, I have nothing to offer you but hunger, thirst, hardship, and death. Let all who love their country, follow me!" He knew many gallant men would follow him, accepting what he offered—even death. Through the ages many others, including government leaders, daring explorers, and medical researchers, have heard and heeded the same type of call—some at great personal cost.

Whittier's advice to a youth who sought his counsel is right to the point: "Young man, if you should make the most of your life, join yourself to some righteous but unpopular cause." When I read of an Englishman, William Wilberforce, who stood up before the British Parliament and lobbied nearly to his deathbed that slaves would not be bought and sold like animals, I thought of this unpopular, but certainly righteous, cause.

Jesus also offered this type of challenge to His followers. It was not for *love of country* as was Garibaldi's call but for the love of God. Yet, the *love of country*—the new earth—did have a drawing influence on those who answered His call. Garibaldi's call offered the possibility of hunger, thirst, danger, and death. However, Jesus included the promise of eternal life. "For whosoever will save his life shall lose it; but whosoever shall lose his life for my sake and the gospel's, the same shall save it" (Mark 8:35). The great secret is that those who find this truth realize it is for both the *here* and the *hereafter* (see John 10:10). Paul tells us, "While we look not at the things which are seen, but at the things which are not seen: for the things which are not seen are temporal; but the things which are not seen are eternal" (2 Cor. 4:18).

A Revolutionary Challenge

Jesus' disciples misunderstood His mission to planet earth and were eager for prominent places in His kingdom, not recognizing that His Father would be the one to give high places in heaven. Even the mother of James and John came to Jesus with this request for her sons: "Grant that these my two sons may sit, the one on thy right hand, and the other on the left, in thy kingdom. But Jesus answered and said, Ye know not what ye ask. Are ye able to drink of the cup that I shall drink of, and to be baptized with the baptism that I am baptized with? They say unto him, We are able. And he saith unto them, Ye shall drink indeed of my cup" (Matt. 20:21-23). Then Jesus introduced the beauty of humility of service to others. He said further: "And whosoever will be chief among you, let him be your servant: even as the Son of man came not to be ministered unto, but to minister, and to give His life a ransom for many" (verses 27, 28). Though the disciples did not know it at this time, they did *drink the cup of suffering* as they continued to follow Jesus. The followers of Jesus were not intimidated by persecution, imprisonment, or death. The resurrection and ascension of Jesus put within their hearts boldness to speak truth.

Jesus often spoke of the terms required to be His follower: "they shall lay their hands on you, and persecute you, delivering you up to the synagogues, and into prisons, being brought before kings and rulers for my name's sake. . . . And ye shall be betrayed both by parents, and brethren, and kinsfolks, and friends; and some of you shall they cause to be put to death. And ye shall be hated of all men for my name's sake" (Luke 21:12-17). The Sermon on the Mount (the Beatitudes) proclaims a blessing on those who are reviled and persecuted, who withstand evil said against them falsely for Christ's sake. "Rejoice, and be exceeding glad: for great is your reward in heaven: for so persecuted they the prophets which were before you" (Matt. 5:12). God's followers refuse to regard "silence" on the part of God as indifference—it's a time for us to wait patiently, a time to reflect and determine to trust God in spite of the circumstances.

Tradition tells us that all the disciples suffered greatly. Some suffered in prison, but most were martyrs for Christ. I could tell in great detail the stories of the deaths of each disciple, but suffice it so say they were true to Christ and the gospel to the end. With joy and satisfaction, they gave their lives for the cause that burned within their hearts. Hopefully we should feel the same if called upon to make a similar sacrifice.

Elisha, who succeeded Elijah, asked for a double portion of his spirit to be upon him as he continued the prophet's calling (2 Kings 2:9). Elijah was translated to heaven without seeing death. Although Elisha was a powerful worker with widespread influence, he died after a lingering illness.

The tragedy of John the Baptist's prison sentence and later his beheading by wicked King Herod was felt keenly by Jesus, yet He never used His power to rescue him. John was satisfied to know Jesus was the Christ and that he had had the privilege to be His forerunner. Jesus never saved Himself or His disciples when it came to martyrdom (Matt. 20:28). John accepted the privilege of fellowship with Christ in sacrifice. Through all the generations since John's death, other sufferers have been sustained by his testimony. Jesus said of John: "Among them that are born of women there hath not risen a greater than John the Baptist" (Matt. 11:11; see also verses 2-15).

Both Elisha and John the Baptist could say with confidence as did the psalmist: "As for me, I will behold thy face in righteousness: I shall be satisfied, when I awake, with thy likeness" (Ps. 17:15). These and other Bible characters did not have the book of Hebrews to gain courage from during their suffering, but thank God that we do! (see Heb. 11).

If one could guarantee a problem-free, suffering-free life by becoming a Christian, many weak, pleasure-loving people would flock to receive this "material insurance." But for those who take into consideration the great controversy between good and evil, they will be completely satisfied with the methods God uses to prepare them to be *safe to save*. "As many as I love, I rebuke and chasten: be zealous therefore, and repent" (Rev. 3:19). Often this includes suffering—physically, emotionally, and spiritually. But those who wait patiently and continue to trust God in all circumstances will realize the answer to the promise: "I am with you always, even unto the end of the world" (Matt. 28:20).

No doubt the hardest trial for us is to witness the suffering of innocent children or family members. "Where was God when my son died?" was the angry question of a bereaved father. A Christian answered: "God was in the same place as when His Son died." Yet it really was not the same. God is near everyone who suffers the death of a loved one, but the sins of the human race

A Revolutionary Challenge

put a barrier between God and His Son. Jesus felt this agony and cried: "My God, my God, why hast thou forsaken me?" (Matt. 27:46). Christ, the adored of heavenly angels, came to this world to save sinners. "He came unto his own, and his own received him not" (John 1:11). Read all the verses of John 1 for a heartfelt experience. Who do we think we are to question our level of suffering when the Creator suffered so much for us? "But he was wounded for our transgressions, he was bruised for our iniquities: the chastisement of our peace was upon him; and with his stripes we [put your own name here] are healed" (Isa. 53:5). The entire chapter of Isaiah 53 is one of the most beautiful prophecies of the life of Christ. It will bless you to read all of it.

If no suffering has come into your life yet, you can count on this experience sometime during your time on earth. It may come to you personally, or it may come as you suffer with others. But the suffering we may encounter for our own mistakes is not something for which to pride ourselves or take credit for patiently enduring. "For what glory is it, if, when ye be buffeted for your faults, ye shall take it patiently? but if, when ye do well, and suffer for it, ye take it patiently, this is acceptable with God. . . . because Christ also suffered for us, leaving us an example, that ye should follow his steps" (1 Peter 2:20, 21).

We'll have to admit that the lifestyle lived by some could be blamed for their suffering, poor health, and the pain connected with it. However, in this unfair world, some who have lived with the knowledge that their bodies are *God's temple* and have tried to live healthfully may still have physical problems and suffering. It would be tempting to complain and say, "Why me?"

I was inspired by a true Christian who found himself in this situation. After a soul-searching reminiscence of God's blessings through his life and the special privileges granted him of serving God and others, the man said to his doctor: "Why *not* me?" I pray I will have that attitude if ever I suffer similar circumstances and be able to say with the apostle Paul, "I reckon that the sufferings of this present time are not worthy to be compared with the glory which shall be revealed in us" (Rom. 8:18).

After reading the life story of Helen Keller, who was deaf and blind from an early age, I find her outlook on suffering a remarkable testimony: "Character cannot be developed in ease and quiet. Only through experiences of trial and suffering can the soul be strengthened, ambition inspired, and success achieved."

It is selfish to waste time feeling sorry for oneself and voicing it to others. Someone may be depending on us for encouragement. Those who have had great sorrows and suffering are frequently the ones who can bring the greatest comfort to others. When we are a blessing to others, we are blessed ourselves.

My heart was touched by the life and experiences of Ralph, a man who lived in a country without religious freedom. Enduring severe hardship, painful sufferings, and threats of death, he remained faithful to God and was *on fire* for His cause. After immigrating to the United States, someone who heard his story told him that he was thankful that Ralph now lived in a country of freedom where he could relax and enjoy his Christian beliefs and lifestyle without fear. Ralph's response was shocking to his American acquaintance. The thought of living in a country with religious freedom bothered Ralph greatly, for he was concerned that he might lose his fervor for the Lord without suffering and persecution.

We must determine to trust God so completely and love so deeply that we will choose to be on His side whatever may happen to us. We can be anchored to the Rock—Christ Jesus—no matter where we are living. Joseph and Daniel were faithful to God as captives in a foreign, heathen land, yet Adam and Eve were unfaithful in *Paradise*!

Testimonies would not be complete without one from Job. Though very confused as to his suffering plight, Job could say, "But he knoweth the way that I take: when he hath tried me, I shall come forth as gold. . . . Neither have I gone back from the commandment of his lips; I have esteemed the words of his mouth more than my necessary food" (Job 23:10-12).

Job knew that good and evil are mingled and calamities come upon all. "Your Father which is in heaven . . . maketh his sun to rise on the evil and on the good, and sendeth rain on the just and on the unjust" (Matt. 5:45). This attitude gives us the secret of Job's faithfulness. Job's other submissive thoughts are recorded in Job 1:21, 19:26, and 42:1-6. Take time now to read these passages—you'll be encouraged!

"Not without a purpose does God send trial to His children. He never leads them otherwise than they would choose to be led if they could see the end from

A Revolutionary Challenge

the beginning, and discern the glory of the purpose which they are fulfilling as workers together with Him. He subjects them to discipline to humble them, to lead them, through trial and affliction, to see their weakness and draw near to Him" (*In Heavenly Places,* p. 267). "For I am persuaded, that neither death, nor life, nor angels, nor principalities, nor powers, nor things present, nor things to come, nor height, nor depth, nor any other creature, shall be able to separate us from the love of God, which is Christ Jesus our Lord" (Rom. 8:38, 39).

It is not what happens to us in life that counts; it is how we relate to it. We can use suffering as an opportunity to grow. Eternal things should be our focus. We should think of the *beyond*. "And God shall wipe away all tears from their eyes; and there shall be no more death, neither sorrow, nor crying, neither shall there be any more pain: for the former things are passed away" (Rev. 21:4). What better thought could give us the courage to stay true to God?

The three young captives in Babylon—Shadrach, Meshach, and Abednego—had this to say about the threat of death: "O Nebuchadnezzar, we are not careful to answer thee in this matter. If it be so, our God whom we serve is able to deliver us from the burning fiery furnace, and he will deliver us out of thine hand, O king. But if not, be it known unto thee, O king, that we will not serve thy gods, nor worship the golden image which thou has set up" (Dan. 3:16-18). Daniel 3:19-30 tells the rest of the story and the reward God bestowed upon them for their faithfulness!

I wish to say to the youth: *May God help you to stand firm and hold fast to upright principles that the most powerful temptations of Satan will not draw you away from your allegiance to Christ.* Here's another word of encouragement from Jesus: "These things I have spoken to you, that in me ye might have peace. In the world ye shall have tribulation: but be of good cheer; I have overcome the world" (John 16:33).

I have found the following quotations very thought-provoking and encouraging, and I hope you will too. These can help bring healing for the emotions of a sufferer:

It is reported that the late Peter Marshall once opened a session of the U.S. Senate with this prayer: "Our Father, when we long for life without trials and work without difficulties, remind us oaks grow strong in contrary winds and diamonds are made under pressure. With stout hearts may we see in every calamity an opportunity and not give way to the pessimism that sees in every opportunity a calamity!"

Here's another great thought from a math teacher to his students, which we can apply to life in general: "We're going to have math [life's] challenges from now on, instead of math [life's] problems. Think of terms to solve them, with easy solutions and call them a game or challenge, but not problems."

From Joseph Fort Newton comes this gem: "We must take time, take pains, have a plan, form spiritual habits, if we are to keep our souls alive; and now is the time to begin. A man to whom religion is a reality and who knows what is meant by 'the practice of salvation;' keeps his balance because the living center of his life is spiritual. He cannot be upset, nor shaken. The same hard knocks come to him as to others, but he reacts to them by the central law of his life. He suffers deeply, but he does not sour. He knows frustration, but he goes right on in his kindness and faith. He sees his own shortcomings, but he does not give up, because a power rises up from his spiritual center and urges him to the best."

Here's a beautiful spiritual challenge to help form a positive attitude and real peace: "Circumstances have but little to do with the experiences of the soul. It is the spirit cherished which gives coloring to all our actions. A man at peace with God and his fellow men cannot be made miserable. Envy will not be in his heart; evil surmising will find no room there; hatred cannot exist. The heart in harmony with God is lifted above the annoyances and trials of this life" (*Testimonies for the Church*, vol. 5, p. 488).

The apostle Paul encourages us to have this beautiful experience: "Speaking to yourselves in psalms and hymns and spiritual songs, singing and making melody in your heart to the Lord; giving thanks always for all things unto God and the Father in the name of our Lord Jesus Christ" (Eph. 5:19, 20).

Suffering comes with disobedience. Can you imagine the pain and grief of Adam and Eve when Cain killed his brother Abel? Suffering has continued through the ages ever since that day and will to the end of time. We have been warned that it is coming so we can be prepared (see Matt. 24).

The period of time before Christ's return has been called "the time of

A Revolutionary Challenge

trouble." John warns us of it in Revelation 12:17. Daniel also speaks of this time, but with the warning of the time of trouble, he promises deliverance for those who are "found written in the book [of life]" (Dan. 12:1). Many people are fearful of this time and speak of it with discouragement and despair. Although it naturally puts fear in the heart to think of the persecution and suffering that could come to those who live during that time, those who have a strong relationship with Christ will be able to go through it. Trust will cause fear to vanish. Some helpful texts about God's faithfulness are found in Deuteronomy 31:8 and Matthew 10:18-20.

Corrie ten Boom, who hid Jews during the Germans occupation of Holland, wondered if she would be subjected to living in a Nazi concentration camp because of the work she and her family did. She was very concerned over her ability to endure this time of great suffering, which could end in death. Her father lifted her spirits by reminding her that a close connection with Christ—which she had—would come to her rescue just when she needed it. Her trust in that thought gave her peace. When the time of her need came, God gave her the strength she needed. She was "found written in the book." What an inspiration and challenge she is for us.

All Christians can apply this beautiful principle to the *time of trouble* and be at peace, knowing that God will support us when we need it. With this attitude we can be an encouragement to other Christians and say with confidence: "And when these things begin to come to pass, then look up, and lift up your heads; for your redemption draweth nigh" (Luke 21:28). "For God hath not given us the spirit of fear, but of power, and of love, and of a sound mind" (2 Tim. 1:7).

This chapter on suffering will hopefully offer relief and courage to those whose trials and sufferings may continue to be part of their current experience. God's timing for healing is not always immediate. If it doesn't come earlier, we know that healing will ultimately come when Jesus returns to take His faithful followers to a place where there will never be pain, sickness, or death. In God's infinite wisdom, there will be a time when all the *whys* will have a fair hearing and an honest satisfying answer. Until then, let us wait and trust.

We can praise God that there are thousands, even millions, of God's healings—some immediate, some soon after prayer, and some after a change of lifestyle. It is common knowledge that the medical profession admits that more people who pray and are prayed for do get well faster than those who do not pray or are not prayed for.

Just recently I read a thrilling story that happened some years ago to a woman who was on the operating table waiting for the surgeon to arrive. Because he was late, she had time to think who was really responsible for a successful operation and her healing. So she prayed earnestly that God would bring glory to Himself by healing her without the scheduled surgery. When her doctor and anesthetist arrived, she was asked what she wanted as anesthesia for the operation. She declined anything. When the surgeon said he would not perform the surgery unless she was asleep, she told him that the surgery was not necessary, for she was already healed. Other doctors were called in, some of whom were Christians, and they gathered around her bed. She asked for a new X-ray with which the former X-ray could be compared. This was done, and all the medical staff was astonished to admit she was healed!

The surgeon was not a Christian, but he was so very impressed by this miracle that the next day he called the patient at her home and arranged for a visit by him and his wife. She was ready with a list of verses from the Bible to get them acquainted with the *Great Physician*—God! Several times these sincere seekers came to get more *spiritual food* to continue their study at home. Because of this experience, the doctor and his wife became believing Christians. "To God be the glory" was the healed woman's joyful response. She was thankful to have had the great privilege of planting seeds of truth in their hearts.

We may hear of healing services, many of which can be seen in theatrical sessions on television. Many will question, "Are these for real?" Not judging, yet we have warnings that may fit: "And many false prophets shall rise, and shall deceive many" (Matt. 24:11). There is much guidance in the Bible that will help reveal true miracles from the false so we will not be deceived. This study is most important during *the time of the end* before Jesus Christ comes the second time. For everything genuine, Satan puts out a counterfeit to attract those who will be swept away by the existence of the supernatural (see Isa. 8:20; Matt. 7:22, 23; Luke 6:44; 1 Cor. 10:31; 2 Cor. 10:17, 11:14; 2 Thess. 2:9, 10; 1 Peter 5:8; 1 John 4:6; Rev. 13:14, 16:13, 14). The Bible must be our ultimate standard of truth.

Reports of true healing can be repeated multitudes of times from all generations in all places of the world. My husband's father, Eric Beavon, who was a missionary in Africa, asked a faithful native who had crawled long distances to church each Sabbath if he would like to have a special prayer for healing. With sincere faith, he was pleased to have him do so. A prayer was offered, and God saw fit to glorify His name by an immediate healing. The grateful sufferer gave God his service for the rest of his life!

God still cares for us and our healing as much as He did while He lived on earth and healing was His main *tool* of sharing God's love. We can trust His timing and can be thankful for healing that goes on in our bodies daily from cuts, bruises, accidents, and sickness. We often take these healings for granted. Healing is part of God's plan. My family and I survived and were healed from a very serious automobile accident, as well as other accidents throughout the years. We personally have much to praise the Lord for.

Let me bring to a close this chapter on suffering by quoting an e-mail that was passed along to me titled "God Said." It conveys beautifully the blessings of this *revolutionary challenge*:

God Said

>"If you never felt pain, then how would you know that I'm a Healer?"
>"If you never went through difficulties, how would you know that I'm a Deliverer?"
>"If you never had a trial, could you call yourself an 'overcomer?'"
>"If you never felt sadness, how could you know that I'm a Comforter?"
>"If you never made a mistake, how would you know that I'm forgiving?
>"If you knew it all, how would you know that I will answer your questions?"
>"If you never were in trouble, how would you know that I will come to your rescue?"
>"If you never were broken, then how would you know that I can make you whole?"
>"If you never had a problem, how would you know that I can solve them?"
>"If you never had any suffering, then how would you know what Jesus went through?"

"If you never went through the fire, then how would you become pure?
"If I gave you all things, how would you appreciate them?
"If I never corrected you, how would you know that I love you?
"If you had all power, then how would you learn to depend on Me?
"If your life was perfect, then what would you need Me for?
"Thank you, God!" ♥

Chapter 15

It Pays!—To God be the Glory

Conversion

The youth groups of the local churches were astir ever since an announcement of a youth rally featuring a well-known rock star who had turned his life around and become a Christian. A good audience was assured to hear his story. The young man, we'll call him Tim, was the son of a Christian college professor. He had grown up in a home with loving, dedicated parents.

As with many young people, the influence of unconverted worldly friends, the pull of the media, and time spent in tainted places of amusement proved too much for Tim. He joined a group of musicians and for years played music for dances, rock concerts, and other places where this type of music was appreciated. His false pleasure was always accompanied by the pain of guilt. His life was swirling downhill with alcohol, drugs, immorality, and many more of Satan's attractions.

Because Tim had once tasted a better way, as well as being the subject of the Holy Spirit's convictions, he finally pled for God's deliverance from the empty life he had chosen. He thought often of his former Christian companions and the meaningful pleasure they were enjoying serving God. The many heartfelt prayers of family and friends were answered when Tim made his choice to come back to God, dedicating his life for His service.

The sharing of his experience was overpowering, for he dwelt on God's call and His compassion on his homeward journey. He used only enough descriptions of his wayward life to make a point of the wisdom of his new choice and desire to *come back home.* The purpose of his witness was meant to stir the listener to a prayer of thanks for his deliverance and to make a determination themselves to go with God and remain faithful, thus sparing themselves the many scars of life and guilt from wasted years.

We often hear, read, or see for ourselves the conversion of those whose backgrounds were unbelievably sinful. Their response to the Holy Spirit's call and the circumstances that led to their decision make for spiritual thrills beyond description. We greatly rejoice and heaven does too over their true conversion (Matt. 18:12-14).

Conversion is truly *turning around* one's life from the choice of sin and its consequences to one of loving service to God and its rewards. Conversion is a miracle regardless of one's background. Ever since sin entered the world there has been a great controversy between man's choice of good or evil. With loving invitations from God versus the evil temptations of the devil, we have suffered *heart trouble*. "The heart is deceitful above all things, and desperately wicked: who can know it?" (Jer. 17:9). This describes the heart condition of the converted as well as the unconverted! If one questions this thought, consider the life of God's friend Abraham by reading the record in Genesis 12:12 and 13 (see also James 2:23 and John 15:14). In fact, Abraham committed the sin of deception on two occasions. Also, check out the life of David in 2 Samuel 11 and 12, which describes his *desperately wicked* deeds of adultery, deception, and murder. So, conversion does not make one sinless, for "all have sinned." We need to "die daily to sin."

We are not to place our sole attention on the sins in people's lives but more so pay heed to the sorrowful repentance and conversion needed. "The character is revealed, not by occasional good deeds and occasional misdeeds, but by the tendency of the habitual words and acts" (*Steps to Christ,* pp. 57, 58). David was called a "man after mine [God's] own heart" (Acts 13:22), not in his great sin, but when he followed God with all his heart and was deeply repentant of his sins and turned from them. "Create in me a clean heart, O God; and renew a right spirit within me" (Ps. 51:10) was David's prayer. The entire chapter of Psalm 51 has been called a *spiritual bath.* It's a cleansing for all God's followers.

Another type of conversion that is seldom discussed is the conversion of persons who come from a background of Christianity, often times from many generations of Christians. They have attended church all their lives, and do the so-called *right things*. Still, they may not really know, value, and love their beliefs. It's just, for some, a religion of habit. They neither indulge in bad habits or have a lifestyle that brings obvious regret. With all their wise choices, they might consider themselves converted, just as in the biblical example of the rich young ruler. In his brief conversation with Jesus, Jesus answered his question of how to obtain eternal life by referring him to the obedience of God's law. (The story is recorded in Luke 18:18-24).

But the rich young ruler had a question that seemed unsolved, even if he could say to Jesus "All these have I kept from my youth up" (Luke 18:21). It is obvious that one can consider oneself a law-abiding individual while ignoring the fine points of obedience (see Matt. 5:28). Being a shallow keeper of the law had left the ruler unsatisfied; yet when the deeper meaning of the eighth commandment was brought to his attention by Jesus—"sell all that thou hast, and distribute unto the poor . . . and come, follow me" (verse 22)—the ruler turned away sorrowful, for he had great riches.

Had this rich ruler allowed this experience to bring about his true conversion by following Jesus, no doubt we would have read of exciting experiences he had gained sharing the gospel. He failed the test! How sad to have traded eternal life for his riches. Jesus, too, was very disappointed, for He loved the young man and saw his spiritual potential if love for God had taken place over his love for material possessions (John 14:15). Jesus has this great love and desire for us too!

Is it possible that some who have gone to church all their lives may be a formal Christian in need of being *born again*? There is a vast difference in just knowing and believing about God and that of a personal experience of loving obedience to Him (see Jer. 24:7; 29:12, 13; 31:33). Habitual time with God produces a relationship of love and obedience (see Job 23:12). A positive, growing attitude is needed.

No doubt the difficulty of true conversion for any person is that one may not know their true condition or see their own need: "Because thou sayest, I am rich, and increased with goods, and have need of nothing; and knowest not that thou art wretched, and miserable, and poor, and blind, and naked" (Rev. 3:17). God has good advice for people in this condition if they will only heed it: "I counsel thee to buy of me gold tried in the fire [to purify it], that thou mayest be rich; and white raiment, that thou mayest be clothed, and that the shame of thy nakedness does not appear; and anoint thine eyes with eyesalve, that thou mayest see. As many as I love, I rebuke and chaseten; be zealous therefore, and repent" (verses 18, 19). These verses tell of the need to see ourselves as we really are and allow the Holy Spirit to do His work in us. Then we can joyfully open the door that Jesus is knocking on as described in Revelation 3:20-22. The result will be fellowship with Him—a relationship that is needed to overcome sin—and the corresponding joy of association with our Savior now and throughout the ceaseless ages of eternity! Conversion, in any form, is truly a miracle!

We may claim any of these acts of conversion—leaving the depths of sin, coming home, and choosing to be what we need to be by God's grace—but to refuse any of these is of great loss, not only losing out on eternity to come but also the part of living abundantly in Jesus NOW! (John 10:10).

We must not overlook the Christians who see themselves and God in their true light and have remained faithful from start to finish. Though still sinners in need of salvation, they have been ambassadors and heroes for God. A few such people, among the many Bible characters, are Enoch, Joseph, Samuel, and Daniel. Through the ages following there have been many who have always been faithful to the end amid wicked surroundings.

Here are some thoughts on conversion to consider, cherish, and apply. First, one must see his/her need. One must choose to let the only solver of our needs—Jesus—take over our lives. That's full surrender! To the world, and to earthly warriors, the word surrender means defeat, but to the Christian warrior, total surrender to God means victory over sin! Surrender is total commitment, allowing God complete control of every area of our lives: our time, our influence, our lifestyle, our money, our entire being. Then, He is our Lord. This should be our first prayer of the day. Just as the greatest accomplishments we've made in life have taken time and great effort, so our discipleship to Christ is no different. It's a day-by-day joyful, challenging, and difficult effort of a lifetime.

Christians have a vocabulary that is strange and not understood by non-Christians. The following is just one example: *Surrender is victory!* Another:

We who are weak in ourselves can be strong in Christ's strength. Weakness is needed for strength (2 Cor. 12:10). These contrasts of meaning in the vocabulary of a Christian remind us that although we have citizenship in this world on paper as a song says, *"this world is not my home, I'm just a passing through."* I have eternity to live in my real home in heaven. My real citizenship is there!

We are judged by our works. "Even so faith, if it hath not works, is dead, being alone" (James 2:17; see also Matt. 16:27 and Rev. 22:12). Yet, we do not earn salvation by our works because we are finite beings and it is impossible for us to earn something infinite—only God can do that, which was done freely out of His great love for us. In response, the service of obedience we give to God comes from our love, appreciation, and respect for what He is and has done for us (Mark 8:35). Roy Adams wrote, "Even then it becomes clear that following Jesus cannot be a halfway thing. Either we give ourselves to Him completely, regardless of the cost, or we do not give ourselves to Him at all."

We are told that God accepts us just as we are, but fortunately He loves us too much to leave us that way! We must be willing to be the clay and allow God, as the Potter, to form us to His design. "But now, O LORD, thou art our father; we are the clay, and thou our potter" (Isa. 64:8). "God never issues a command without furnishing the grace sufficient for its fulfilment" (*The Signs of the Times,* July 26, 1899). "Without me ye can do nothing" (John 15:5). "I can do all things through Christ which strengtheneth me" (Phil. 4:13).

Here is what the works that we are judged by do: "Let your light so shine before men, that they may see your good works, and glorify your Father which is in heaven" (Matt. 5:16). Our good works bare witness as to whose side we have chosen to be on. Philippians 2:13 tells who is responsible for our good works: "For it is God which worketh in you both to will and to do of His good pleasure."

I found the following thought by Pastor Ken Coleman quoted in the September 21, 2006, *Adventist Review*. It is a beautiful way to describe the difference between two types of obedience. "Sometimes there is very little outward difference between a *legalist* and a *loyalist.* The *legalist* asks, 'What do I have to do?' The *legalist* is trying to earn brownie points—to gain God's love and salvation. The *loyalist* asks, 'What more can I do?' The *loyalist* is so thankful for what God has done, that he longs to do anything God might want him to do—whether or not it is required."

Since we do not read the hearts of others, we should leave the judgment to God. "Consecrate yourself to God in the morning; make this your very first work. Let your prayer be: 'Take me, O Lord, as wholly Thine. I lay all my plans at Thy feet. Use me today in Thy service. Abide with me, and let all my work be wrought in Thee.' This is a daily matter. Each morning consecrate yourself to God for that day. Surrender all your plans to Him, to be carried out or given up as His providence shall indicate. Thus day by day you may be giving your life into the hands of God, and thus your life will be molded more and more after the life of Christ" (*Steps to Christ,* p. 70).

Christianity

Our young friend decided that the best way to answer a certain question was to ask the questioner another question. The question really needed a definition. Could it be that the one asking and the one being questioned had two different definitions? The question: "Are you a Christian?" The response question: "How do you define a Christian?" It's amazing how many answers one will receive with this approach.

Most people equate a Christian with a person who attends church on a regular basis. A non-Christian will judge Christianity by the ones they are acquainted with. If a follower of Christ really "walks the talk," Christianity will be defined positively. "He that saith he abideth in him ought himself also so to walk, even as he walked" (1 John 2:6). If the opposite is true, Christianity, or religion, is given a black eye.

Some who claim to be Christian bring a reproach upon Christianity. God desires spiritual fruit from Christians, not religious nuts. It is not wise or fair to judge Christianity by the mistakes and failures of those who claim to be Christians. We must also remember that God is not through with them yet. He knows the heart. Those who make this an excuse and have a negative attitude toward Christianity for this reason may be covering up for themselves. When we know what is right in God's eyes, we need to do it even if we are the only one. It's a no-regret decision!

If religion makes us arrogant or unkind to those who think different than we do, we have not demonstrated true Christianity. If we claim to believe in God's *grace*, we must be *graceful* to others. We must remember the admonition in Romans 14:5: "Let every man be fully persuaded in his own mind." We are not saved by the religion of our parents or other people. Our belief system and our walk with God should be the result of prayer and a deep, personal study of God's Word.

A friend shared this heart-searching story with me, and I want to share it with you:

"Several years ago, a preacher from out-of-state accepted a call to a church in Houston, Texas. Some weeks after he arrived, he had an occasion to ride the bus from his home to the downtown area. When he sat down, he discovered that the driver had accidentally given him a quarter too much change. As he considered what to do, he thought to himself, *You'd better give the quarter back. It would be wrong to keep it.*

"Then he thought, *Oh, forget it, it's only a quarter. Who would worry about this little amount? Anyway, the bus company gets too much fare; they will never miss it. Accept it as a 'gift from God' and keep quiet.*

"When his stop came, he paused momentarily at the door, and then he handed the quarter to the driver and said, 'Here, you gave me too much change.' The driver, with a smile, replied, 'Aren't you the new preacher in town? I have been thinking a lot lately about going somewhere to worship. I just wanted to see what you would do if I gave you too much change. I'll see you at the next church service.'

"When the preacher stepped off of the bus, he literally grabbed the nearest light pole, held on, and said, 'Oh God, I almost sold your Son for a quarter.'"

Our lives are the only Bible some people will ever read. This is a sobering example of how much people watch us as Christians and will put us to the test. Always be on guard—and remember—you carry the name of Christ on your shoulders when you call yourself Christian.

"Watch your thoughts; they become words.

Watch your words; they become actions.

Watch your actions; they become habits.

Watch your habits; they become character.

Watch your character; it becomes your destiny."

Just what is a Christian? The dictionary defines a Christian a someone "professing belief in Jesus as Christ and following the religion based on His teachings." It goes on to add: "Manifesting the qualities or spirit of Christ—Christ-like." I like that addition! A disciple is one who is a follower of Christ, and spreading the word is his chief desire. Every Christian should be a disciple and carry out the gospel commission found in Matthew 28:19 and 20: "Go ye therefore, and teach all nations, baptizing them in the name of the Father, and of the Son, and of the Holy Ghost: Teaching them to observe all things whatsoever I have commanded you: and, lo, I am with you always, even unto the end of the world."

It is repeated as marching orders to the new church in Acts 1:8: "But ye shall receive power, after that the Holy Ghost is come upon you: and ye shall be witnesses unto me both in Jerusalem, and in all Judea, and in Samaria, and unto the uttermost part of the earth." These were the farewell words Jesus spoke before He left His disciples to go back to His heavenly home! In our generation and location, we might consider "Jerusalem" our family; "Judea" our friends and neighbors; "Samaria" our country; and the "uttermost parts" the world! "Not more surely is the place prepared for us in the heavenly mansions than is the special place designated on earth where we are to work for God" (*Christ's Object Lessons*, p. 327).

Knowing Jesus personally is vital to being a disciple. Our relationship must be close. This comes by spending time with Him, hearing what He has to say, and acting upon it. Let's not allow the *earthly urgent* to crowd out the *eternal important*. We must be balanced.

The Bible has another requirement for a disciple: "By this shall all men know that ye are my disciples, if ye have love one to another" (John 13:35). Our love for others is based on our love for God. Jesus told the questioning lawyer it is the "great commandment." Jesus divided the Ten Commandments into two parts, which are both based on love: "Thou shalt love the Lord thy God with all thy heart, and with all thy soul, and with all thy mind. This is the first and great commandment [encompassing the first four commandments]. And the second is like unto it, Thou shalt love thy neighbour as thyself [as revealed in the last six commandments]" (Matt. 22:36-39). Jesus also tells us how to love Him with all our hearts: "If ye love me, keep my commandments" (John 14:15). True obedience comes from love—Christianity is based on love.

The word love is used very loosely these days. The definition of true love, also known as *charity*, found in 1 Corinthians 13, is a very tall order for sinful humanity. We should daily pray to have these character traits rule our lives. It is so important to keep the Bible always in our minds. We must read and absorb it until it takes possession of us.

My personal definition of Christianity is also one based on love. Christianity is a passionate love affair—loving our *Creator* and *Redeemer* with all our heart and striving to please Him and bring Him glory. "I delight to do thy will, O my God: yea, thy law is within my heart" (Ps. 40:8). As His followers, we should seek a deep relationship that finds joy in His presence (Ps. 84:10). How could we keep from desiring to have and to share with others something so important and so dear to our lives? How humbly grateful we should be for the privilege of being a Christian, and we should gladly admit to being one. Christianity transforms those who take it seriously. They find courage to face hardships, including death itself. True Christianity brings out the best in us. It makes people willing to make great sacrifices to help the less fortunate. Meaning, purpose, direction, peace, and hope add to the life of a true Christian. What a great privilege to be a follower of Christ. What an awesome responsibility to live in a way to bring glory to God!

With the rapid growth of Far Eastern religions in our country, engaging even former Christians, one might wonder if Christianity has failed them. Considering the biblical definition of Christianity and its great benefits, it really could be said that humanity is what has failed Christianity. The fault is not in Christianity, but in the heart. Hearts have been hardened by materialism and intellectualism. True intelligence is to see our spiritual need.

It's easy to find fault with something we really don't know about. It was said of one man who claimed to be Christian: "He had enough religion to make him miserable." Maybe he also made everyone around him miserable, too! He failed to get the message and failed to fulfill his responsibility to be a good advertisement for the Christ-filled life. True Christianity should make people have peaceful happy attitudes, and they will show it! Speaking of Christianity,

William Johnsson wrote, "It has never been tried and found wanting, but with many it is unwanted and untried."

We are always eager to know the possible side effects of things we use; much could be said for the beneficial side effects of true religion. First, it teaches us how to live a meaningful life from start to finish. Lusts of the world such as the use of liquor, drugs, illicit sex, or any other type of *idol* have painful side effects that bring guilt, sickness, disappointment, deep regret, grief, and death. Some unbelievers label Christianity as a *crutch*. I could go along with this if the crutch is the *Shepherd's rod,* giving God's guidance and protection throughout life.

In spite of sin in our world and the great controversy going on between good and evil, we can be thankful that God created us with the desire to worship Him. A vacuum is within us, and it can be filled only with the Spirit of God. If we worship anything but our Creator, we will still be dissatisfied and feel emptiness in our soul and life.

In Hebrews 10:23-25 Paul reveals the importance of church attendance: "Let us hold fast the profession of faith without wavering; (for he is faithful that promised;) and let us consider one another to provoke unto love and to good works: not forsaking the assembling of ourselves together, as the manner of some is; but exhorting one another: and so much the more, as ye see the day approaching."

Some have an aversion to becoming a Christian and attending church. They often make excuses. Since the beginning of time, wars have been fought and lives lost over "religion." Since the Prince of Peace is the true head of the church, this can be puzzling. Just a bit of a reminder from Romans 3:1 and 2: "What advantage then hath the Jews? . . . Much every way: chiefly, because that unto them were committed the oracles of God." In many cases, the wars preserved the oracles of God that the heathen nations were trying to destroy. You might want to review additional thoughts regarding these wars in Deuteronomy 7—the entire chapter is good.

Another reason given for avoiding Christianity and church attendance is that many who profess Christianity are hypocrites. Jesus met hypocrites in His day too. They were acting a lie. "This people draweth nigh unto me with their mouth, and honoureth me with their lips; but their heart is far from me"

(Matt. 15:8). Others who claimed to be Christ's followers did not have the right motive for their "good deeds." They wanted to look good to make an impression. "Not every one that saith unto me, Lord, Lord, shall enter into the kingdom of heaven; but he that doeth the will of my Father which is in heaven. Many will say to me in that day, Lord, Lord, have we not prophesied in thy name? and in thy name have cast out devils? and in thy name done many wonderful works? And then will I profess unto them, I never knew you: depart from me, ye that work iniquity" (Matt. 7:21-23). Perhaps the doers of good deeds were doing it for *brownie points*, striving to gain salvation by their works. But thanks be to God that salvation is a free gift made possible by Jesus' sacrifice at Calvary.

A friend once said, "I only wish I was as good as people think I am—or as I want to be!" No doubt everyone has a thread of hypocrisy in their veins—we often look better than we are. The church is a *hospital for sinners,* offering healing as we become genuine *practicing saints*. We need the prayers and understanding of one another for this healing process to take place. Instead of concentrating on the mistakes of others in the church, how much better is it if we look for the good in others? Since man looks on the outward appearance and God looks on the heart, let's let Him do the judging while we make an effort to think the best of others. If we do this we will never be tempted to leave the church by deeming it to be hypocritical. God loves hypocrites and wants to transform them into genuine Christians.

Another complaint some have about the church is that all Christians think about is going to heaven so what's happening on earth really doesn't seem to matter to them—the worse the world becomes, the sooner they'll go home to a better world! It's been described this way: "They're so heavenly minded, they're of no earthly good!" We may long for deliverance from sin and its results, but rather than sit and dream about the future, a true believer actively gets involved with those who need help now. Those who blame Christians for sitting back must see that *true* followers look at the world and do something about its needs. They use knowledge, resources, and opportunities around them to make the world a better place. True, there are nonreligious organizations that help people, but they lack an important motive that Christians add to their love and compassion and that is to help prepare people for their eternal destiny. Our earthly life is meant to make sure we—and those we help along the way—are ready for the world to come. We have citizenship in two worlds, and we should make every effort to be good loyal citizens! When we work to help others, we are also doing it for Jesus (Matt. 25:40).

Most Christian organizations have church entities that provide opportunities for their members to reach out to help those in need. Seventh-day Adventists are no exception. Christian Record provides Bibles and other spiritual material in Braille for the blind. They operate special camps for blind children as well as concentrating their efforts in many other ways to help the sightless. Community Services, formerly called *Dorcas Societies,* provide clothing, furniture, food, and other help to the needy. ADRA (Adventist Development and Relief Agency) does much to give help around the world, responding to emergency and disaster needs, digging wells in third-world countries, helping to plant gardens, assisting under-privileged people get back on their feet, helping with education, training people in healthful living, and coordinating a host of other projects too numerous to list.

Another service-oriented institution is called Project PATCH. Located in Vancouver, Washington, the organization offers assistance to troubled children and youth in crisis. Many of the formerly troubled ones give their testimony of finding Christ and a meaningful way to live while associated with Project PATCH.

Adventists also respond by ministering to prisoners (see Matt. 25:26). United Prison Ministries works worldwide to share God's Word and suggest practical ways to enter back into society and reunite with their families. Native Americans are ministered to by the Holbrook Indian School. Many more organizations and personal work could be added to this list.

Seventh-day Adventists take seriously the gospel commission to share the Word of God with the world, and the church often uses its numerous radio and television stations around the world to accomplish this goal. They herald the good news of Jesus soon return, having a God-given task to spread the message to every person and nation—the last message God has given to the world for this end time! (Rev. 14:6-12).

There is ample opportunity for church members and interested friends to join in united efforts to help the needy, and if we are truly Christians, we will

It Pays!—To God be the Glory

want to support the activities of one or more of these service entities as well as reaching out individually to assist others in need.

To emphasize again the mission of Christians is this added thought, which *rings a bell* with me: "We who follow Him do not contemplate mercy—we practice it. We do not meditate on purity of heart—we live it in everyday relations. We do not talk about peace—we seek to bring peace, from God among men and women. We don't ask if those who need us are worthy, but what can I do to benefit them." No Christian can be at peace when others are suffering.

If one wants to live a meaningful and exciting life, join Christians in doing to others what Jesus would do! The keys to the kingdom are how we treat others (see Matt. 25:31-40). Yes, we are our "brother's keeper." The admonition in Hebrews 10:24 and 25 about fellowshipping with fellow-believers in church adds this reasoning: "to provoke [take action] unto love and to good works … exhorting [encouraging] one another." Now who wouldn't wish to be part of this divine organization?

What a great blessing we receive from the words we hear and share in our Bible study and the message of the church service. These become the source of our inspiration for loving obedience and service and the hope that burns within a believer's heart for a *new earth* where there will be no more sickness, pain, or suffering. The very first sanctuary built, and later the temple built by Solomon, as well as the one rebuilt after the destruction of Jerusalem, were made for God to dwell among His people. The life of Jesus on earth was the greatest example of God with us.

Why do we go to church? We do it to praise, honor, and worship God our Creator. That will be our first blessing. Next, we'll want to share the blessing with our church family, not only in the fellowship of the worship hour, fellowship meal, or times together in our homes, but also during the coming week as various needs require. To feel part of a loving, caring church family is very rewarding. "A man that hath friends must shew himself friendly: and there is a friend that sticketh closer than a brother" (Prov. 18:24). If ever we feel a friendship is one-sided—*our-sided*—be encouraged with the last part of the quoted verse and realize that best of all Jesus, Himself, sticks closer than a brother! Read Proverbs 17:17 to learn what a brother does!

Think on These Things

A very meaningful part of our Sabbath School study hour starts with a time for sharing spoken and unspoken prayer requests. We pray for courage and strength to remain faithful. We feel the warmth and care of our church family. Church attendance is a gathering of people who are committed to God and each other. We are family growing together in Christ to be a blessing to others. This is the ideal fruit of church attendance and is a *tie that binds*. If in our membership in a church body we put our hearts and actions into service for others, we form a brotherhood that helps keep us faithful. If ever tempted to leave, we'd ask ourselves, "Where else would we go?"

Just a word of warning. We must realize that Satan, a diligent worker, throws in some great challenges of conflict that can hurt relationships with others within our church family. We must ask the question "Is it possible, at times like this, when people feel hurt and slighted, misunderstood, and/or misused to innocently be a part of the cause?" We need to pray daily that our influence in the church is positive rather than negative and that we right our wrongs promptly.

We are not responsible for the actions of others, but we do have a great responsibility to maintain a sweet spirit and attitude ourselves. It's a gift God is eager to give us if we ask for it. When there is a *conflict* among people, we should pray for those involved. Let us pledge to be part of the solution—in love—and not part of the problem (see Eph. 4:13; Rom. 12:18; John 13:35). We should never, never give up. "And let us not be weary in well doing: for in due season we shall reap, if we faint not" (Gal. 6:9). "It is the will of God that union and brotherly love should exist among His people. The prayer of Christ just before His crucifixion was that His disciples might be as one as He is one with the Father, that the world might believe that God had sent Him" (*Mind, Character, and Personality,* vol. 2, p. 797). What wise counsel Paul also gives us in Ephesians 4:3: "Make every effort to keep the unity of the Spirit through the bond of peace."

"Harmony and union existing among men of varied dispositions is the strongest witness that can be borne that God has sent His Son into the world to save sinners. It is our privilege to bear this witness" (*God's Amazing Grace,* p. 210). This does not mean that unity is to be gained at the cost of principle or the yielding of identity of character, for persons of differing opinions and tastes may, in Christ, arrive at a basic unity that will tie them together in a very real communion. What a witness for God!

A goal for every Christian is described in the words of a little song by an unknown author:

> "I love this family of God
> so closely knitted into one.
> They've taken me into their hearts,
> and I'm so glad to be a part
> of this great family."

We need to be on both sides, giving this type of love and receiving it.

Worship by Knowing God

During church family time, a young fervent Christian parent expressed a deep concern: "Do I really worship God in a way that would be pleasing to Him?" Since that time I often ask myself a like question: "Do I bring glory to God as I worship Him?"

After reading an eye-opening article in the *Adventist Review* by Ivan C. Blake titled "Does God Get A Lift?", I have great reason to wonder about my worship. The article presented a wonderful goal to aim for. We need to worship God because we have learned who He is. Is our worship about us or is it about God? The following thoughts have been gleaned from the article. Maybe these thoughts will leave you with the same questions and longing.

It's a great assignment to focus on the attributes of God. We often think of God's mercy, compassion, grace, and forgiveness. These character traits are His *goodness*. We must also think of His greatness, power, and majesty. To worship is to connect with God. The center of our worship *is* about God—not ourselves. Contemplate the story of Elijah and the prophets of Baal on Mount Carmel as recorded in 1 Kings 18:16-40. There is a great difference in how the prophets of Baal worshipped their god and the way Elijah worshipped his God. The center of Baal worship was about themselves. When Elijah worshipped, everyone received an overwhelming awareness of God and who He was. The people fell prostrate and cried, "The LORD—he is God! The LORD—he is God!" (verse 39). God, not Elijah, was the center of the worship experience.

God's greatness brought Elijah great satisfaction. Elijah had prayed that the people would know that he was God, and he described the Lord as the One turning their hearts back again. True worship begins with knowing who God is and celebrating His saving power.

"A real sense of awe and godly fear is appropriate and necessary in our worship of God. Without it, we can still have a 'good time' at church, but God will not be lifted up, He may even be missing" ("Does God Get A Lift?", July 19, 2007). "Like Thomas, we too can fall at His feet [in our hearts] and say with all the emotion and depth we can muster: 'My Lord and my God.' This is worship and God, appropriately, will receive the greatest Lift from it" (*ibid.*).

Ivan Blake goes on to describe an experience I long to have. "We need to strive for a clear view of God, for once we've grasped the truth of His greatness, His holiness, His awesome majesty, we will be filled with enthusiasm of expression in worship. Such a clear view can generate more joy and vitality in worship as we praise a God who at the same time is intimately involved in the life of the worshipper. Stiff formality and meaningless expressions in worship can't exist in such an atmosphere. When a high sense of the holiness of God governs worship, there will be no boredom, cold formality, mere entertainment, or an emphasis on emotionalism—all the common problems experienced in worship today" (*ibid.*).

As we worship we focus on the attributes of God—His love, compassion, and forgiveness—that draws us to Him. We must also focus on His greatness, power, majesty, purity, and wisdom. "Who among the gods is like you, LORD? Who is like you—majestic in holiness, awesome in glory, working wonders?" (Ex. 15:11, NIV). There is none like Him, yet He wants to be involved with us! Close to us! And personally in us! "For this is what the high and exalted One says . . . I live in a high and holy place, but also with the one who is contrite and lowly in spirit, to revive the spirit of the lowly and to revive the heart of the contrite" (Isa. 57:15, NIV). Knowing this puts within our minds a sense of our unworthiness. This is the proper attitude in which we should approach God in worship.

There are many experiences in Scripture that bring out man's reaction to God's holiness and power. Take a look at what God's Word says. Jacob in Bethel: "Surely the LORD is in this place; and I knew it not" (Gen. 28:16). Jacob was afraid and said, "How dreadful [sacred] is this place! there is none other but the house of God, and this is the gate of heaven" (verse 17). Moses at the burning bush (Ex. 3:1-6), and Moses in front of the glory of God (Ex. 33:12-34:8): "And Moses made haste, and bowed his head toward the earth, and worshipped" (Ex. 34:8). In the New Testament the calming of the sea led the disciples to exclaim, "What manner of man is this, that even the wind and seas obey him?" (Mark 4:41). When Jesus filled the fishermen's nets with fish that had previously evaded them, Peter was humbled and said, "Depart from me; for I am a sinful man, O Lord" (Luke 5:8). My favorite experience is the one where doubting Thomas exclaimed, when he came to understand who Jesus was after seeing the nail prints in His Savior's hands, "My LORD and my God" (John 20:28).

The balance spoken of in this article is necessary, not only in church messages but also in our personal spiritual study. Dietrich Bonhoeffer, a German Lutheran theologian and martyr, had this to say of an imbalance in knowing who God is: "Cheap grace is the preaching of forgiveness without requiring repentance, baptism without church discipline, communion without confession, absolution without personal confession. Cheap grace is grace without discipleship, grace without the cross, grace without Jesus Christ, living and incarnate. Cheap grace is the deadly enemy of our church. We are fighting today for costly grace. Cheap grace is to undervalue the greatness of the gift of salvation."

Attending church is hopefully not the only spiritual food people get. If it were, they would be spiritually thin and weak! The purpose of the spiritual fellowship during the church service is to promote a desire for daily study at home. Granted, people have different schedules and obligations of employment, and some have families at home. Some have more time than others for reading and study. However, we can usually find time to do what is a top priority for us. If we cannot find this time, there may be a need to *reevaluate* our schedule.

Many super-busy *disciples* have experienced times in their lives that they were so busy *working for the Lord* that the Lord of the work was almost forgotten—or at least was not a top priority. Putting life into balance requires a mountaintop experience of prayer. See Jesus' experience recorded in Matthew 14:23. God will nudge you when to say *yes* and when to draw back. We'll never regret putting God and His word first in our lives. However busy a person is, his mind can be set on spiritual themes. It is like *background music* to our soul.

Some employment calls for technical sharpness in thought and planning; however, the mind needs to take a break, and at that time it can be filled with God's guidance and love. We need His help in controlling our thoughts, and if we choose His help, it will be there for us. Here are some wonderful thoughts on the mind: "And be not conformed to this world: but be ye transformed by the renewing of your mind, that ye may prove what is that good, and acceptable, and perfect will of God" (Rom. 12:2; see also Phil. 2:5, 6; 4:7). This is a mind worth praying to receive.

When we contemplate joining an organization or looking for needed employment, we normally check out a lot of details to be sure our choice is satisfactory. If it is employment we are seeking, we check on the hours of work and the salary paid. No doubt we consider the benefits offered. When we decide to become a Christian and join God's family, we do not carry a checklist of benefits. In fact, as the chapter on suffering revealed, our new life will not necessarily be a *bed of roses*. There is no insurance that all will go well. If by becoming a Christian we were promised a life of ease, material prosperity, freedom from physical problems, no suffering and no setbacks, many would be attracted to Christianity for these reasons alone. There is no such assurance or insurance; however, there is something much better—the promise and experience of eternal life in the home of the saved. Eternal life—what could be better?

Worship by Discipleship

To be a real disciple and follower of Jesus Christ, all must deny themselves, take up their cross, and follow Him (Matt. 16:24). That may sound like a negative advertisement for Christianity, but as we contemplate the exciting blessings money can't buy, we will find it well worth it. "Whosoever shall seek to save his life shall lose it; and whosoever shall lose his life [for My sake] shall preserve it" (Luke 17:33). "But the law of self-sacrifice is the law of self-preservation" (*Christ's Object Lessons,* p. 86). Bearing our cross and receiving blessings go hand in hand.

"Now unto him that is able to do exceeding abundantly above all that we ask or think, according to the power that worketh in us" (Eph. 3:20). Good, better, and best is a progressive scale and to add "exceedingly abundantly" makes it out of this world!

Worship in Creation

Let me share some of the aspects of being one of God's children that brings much happiness to me. First, I'm so happy to be a result of creation. Most of creation came about by the voice of God. He spoke, and there it was! The exception was the creation of mankind. He formed man from the dust of the ground (the foundation of the earth), and then breathed into man's nostrils the breath of life. With this *kiss from God*, "man became a living soul" (Gen. 2:7). It is exciting for me to know I was made in the image of my Creator! Being made in God's image is an inspiring thought, and believing in a masterful Creator gives me Someone to thank and praise.

The front lobe of our brain holds our spiritual and personality traits. I believe that in this area of our brain we, first, desire to worship our Creator; second, seek to make good decisions for right choices; third, desire to do good works for others; fourth, explore creativity in many areas; fifth, long to go home to heaven; and sixth, accept and use the gifts of the Spirit that were placed in this extraordinary place in our brain by our Creator. It's an awesome thought that our Creator wants a close relationship with us, His created beings. Knowing this gives me a lot of self-worth and self-value. True self-esteem stems from self-respect, self-acceptance, and self-confidence. It is a gift that should be shared or passed on by example to others who are suffering from a poor sense of self-worth. This God-given gift comes from a belief that we are created in God's image. No matter the circumstances of birth, God has given us this birthright. What matchless love and grace for each of us.

God gave the human race an expensive gift when He created us as free moral agents. We have the choice to accept, obey, and love Him, or to reject Him. With the freedom of choice God has given us, we can be a Hitler or a Mother Teresa. The only way to correctly make this weighty responsibility of choice is to stay humbly close to our Creator, asking Him for wisdom to use our freedom of choice for His glory (see Zeph. 2:3). How foolish, how incredibly shortsighted, to squander that gift on anything that this world offers us. Daily let us choose for eternity!

Think on These Things

I also thank and praise the Creator for our marvelous fearfully-and-wonderfully-made bodies. Our eyes, brain, and all other organs are beyond description and call for the work of a wise and powerful Creator. Because most Christians take seriously 1 Corinthians 6:19 and 20—our bodies are a temple for God; we are not our own; we are bought with a price—the result should be a willingness to glorify God in all we do. We should choose a lifestyle that brings God glory, and in most cases this lifestyle gives us health. Yet Christians get sick as do non-Christians, for this sinful world is not fair. While there is peace in the heart when we realize that our choices were the best we could do, we still must suffer the effects of sin.

Saint Augustine had this to say: "Thou hast formed us for Thyself, and our hearts are restless till they find rest in Thee." We were made to worship our Creator. J. N. Andrews wrote this important insight regarding worship: "The true ground of divine worship, not of that of the seventh day merely, but of all worship is founded in the distinction between the Creator and His creatures. This great fact can never become absolute, and must never be forgotten."

We can ask ourselves who or what we worship—money, power, sports, entertainment, people, immorality, our own opinions, or our appetite as described in Romans 16:18 and Philippians 3:19—but what good do these *other gods* do for us? "For what is a man profited, if he shall gain the whole world, and lose his own soul? or what shall a man give in exchange for his soul?" (Matt. 16:26).

Worshipping and serving God requires us to make priorities in our lives: "But seek ye first the kingdom of God, and his righteousness; and all these things shall be added unto you" (Matt. 6:33). There just isn't another way to serve God. "No man can serve two masters: for either he will hate the one, and love the other; or else he will hold to the one, and despise the other. Ye cannot serve God and mammon [money]" (Matt. 6:24). "For where your treasure is, there will your heart be also" (Luke 12:34).

We will never, never regret putting God first in our lives, but it takes courage, especially when we think we are standing alone. When we stand for God we really never stand alone, for He stands with us. It takes more courage than we have on our own, but God will help us with this need. Reading the book of Daniel shows us how God stood by Daniel, giving him courage, faith, and integrity.

Worship by Sabbath Observance

Sabbath is to be celebrated as a weekly memorial. Ellen G. White tells us: "It was to keep this truth ever before the minds of men, that God instituted the Sabbath in Eden; and so long as the fact that He is our Creator continues to be a reason why we should worship Him, so long the Sabbath will continue as its sign and memorial. Had the Sabbath been universally kept, man's thoughts and affections would have been led to the Creator as the object of reverence and worship, and there would never have been an idolater, and atheist, or an infidel. The keeping of the Sabbath is a sign of loyalty to the true God, 'Him that made heaven, and earth, and the sea, and the fountain of water!' It follows that the message which commands men to worship God and keep His commandments will especially call upon them to keep the fourth commandment" (*The Great Controversy,* p. 438). We may not have any trouble remembering that the seventh day is the Sabbath, but we may need to remind ourselves to keep it holy (see Isa. 58:13, 14). Our love for God will make it our joy to keep the Sabbath holy.

As a child I remember Sabbath being the *best day of the week*. I could say it again through the years when our sons were growing up. It will be the *best day of the week* for the rest of my life. It's a day to lay aside work that often brings the cares and stresses of everyday life. It's a day to delight in the Lord (Isa. 58:13, 14). It's a great family day! It provides a wonderful opportunity to introduce our children to the beauties of the world our Creator and Redeemer made. From nature we can learn lessons of obedience and trust in God.

Of all the experiences of life, this special day brings back more pleasant memories of time with family than any other occasion. Looking back through the years, here is a glimpse of our life and the joy we found in Sabbath. We looked forward to the Sabbath all week long. To keep from making Friday, *preparation day* (Luke 23:54), from being hectic, we started to prepare earlier in the week for this *special day*. There were clothes, worn only on Sabbath, to have ready, the house made clean and orderly, and food prepared ahead of the Sabbath. Our baths were taken on *preparation day,* and to have clean bed sheets was another plus for the beginning of God's special day.

I recall the simple Friday evening supper of tasty homemade chili, and Sabbath morning we continued this special day by singing our blessing song,

"Father We Thank Thee," before we ate our breakfast. It was the blessing song used at summer camps, and the tie between the camp and our hearts made our use of this song an extraordinary blessing for Sabbath. There was extra joy when my husband, Fred, was home to enjoy this time with me and our sons—Eric, Fred, and Ted. Often his youth leadership responsibilities required weekend travel that took him away from home.

From Friday sunset through all day Saturday, the hours of the Sabbath were spent on very special activities reserved for this time only. Sunset on Friday and Saturday evenings found our family together singing or playing instruments. Favorite songs of the boys included: "Lift Up the Trumpet, Loud Let it Ring"; "Jesus is Coming Again"; "Make Me a Blessing"; "If I Have Wounded Any Soul Today, Dear Lord Forgive." And we always sang "Day is Dying in the West" as our first song.

Part of our Sabbath pleasure was in attending Sabbath School and church. While our boys were growing up we attended the Pioneer Memorial Church on the campus of Andrews University, Berrien Springs, Michigan. I had the pleasure of teaching a kindergarten Sabbath School class using a sandbox for illustrations of our Bible lesson. The church was also known by the beautiful words engraved above the entry of the sanctuary, "An house of Prayer for All People." The fellowship of students and families from around the world was inspiring. The beauty and order in which the services were conducted added to the reverence and sacredness we felt on these very special occasions.

In our home on Sabbath afternoon there were nature games to play, stories to be read or told, Bible games and quizzes, and charades based on scriptural stories, which caught everyone's attention, both when planning the story to the acting out or the fun of guessing. We practiced our artistic skills by drawing on the chalkboard various scenes to depict gospel hymns, a Bible experience, or a memory gem from Scripture, while others guessed what was being represented. Artwork, done by each son on his favorite nature or Sabbath subject, was often shared with an elderly individual during an afternoon visit.

One of our favorite Sabbath games, which is still used with Sabbath guests today, is called Clue In a Bag. It was special to share these pleasures with Sabbath guests and with my parents—Ted and Florence Boelter—in our home or in my parents' home on a nearby fruit farm. A copy of the directions is included with this chapter in the event you are interested in enjoying it too.

Being nature lovers, our family enjoyed being outside, taking walks to see farm animals, swinging on sturdy vines hanging from the trees, enjoying the beautiful sand of Lake Michigan's sand dunes, or—after moving West—hiking in the mountains. The locations where we lived offered us a wonderful variety of enjoyable outdoor activities. We would collect specimens of plants (where it was lawful) to dry and put in a book in which we also included interesting details about our specimens.

Now, in our later years, we endeavor to continue following the example of Jesus as recorded in Luke 4:16: "As his custom was, he went into the synagogue on the sabbath day." Sabbath afternoons, when spending time amidst the beauties of nature, our minds become focused on the joy, beyond our imaginations, awaiting us as we contemplate walks in heaven with our Creator (see 1 Corinthians 2:9).

Another pleasure we continue to enjoy on this *best day* is to again follow Jesus' example by going about doing good on the Sabbath. This brings great pleasure to the giver and the receiver as encouragement, healing, and joy are shared with those who need it. We'll never run out of those who are in need.

No wonder the Sabbath is the best day of the week!

Clue in a Bag

Clue In A Bag is a favorite game that generates a lot of discussion and conversation. It is a great icebreaker, but it is also a spiritually profitable learning and sharing experience. This game is for all ages. Often, it is amazing the insights brought out by children and youth.

Use a cloth tote or shopping bag approximately 16" x 14", preferably with handles, as a container to fill with small bags (size no. 2), each containing an item to remind the contestant of something in the Bible. The large bag is taken around to each person, and without inspecting items in the small bags, the player chooses one bag. Each player chooses a small bag before the game begins. Then, the first player who selected a bag, having had some time to think, begins the game by revealing the article in his bag and telling—by way of Bible story, text, quote, or spiritual insight—what the object evokes from his heart or memory. In case inspiration is needed, Bible references are written on the outside of each small bag, which the player may refer to for assistance. When a person is finished with their contribution, other players, in turn, present additional stories

Think on These Things

or ideas. Then, the second player begins, and the game goes on.

To save you time, I have listed the items and verses used in our bag. You may think of others to add. You may not use all the little bags in one game since the amount of people taking part and the times the big bag is passed around for additional turns will determine the items used. There is no time limit on this inspirational game of sharing and fellowship.

1. Pen and paper: 3 John 13	2. Plastic serpent: Gen. 3:1, 13, 15; Rev. 12:9
3. Ten ribbons pinned together and two ribbons pinned together: 2 Chron. 10:3-11, 19 (dividing of the twelve tribes)	4. Bunch of plastic grapes: Num. 13:23; Mark 14:24, 25; John 15:5
5. A small flask of perfume: Luke 7:37-50; Eccl. 10:1; 2 Cor. 2:14, 15	6. Small knife in plastic bag: Gen. 22:1-13; Heb. 4:12
7. A baggy with a slice of bread: Gen. 3:19; Prov. 22:9, Isa. 33:16, 55:2	8. Strong rope (short) with a rag tied around it: Jer. 38:6-13
9. Matches: 1 Peter 1:7; James 3:5; Rev. 3:18, 20:9, 10	10. Circle of paper, manger scene sticker, and a cross: John 3:16
11. Container of salt: Gen. 19:26; 2 Kings 2:21; Matt. 5:13; Mark 9:50; Col. 4:6	12. Your choice
13. Soiled rag: Isa. 64:6	14. Set of keys: Matt. 16:19; Rev. 20:1-3
15. Foreign language dictionary: Gen. 11:1-8; Acts 2:4	16. Rainbow picture: Gen. 9:13-16; 2 Peter 1:4
17. Small sandal: John 13:12-17; Eph. 6:10-17	18. Paper chain (golden); 3 circles (Trinity): Matt. 28:19
19. Fruit (raisins), nuts, grain: Gen. 1:29	20. Stone in shape of heart: Eze. 36:26
21. White stone: 1 Peter 2:5; Rev. 2:17	22. Paper chain; 2 circles (marriage): Gen. 2:23
23. Coins, money: Gen. 42:25; Matt. 21:12, 13; Matt. 22:24	24. Small cardboard circles (4") with stickers for each day of Creation: Gen. 1 and 2; John 1:3

Worship Through Music

Another special pleasure of worship as one of God's followers is music. There has always been music in heaven, and it is recorded that it began on earth during Creation. Job refers to this time in Job 38:7: "When the morning stars sang together, and all the sons of God shouted for joy?" Scripture reveals that music was used on many occasions, including choirs singing in celebration of victories won. (2 Chron. 20:21).

Zephaniah 3:17 certainly demonstrates how valuable we are to God: "The LORD thy God in the midst of thee is mighty; he will save, he will rejoice over thee with joy; he will rest in his love, he will joy over thee with singing."

The early church often sang songs of thanksgiving and praise to God. Two disciples had such trust in God that they could sing while in prison for Jesus' sake! The greatest song recorded in Scripture has yet to be sung. It will be sung at the second coming of Christ: "And they sing the song of Moses the servant of God, and the song of the Lamb, saying, Great and marvellous are thy works, Lord God Almighty; just and true are thy ways, thou King of saints" (Rev. 15:3).

There's a song that moves me to tears of joy as I sing it: "Holy, Holy is What the Angels Sing." Written by Johnson Oatman, Jr., verse four reads:

> "So, although I'm not an angel, yet I know that over there,
> I will join a blessed chorus, that the angels cannot share;
> I will sing about my Saviour, who upon dark Calvary,
> Freely pardoned my transgressions, died to set a sinner free."
>
> Refrain:
> "Holy, holy, is what the angels sing,
> And I expect to help them make the courts of heaven ring;
> But when I sing redemption's story, they will fold their wings,
> For angels never felt the joys that our salvation brings."

Let us make a pledge to be there to sing this song together.

Music can change hearts like nothing else can. It has incredible power to touch people's hearts and cause a desire to bring glory to God. After hearing the song "Give of Your Best to the Master," a friend told me that the words spoke to her heart. She determined to wear her best in church while worshipping God. It was a change from her ordinary clothes—jeans—to an attractive, modest dress.

Disadvantaged children from challenging surroundings have been taken under the wing of very caring, thoughtful orchestra conductors. The results after some time of practicing together have been astonishing! One of the young boys said it was the first time in his life when he was involved in something that was not competitive where he wanted to outdo someone else. He felt very good about the unity he felt by being involved with others producing good music.

I was thrilled to hear this story on the news. These conductors reported excitedly that the music the youth played was classical or semi-classical. Jazz or rock music would not work. I have read of this opinion expressed by conductors in other countries as well as in the United States of America. These men are passionate about helping disadvantaged children and youth develop plans for their lives that do not include drugs or crime! When I read or hear about such caring professional people, my heart goes out in joyful, thankful prayer for them and their work for and with youth.

Gospel music brings comfort, encouragement, strength for trials, and courage to make life-changing decisions. There are many authors of hymns who wrote them due to some glorious or tragic experience they encountered. It was a disastrous happening that inspired Horatio Gates Spafford to put his thoughts into verse two years after his four daughters—aged 2 to 11 years—were drowned at the time of a disastrous collision of their ship with another vessel. Their ship sank in half an hour.

"It Is Well With My Soul" has encouraged and comforted others who have gone through a tragic bereavement. Trust and confidence in God, in spite of deep personal sorrow, sustained these parents. The hymn says:

> "When peace, like a river, attendeth my way,
> When sorrows like sea billows roll;
> Whatever my lot, Thou has taught me to say,
> It is well, it is well with my soul."

> "Though Satan should buffet, though trials should come,
> Let this blest assurance control,
> That Christ hath regarded my helpless estate,

It Pays!—To God be the Glory

And hath shed His own blood for my soul."

Many Christian composers write their songs as prayers. Singing is a part of worship as much as prayer. Many can testify to the encouragement and blessing it is to sing when times are dark and discouraging or when temptations come. What could be better than to sing praises when the heart is filled with joy? What a treasured gift is music.

Worship Through Prayer

After their creation, Adam and Eve visited with their Creator face to face, but when sin entered, they were afraid of their Maker and hid from Him. What a sad change from their former face-to-face fellowship. When humanity could no longer meet this way, they were given the gift of prayer in its place: "then began men to call upon the name of the LORD" (Gen. 4:26).

In Bible times people used various physical positions as they prayed: standing, bowing down, kneeling, and some—in great anguish or fear—falling on their faces. God hears us in any position. We can pray on any occasion. We are told to "pray without ceasing" (1 Thess. 5:17). To me, I liken this to having, in my mind, the background of an attitude of prayer. Surely, this attitude will help us resist temptation. When we are healthy Christians, we won't have to decide to pray without ceasing—it will happen automatically. Our prayer life will increase when our activity for Christ does.

Prayer is speaking sincerely from an open heart and a humble attitude to God as to a friend. The Lord's Prayer was given as a guide or model. Each phrase can be made personal. Someone has prepared the word **ACTS** as an acronym for a prayer guide which truly covers a complete prayer:

Adoration
Confession
Thanksgiving
Supplication

God speaks to us by things we see in nature, by the influence of the Holy Spirit, by His work, and by experiences that come to us. While Jesus was here on earth, He depended on His Father and felt the need of much prayer. God's heart of love longs to help and is eager to hear our petitions. We are in danger of giving in to temptations when we cease to ask for God's help. He cares about all our desires and needs. "He that spared not his own Son, but delivered him up for us all, how shall he not with him also freely give us all things?" (Rom. 8:32).

There are many prayers of God's followers recorded in Scripture. Moses and other leaders prayed for the people, for guidance, for forgiveness. Some of these prayers make an indelible impression on my mind. The story found in Exodus 32:1-14 was a test for Moses. His prayer for the rebellious people proved he passed the test. Moses was more eager for God's reputation than for any benefit on his part.

Any reader of the book of Daniel can't help but admire and love this young captive who was taken to Babylon. He was faithful to God at all costs. In his humble prayer recorded in Daniel 9:3-19, he counted himself among the sinners. He, too, was eager for God's people to represent Him. No wonder Daniel was "greatly beloved" by God.

The prayer of all prayers is the one Jesus offered to His Father for the apostles and believers of all times. It is recorded in John 17. Some outstanding thoughts are as follows: "And this is life eternal, that they might know thee the only true God, and Jesus Christ, whom thou hast sent" (verse 3); "I pray not that thou shouldest take them out of the world, but that thou shouldest keep them from evil" (verse 15); "Sanctify them through thy truth: thy word is truth" (verse 17); "Father, I will that they also, whom thou hast given me, be with me where I am" (verse 24). Read the entire prayer for a heartfelt experience.

The following are thoughts on the gift of prayer: "Prayer does not change God, but it does change us and our relation to God." Also, "prayer is the breath of the soul. It is the secret of spiritual power. No other means of grace can be substituted and the health of the soul be preserved" (*Messages to Young People,* p. 249). And we often use the expression, "I breathed a prayer" (see Lam. 3:55, 56).

The following quotes are from a godly woman who believed in the power of prayer. Ellen White wrote:

> "Keep your wants, your joys, your sorrows, your cares, and your fears before God. You cannot burden Him; you cannot weary Him" (*Steps to Christ,* p. 100).

"In the future life the mysteries that here have annoyed and disappointed us will be made plain. We shall see that our seemingly unanswered prayers and disappointed hopes have been among our greatest blessings" (*The Ministry of Healing,* p. 474; see also Rom. 8:28).

"Why should the sons and daughters of God be reluctant to pray, when prayer is the key in the hand of faith to unlock heaven's storehouse, where are treasured the boundless resources of Omnipotence?" (*Steps to Christ,* pp. 94, 95).

"Although there may be a tainted, corrupted atmosphere around us, we need not breathe its miasma, but may live in the pure air of heaven. We may close every door to impure imaginings and unholy thoughts by lifting the soul into the presence of God through sincere prayer" (*Steps to Christ,* p. 99).

We should also make "Turn Your Eyes Upon Jesus" our theme song. The source of Jesus' spiritual power while on earth was His relationship with His Father through prayer. Jesus spent time between the mountaintop where He went for prayer and strength and the multitude where He met the needs of others.

"He that cometh to God must believe that he is, and that he is a rewarder of them that diligently seek Him" (Heb. 11:6(. "The effectual fervent prayer of a righteous man availeth much" (James 5:16). "Our heavenly Father has a thousand ways to provide for us of which we know nothing. Those who accept the one principle of making the service of God supreme, will find perplexities vanish and a plain path before their feet" (*The Ministry of Healing,* p. 481).

There are certain acts on our part that will be a deterrent to answered prayer: "If I regard iniquity in my heart [if we cling to any known sin], the Lord will not hear me" (Ps. 66:18). Some people snuggle with their sins—they really don't choose to part with them. Some of us struggle with sin. God is on the side of strugglers and will bring victory through Jesus. When all known wrongs are righted, we may believe that God will answer our prayers. "He that turneth away his ear from hearing the law, even his prayer shall be abomination" (Prov. 28:9).

"Forgive us our debts, as we forgive our debtors" (Matt. 6:12)—this was Jesus' recipe for our forgiveness. We can have trust and confidence in knowing we have forgiveness when we repent: "If we confess our sins, he is faithful and just to forgive us our sins, and to cleanse us from all unrighteousness" (1 John 1:9). It gives us a feeling of triumph when we can say at the close of the day: "Thank you, God, for a day of victory." Yes, God accepts us just as we are, but He's just as eager to give victory as to forgive. James tells us: "Ye ask, and receive not, because ye ask amiss, that ye may consume it upon your lusts" (James 4:3). Peter urges husbands and wives to take note of his very important counsel found in 1 Peter 3:7 "that your prayers be not hindered."

God wants us to pray for those who despitefully use us and persecute us (Matt. 5:44). If these prayers are slow at changing the *perceived enemy*, let them be answered quickly by changing us! Our change may make a good change in those who are unkind to us.

We need to praise God more "for his goodness, and for his wonderful works to the children of men!" (Ps. 107:8). "In every thing by prayer and supplication with thanksgiving let your requests be made known to God" (Phil. 4:6). When we understand our part in the act of prayer, it makes for a good time of *soul searching and cleansing*. The greatest benefit of prayer is to strengthen our love and trust relationship with God. We are talking to our forever Friend. We can trust His answers to be for our best.

We can often help in answering our own prayers. If we sincerely pray for health, we must seek to live by God's laws of health. If we sincerely pray for a discouraged, sick, or destitute person, we can visit them and help answer our own prayers (see James 2:15-17). If we sincerely want to strengthen our Christian walk and ask God for this experience, we can help answer this prayer by spending time with Him a daily habit. "If we thought and talked more of Jesus, and less of self, we should have far more of His presence" (*Steps to Christ*, p. 102).

There are times I need to repent for lack of trust, forgetting how God has answered my prayers in the past. In these instances, I have allowed fear to take over. The trust in my prayer life strengthens as I grow spiritually. Let us not get discouraged if our prayers are not answered to our satisfaction as quickly as we wish. God has asked us to patiently wait (Rom. 8:25). "We are so erring and short-sighted that we sometimes ask for things that would not be a blessing to us" (*Steps to Christ*, p. 96).

It Pays!—To God be the Glory

One of Jesus' own prayers was not answered. Yet, He added "nevertheless not as I will, but as thou wilt" (Matt. 26:39). We too should pray according to God's will (see 1 John 5:14, 15). Many answers to prayer come before a prayer is offered! "And it shall come to pass, that before they call, I will answer; and while they are yet speaking, I will hear" (Isa. 65:24). How grateful we can be that God's ear is always open to our petitions, said or unsaid!

Skip McCarty has these encouraging, helpful thoughts to ponder: "For some, unanswered prayers are devastating because of the high expectations Bible promises raise. How do we cope with unanswered prayer?
1. Talk openly to God about your disappointment and disillusionment.
2. Seize the opportunity to grow.
3. Recognize that an 'unanswered prayer' may be a blessing in disguise.
4. Realize that your unanswered prayer might benefit someone else.
5. Consult past evidence."

When there are unanswered prayers, it would be wise to check if there are things in our life that we need to confess and repent of.

Some of the most meaningful stories told or written are those of answered prayer. George Müller established orphanages in England in the mid-1880s. All the funds needed for the children's care were miraculously provided through his constant prayers for his project. He never had to ask people to help with finances for the care of his children. This great man of faith learned many things while talking to God for more than sixty years. His concentration was increased when he chose a Bible verse to think upon when he prayed. He would trust God's promises and claim them in his prayers. God never failed Müller. He impressed people of the children's needs and, consequently, funds and food were sent just at the right time.

We have many role models from the days of the first prayer offered until now. All sincere Christians have heartwarming answers to prayers for their own salvation and that of others for whom they have labored and prayed—answers, also, for physical, emotional, social, and many other needs common to the human race. I could tell many personal stories of answered prayer, but the story I'm choosing to include is one I found very special about the needs of a little child. It goes as follows:

"An eyewitness account from New York City, on a cold day in December, some years ago: A little boy, about ten-years-old, was standing before a shoe store on the sidewalk, barefooted, peering through the window, and shivering with cold.

"A lady approached the young boy and said, 'My, but you're in such deep thought staring in that window!'

"'I was asking God to give me a pair of shoes,' was the boy's reply.

"The lady took him by the hand, went into the store, and asked the clerk to get half a dozen pairs of socks for the boy. She then asked if he could give her a basin of water and a towel. He quickly brought them to her.

"She took the little fellow to the back part of the store and removing her gloves, knelt down, washed his little feet, and dried them with the towel. By this time, the clerk had returned with the socks. Placing a pair upon the boy's feet, she purchased him a pair of shoes. She tied up the remaining pairs of socks and gave them to him. She patted him on the head and said, 'No doubt, you will be more comfortable now.'

"As she turned to go, the astonished child caught her by the hand, and looking up into her face with tears in his eyes, asked her: 'Are you God's wife?'"

I don't know how the woman reacted, but I'm sure amid my own tears I would have put him in my arms and said, "God loves you, and I love you, too!"

Two old gospel songs come to my mind that remind me there is a time coming when no longer will we need the comforting gift of prayer. The last verse of "Sweet Hour of Prayer" closes with this thought: "Farewell, farewell, sweet hour of prayer." An important part of the redemptive act will be when we go back to the original way of communication with God: "Face to face with Christ my Saviour, Face to face what will it be, When with rapture I behold Him, Jesus Christ, who died for me."

The following encompasses various times and ways we can communicate with God while we're still on this planet:

Moments with God

Happy moments	*Praise God*	*James 5:13*
Difficult moments	*Seek God*	*Psalm 63:1;*
		Matthew 26:41
Quiet moments	*Worship God*	*Psalm 4:4*
Painful moments	*Trust God*	*Psalm 32:7*
Every moment	*Thank God*	*Psalm 100:4;*
		Philippians 4:6

"O thou that hearest prayer, unto thee shall all flesh come" (Ps. 65:2).

Let us always remember that it is impossible for the soul to flourish while prayer is neglected. Prayer is a beautiful subject that merits much contemplation. A concordance is helpful for further study.

Worship Through Stewardship

Our loving God is familiar with the selfishness of humanity. To bring this to our mind, Jesus used the subject of money in two-thirds of His parables: how we use it and our attitude toward it. The use we make of our money tests our character. There are more than 2,000 references to money matters in the Scriptures. It was God's intention that we have our mind and money both converted—one story goes that a man wanted his wallet in his pocket when he was baptized!

We may not think of this often, if ever, but giving offerings is part of the pleasure and privilege of worship. Besides the returning of tithe (which already belongs to God), we give offerings used for the furtherance of God's work. We will be helping to answer our own prayers for the gospel commission to be fulfilled if we are generous with God's work (see Matt. 28:19, 20). "Lay not up for yourselves treasures upon earth . . . But lay up for yourselves treasures in heaven, where neither moth nor rust doth corrupt, and where thieves do not break through nor steal: For where your treasure is, there will your heart be also" (Matt. 6:19-21). "Every man [person] according as he purposeth in his heart, so let him give; not grudgingly, or of necessity: for God loveth a cheerful giver" (2 Cor. 9:7).

A Danish proverb states that "When it comes to giving, some people stop at nothing."

Stewardship is a total lifestyle. We often think it involves only finances, but it involves our time, talents, health, relationships, spirituality, and environment. When we love God with all our heart, giving becomes a pleasure!

Keep your lives free from the love of money, and be content with what you have because God has said, "I will never leave you, nor forsake thee" (Heb. 13:5). That's an investment, a value, that can't be bought at any price. "Moreover it is required in stewards, that a man be found faithful" (1 Cor. 4:2).

Worship in Hope

After telling the children's story at a worship services during one Thanksgiving season, I asked what they were especially thankful for. The thoughtful answers were a blessing to those who heard them: "Health"; "Living in a free country"; "Belonging to a Christian family who worships God"; "Thanks for enough food, a warm home filled with love, and parents to care for and trust me."

I was greatly impressed with one small boy's unforgettable reply, which he said in only one word: "HOPE." I wondered about his reason for this answer and regret not asking "Why hope?" But we did talk about the great value of hope and went home with something new to think about. Hope is wonderful, especially if we have great confidence that it will become a reality someday!

Hope kept Christ going in an unfriendly world with thoughts of His followers through the ages who would accept His gift of eternal life and live with Him in the home He would prepare for them! (John 14:1-3). *Hope* has placed confidence and trust in the hearts of those who may have nothing else to carry them through. *Hope* can be for all of us who love, obey God, and look forward to His second coming.

The Christian's hope is revealed in Titus 2:13 and 14: "Looking for that blessed hope, and the glorious appearing of the great God and our Saviour Jesus Christ; Who gave himself for us, that he might redeem us from all iniquity, and purify unto himself a peculiar people, zealous of good works."

Of course, the hope of all of Jesus' followers is in the resurrection from the sleep of death. "But we would not have you ignorant, brethren, concerning those who are asleep, that you may not grieve as others do who have no hope. For since we believe that Jesus died and rose again, even so, through Jesus, God will bring with him those who have fallen asleep. For this we declare to you by the word of the Lord, that we who are alive, who are left until the coming of the Lord, shall not precede those who have fallen asleep. For the Lord himself will descend from heaven with a cry of command, with the archangel's call, and with the sound of the trumpet of God. And the dead in Christ will rise first; then we who are alive, who are left, shall be caught up together with them in the clouds to meet the Lord in the air; and so we shall always be with the Lord. Therefore comfort one another with these words" (1 Thess. 4:13-18, RSV).

We are told "which hope we have as an anchor of the soul, both sure and steadfast" (Heb. 6:19). This "hope" will keep God's followers true to principle and keep them so firm that the most powerful temptation of Satan will not draw them away from their allegiance to Him. "And every man that hath this hope in him purifieth himself, even as he is pure" (1 John 3:3). "Be of good courage, and he shall strengthen your heart, all ye that hope in the LORD" (Ps. 31:24). "And we desire that every one of you do shew the same diligence to the full assurance of hope unto the end" (Heb. 6:11).

We worship the Creator God even if we can't see Him. Hebrews 11:1 says: "Now faith is the substance of things hoped for, the evidence of things not seen." God's creative power is all around us in nature, giving evidence of His existence.

Hope is a powerful blessing to God's followers. It deserves to be placed among the "exceedingly abundant" thoughts that bring peace and happiness.

A Timely Gift

Another of the "exceedingly abundant" gifts to be blessed by as God's followers is a very *timely gift*. This gift is one of the identifying marks of God's followers: "And the dragon [Satan] was wroth with the woman [the church], and went to make war with the remnant of her seed, which keep the commandments of God, and have the testimony of Jesus Christ" (Rev. 12:17). To identify the "testimony of Jesus Christ" as the timely gift, see Revelation 19:10: "for the testimony of Jesus is the spirit of prophecy." With this understanding, let us consider more about this gift.

I am grateful and humbled to know how much God loves His followers! When He knew He was soon to leave His disciples, His thoughts were on them: "He loved them unto the end" (John 13:1). This love included giving guidance to His followers to help them prepare their lives to be ready to live with Him through eternity. God has bent over backward to do all that is possible to win, by His love, His created beings. What more could He do?

Through the ages, God, in His wisdom and love, has called a messenger with a message to meet every need of the human race. The Scriptures record many instances of God's messengers. At the time of the Flood God used Noah to save the human race (Gen. 6-9); He used Joseph to save Egypt and his own family during a seven-year famine (Gen. 37:14-36; 41-47); He used Moses to deliver His chosen from slavery and lead them to the Promised Land (Ex. 3-16); and John the Baptist was a forerunner of Jesus, our Savior. It is recorded in the Old and New Testaments how God used prophets as messengers to lead, guide, and reprove His people.

Would He leave His followers at the challenging, fearful end-times without a messenger and a message? Notice the prophecy in Joel 2:28 and 29, which is also repeated in Acts 2:17 and 18: "And it shall come to pass afterward, that I will pour out my spirit upon all flesh; and your sons and your daughters shall prophesy, your old men shall dream dreams, your young men shall see visions: and also upon the servants and upon the handmaids in those days will I pour out my spirit." These words were written for those living in "the day of the Lord"—the end times.

If God's people had always made the principles of the Scripture their influence, He would not have had to repeat the guidance through a later prophet. Isn't it just like a loving *heavenly Father* to always come to our rescue in spite of our careless neglect? The goal of Scripture and prophecy is to help us understand the character of God and His desire for a loving relationship with us, thus inspiring the love of obedience in His followers.

The last book of the Bible, the prophetic book of Revelation, starts with these words: "The Revelation of Jesus Christ." It doesn't say the revelation of "things to come." However, this book does have plenty to say about the future. All the predictions of the future are summarized in the last two chapters of Revelation, telling us that God is vindicated and His followers are worthy to inhabit through eternity the magnificent home in heaven that is described in Revelation 21 and 22.

Prophets do more than reveal future events. They give God's guidance in all matters. They are God's mouthpiece of encouragement, rebuke, discipline, and a call to repentance. The prophets must be obedient servants of God. They were often very unpopular. Note 2 Chronicles 36:15 and 16: "And the LORD God of their fathers sent to them by his messengers, rising up betimes [continually], and sending; because he had compassion on his people, and on

It Pays!—To God be the Glory

his dwelling place: But they mocked the messengers of God, and despised his words, and misused his prophets, until the wrath of the LORD arose against his people." Jesus added this disappointing end to His discussion of the fact that prophets are often not recognized or accepted by their own community! "A prophet is not without honour, save in his own country, and in his own house" (Matt. 13:57). Jesus was actually convicted of evil: "He casteth out devils through the prince of devils" (Matt. 9:34). Be sure to also read Luke 13:34 and 35 and Acts 7:52.

But encouragement was given to support those who spoke for God (see Isa. 51:7). Encouragement was also given to the people to listen: "Hear me, O Judah, and ye inhabitants of Jerusalem [this includes "modern" Israel—those who are Christ's—as shown in Gal. 3:29]; Believe in the LORD your God, so shall ye be established; believe his prophets, so shall ye prosper" (2 Chron. 20:20). It is said that "true prophets tend to be overused or underused, abused or misused." One way or another, prophets have never been popular people with the majority—from the first prophet to the last one. "Yea, they made their hearts as an adamant stone, lest they should hear the law, and the words which the LORD of hosts hath sent in his spirit by the former prophets" (Zech. 7:12). Jesus lamented: "O Jerusalem, Jerusalem, which killest the prophets, and stonest them that are sent unto thee" (Luke 13:34).

Some prophets complained about their *calling,* which is understandable. When God promised the guidance of a prophet for the end times, is our response one that God would appreciate? Do we say "Thank you" or "No thanks"?

The Seventh-day Adventist Church considers Ellen G. White (1827-1915) the answer to Joel 2:29: "And also upon the servants and upon the handmaids in those days will I pour out my spirit." The following verse, which was already referred to, was spoken by Jesus: "A prophet is not without honour, save in his own country, and in his own house" (Matt. 13:57). Jesus experienced this even among His own disciples. Two were untrue to Him: Peter denied Him three times in a row, and Judas betrayed Jesus to His death. Broken-hearted Peter was forgiven. Conscious-stricken Judas threw back the money he received for being a traitor to Jesus and then went out and took his own life.

This experience was also true of Ellen G. White. Many members of her church dismissed and discarded her testimonies and counsel. Praise God, most members and leaders worldwide have heeded the counsel and writings and been blessed beyond measure!

After research the life and work of Ellen G. White, Roger W. Coon wrote *A Life of Light*. I will share in my own words some of the many convincing thoughts from this book. While some members of her church failed to see the wisdom, beauty, and power of her words, others—not Seventh-day Adventists—have given her due honor. Those who treasured her works were renowned authorities and well-known and distinguished in many areas. One—Clive McCay, Ph.D. in nutrition—was very impressed with her book *Counsels on Diet and Foods*. McCay wondered how an uneducated woman wrote such health teachings so far in advance of the time in which she lived. He was eager to know more about her history, and he came to the conclusion that her findings were more than humanly discovered. Her words were written back in the days when doctors were still *bloodletting* and performing surgery with unwashed hands—an era of medical ignorance bordering on barbarism!

Among the many others who gave her honor and praise was Florence Stratemeyer, a leading educator and professor of education. Of White's book *Education* (published 1903), she said, "This volume is more than fifty years ahead of its time." What is so amazing is that the book was written by a woman with but three years of formal schooling. A childhood accident was responsible for her dropping out. She experienced frail health during her long life of service. Truly God used this "thorn in the flesh" by using the "weakest of the weak" for His glory.

This input by these well-educated people about the writings of Ellen G. White is glowing with amazement and gratitude. I must mention the sixteen-paragraph article featuring Ellen White written by American Broadcasting Company news commentator Paul Harvey. He often remarked about her on his broadcasts and cited her remarkable contributions to nutrition, education, and many other aspects of life. Speaking of her, he called her the "amazing little lady." He asked his listeners, "Do you know Ellen White? If not, get acquainted with her."

One educator was so impressed that she held the opinion that "had Ellen White been a Roman Catholic instead of a Seventh-day Adventist, she might very well be canonized in due course." At the time of White's death, in 1915,

It Pays!—To God be the Glory

she received considerable editorial comment in the secular press. To quote: "Mrs. White . . . early manifested some of the gifts of prophecy. With the formation of the church of the Seventh-day Adventists, she immediately developed an influence, and that influence was maintained to the hour of her death, a period of seventy years. Besides unusual talents as a preacher, she had organizational and administrative powers. These were all given to her church. It prospered and grew until it has spread through many lands, universities were founded, medical schools, hospitals, and schools for teachers and missionaries. Mrs. White was a remarkable woman. . . . She was the flesh of which saints are made."

There are many reports of her noble record in which she deserved and was given honor. Had she heard all these commendations, she—with her humble attitude—would, no doubt have replied "To God be the glory." She considered and called herself "God's messenger." Quoting from the *Independent* in 1915: "She was absolutely honest in her belief in her revelations. Her life was worthy of them. She showed no spiritual pride and she sought no filthy lucre. She lived the life and did the work of a worthy prophetess, the most admirable of the American succession."

There are many more books written about the life and work of Ellen G. White. One that I have read to glean from to share thoughts from is titled *They Were There* by Herbert E. Douglass. It includes many stories of those who witnessed her prophetic gift and believed. The stories reveal how God used her visions to convince doubters of her authenticity. One will develop great confidence in God and His gift of prophecy through Ellen White as you read Douglass' stories in detail.

Joseph Bates, a converted sea captain, was a doubter. But God gave Mrs. White a vision in Mr. Bates' presence where she saw and described views of different planets. What is extraordinary is that she knew nothing of astronomy. She didn't name the planets, but Bates could tell which ones she was describing with glowing descriptions. What astounded Bates was her description of the "opening heavens"—a reference to the so-called "open space in Orion." He felt it surpassed any description made by contemporary astronomers. This interesting *astronomy vision* corresponded to Bates' knowledge of what telescopes showed in 1846. It gave him great confidence in Ellen White's ministry.

God gave dreams and visions to Ellen White to guide in the establishing of health, publishing, and educational institutions around the world, as well as messages that exposed sin and helped to solve church problems. The stories are both thrilling and remarkable. Often she was given these messages long before the incidents happened. Many times she would forget details of these visions, but the details would come back to her later, causing her to write letters to the people involved at just the right time. She was often some distance away—sometimes overseas—when she sent these timely messages. They usually arrived the day that a decision needed to be made. Those receiving them were awestruck at her amazing accuracy describing people involved as well as the incident itself.

The well-known Dr. John Harvey Kellogg was a member of the Seventh-day Adventist denomination. He was a brilliant man and had great influence over many members and even among the leaders. He wrote *The Living Temple* which seemed to be splitting the leadership of the Adventist church. A full day at the Autumn Council meeting was given to study of the book, which contained pantheistic philosophy and mysticism regarding the personality of God. There were dangerous errors being taught in this book.

Two messages from Mrs. White came just at the right time. Those at this important meeting exclaimed: "Deliverance has come!" As these messages were read to those assembled, many loud "amens" were heard and tears flowed freely. At that point the tide was turned against accepting the pantheistic teaching of the book. Elder A. G. Daniells, president of the General Conference of Seventh-day Adventists at that time, was overwhelmed with these events. He wrote a grateful letter to Ellen White. Gleaning from his letter are these words: "It [your letter] came just at the right time exactly. The conflict was severe, and we knew not how things would turn. But your clear, clean-cut, beautiful message came and stilled the controversy. . . . I do not say that all parties came into perfect harmony, but it gave those who stood on the right side strength to stand and hold their ground!"

These interventions, that kept the denomination on course, happened often. Each time those in leadership positions were gratefully humbled to write letters such as this: "Never in my life have I seen such signal evidences of the leadership of an all-wise Being [God]."

Another letter said, "Your message came on just the right day . . . I read it to the council yesterday and it produced a most profound impression . . . as for myself, when I received this last communication, I could only sit and weep . . . it called our brethren to take their stand, [it] brought great relief to me, and the terrible load that had at times almost crushed me, has, in a measure, rolled off from me."

Another such incident is most interesting to our family. In brief, the much beloved Battle Creek Tabernacle church in Battle Creek, Michigan, which could comfortably seat up to 3,200 people when opened fully, was without a pastor probably due to the struggle in 1907 over the ownership of the church building and the stress involved settling difficult problems. Finally, M. N. Campbell, a 32-year-old newly ordained minister, was chosen as the pastor.

"Close to the church was the world-famous Battle Creek Sanitarium. By 1907, Dr. John Harvey Kellogg and his followers had wrested control of the Sanitarium from the denomination and now their attention was focused on taking over the largest church in the denomination. . . . Strange as it may seem, most of the churches' trustees were inclined to support Kellogg and the Sanitarium.

"God gave young Pastor Campbell great tact and wisdom making friends with the trustees. He talked with them about reincorporating the charter. The charter had expired in 1892 and the trustees had done nothing to renew it. The pastor had done his homework well, seeking legal advice and studying the steps that had to be taken to keep the Tabernacle in the denomination. A little time before the meeting, the pastor called a few of the leading brethren together for prayer. Ten minutes before the meeting was to open, a Western Union messenger came to the door and inquired: 'Is Mr. Campbell here?'

"Campbell said, 'yes,' and reached out for the telegram addressed to him. Opening it, he found this message: 'Philippians 1:27, 28. (Signed) Ellen G. White. (She was in California at that time.) It was a testimony, her shortest testimony ever. Opening the Bible to the reference given, they read: 'Let your conversation be as it becometh the gospel of Christ: that whether I come and see you, or else be absent, I may hear of your affairs, that ye stand fast in one spirit with one mind striving together for the faith of the gospel; and in nothing terrified by your adversaries: which is to them an evident token of perdition but to you of salvation and that of God.'

"Elder Campbell later wrote: 'That settled the question. That was a communication from Sister White we needed right at that time. God knew we were holding that meeting and that we had a group of scared men, and that we needed help from Him, and so He gave us the message that came straight to us in the nick of time . . .' In spite of the fact that every conceivable step was taken by the opposition to block the work of reorganization, the meeting was conducted successfully. A grateful letter was written: 'With much joy I hastily pen you a few lines. Many thanks for the telegram. How appropriate was the Scripture . . .'"

The Lord through His servant had sent warning messages for many months, but nothing could have been more dramatic or timelier than that short telegram. Her timing was impeccable! The Battle Creek Tabernacle was saved for the Seventh-day Adventists—one more reason, among many, to trust the *messenger of the Lord.* We also heard the story directly from Elder Campbell, who was my husband's beloved grandfather.

From the flyleaf of the bestseller by Rene Noorbergen—*Ellen G. White: Prophet of Destiny*—is this description: "a full and fascinating portrait of a truly remarkable, yet strangely little-known woman." She testified: "'Early in my public labor, I was bidden by the Lord, write, write what is revealed to you,' and Ellen White heeded that instruction, producing more than fifty books translated into over a hundred languages, and still being read by millions. In them, she recounted her visions of spiritual matters, of the final end of the great controversy between good and evil, which inspired the young and growing Seventh-day Adventist movement with her revelations of truths concerning life on earth. She wrote of the poisonous effect of tobacco [when the public attitude toward smoking was positive], the dangers of X-rays, the coming pollution of the environment, the drug addiction and unrest of today's youth, the concept of natural diet—all well in advance of her time. Not an astrologer, seer or mystic, Ellen White drew her prophecies from the true source of revelation—divine inspiration."

Ellen White often warned of fanaticism and empty vain emotionalism. She promoted spiritual and biblical common sense. She never claimed perfection, knowing that as a sinner she, too, needed the free gift of salvation. Through her life she, as others, grew in her Christian experience, and her writings urge the same for God's followers.

It Pays!—To God be the Glory

Some of Mrs. White's visions were given to relay personal messages to specific people. They are found in a series of books called *Testimonies for the Church*, which are filled with practical counsel and principles that are appropriate for all Christians. At times her personal visions were delivered in public if the situation or the person's sin or problem affected other people in the congregation. She was often bold with her message, even exposing the errors of leaders who were up front preaching. Of course, many of these messages were given personally by letter or visits with the person in need. These personal contacts were made with much tact, wisdom, compassion, and kindness. Individuals were never again the same. Most recipients of her messages received them positively, some responding immediately, others eventually, and usually gratefully. Here is a sample of her attitude toward erring persons as is written in *Testimonies for the Church*, volume 7: "A word of love and encouragement will do more to subdue the hasty temper and willful disposition than all the faultfinding and censure that you can heap upon the erring one" (p. 266).

The following letters are a part of an autograph album where grateful people wrote daily messages for Mrs. White to read while on a seven-day voyage: ". . . as I must confess that my interest for the truth was growing cold. But thanks be to God, He did not let me go on with them [a secret society] without giving me warning through His servant. I cannot express my gratitude to Him for it. . . . I can praise God with all my might and then I cannot express my gratitude to Him for the love that He has shown me" (N. D. Faulkhead).

Another entry: "It affords me the most sincere pleasure to have the privilege of putting on record my appreciation for Sister E. G. White's work and my gratitude to my Heavenly Father for the messages sent through her to His people. The faithful witness thus revealed to me the means whereby the bondage of Satan was broken when, owing to the influence of spiritualism, I had well-nigh became a spiritual wreck. I have every reason to be positive in my confidence in Sister E. G. White as a true prophet" (N. A. Davis).

It is understandable that during the early years of Ellen White's ministry many questioned the origin of her visions and dreams. Some doubters were sincere Christians. Some felt disappointed that a very young and frail woman was chosen to be God's messenger. During these end times, as well as at all times, we must "try the spirits," for not ever spirit comes from God: "Many false prophets have gone out into the world" (1 John 4:1). Visions have been confused with spiritualistic seances or mesmerism. Some felt Mrs. White's poor health was the reason for her visions and dreams. Most of the doubters, even those whose moral sins were exposed, were eventually convinced and converted.

There is a chapter in *Ellen G White—Prophet of Destiny* by Rene Noorbergen titled "Psychics Versus Prophets" in which the author emphasizes the great need of checking out true versus false prophets. We can imagine the great increase of people being involved in psychic activities and business today. The author has this to say: "At a time when 10,000 professional astrologers control the daily activities of 40 million people in the United States through 1,200 daily astrology columns and 2,350 horoscope computers; when roughly 140,000 fortune-tellers, mediums, clairvoyants and psychic seers have created a 42-million-dollar-a-year business; and when three major universities offer credit courses in witchcraft, magic, astrology and sorcery, a foolproof method to separate the psychics from the prophets has become essential."

The tests for a true prophet, all found in the Old and New Testaments of the Bible, pointedly indicate that those prognosticators not measuring up to these stringent qualifications cannot lay claim to the rare distinction of being true prophets of God. They can be summarized as follows:

1. True prophets do not lie. Their predictions will be fulfilled (Jer. 28:9).
2. True prophets prophesy in the name of the Lord, not in their own name (2 Peter 1:21).
3. True prophets do not give their own private interpretation of prophecy (2 Peter 1:20).
4. True prophets point out the sins and transgressions of the people against God (Isa. 58:1).
5. True prophets warn the people of God's coming judgment (Isa. 24:20, 21; Rev. 14:6, 7).
6. True prophets edify the church, counseling and advising it in religious matters (1 Cor. 14:3, 4).
7. A true prophet's words will be in absolute harmony with the words of the prophets that have preceded them (Isa. 8:20).
8. True prophets recognize the incarnation of Jesus Christ (1 John 4:1-3).

It Pays!—To God be the Glory

9. True prophets can be recognized by the results of their work (Matt. 7:16-20).

A true prophet acts in accordance with the will and approval of God. "To be even more precise, the actions of a true prophet are not in contradiction of basic Biblical doctrines, but rather support and strengthen precepts already outlined" (*Ellen G White—Prophet of Destiny*, p. 21).

For starters, take Paul Harvey's suggestion by "getting acquainted with Ellen White." Read the precious little book *Steps to Christ* (sometimes called the *Happiness Digest*). It is a spiritual classic published in more than 150 languages. It has sold more than 100 million copies. It is perhaps the largest single printing of any religious book in history. Its continued use tells of the timelessness and universality of its simple, direct, and clear message.

Also, a good way to appreciate the Scripture is to read *Character Classics*, a five-part series covering Genesis to Revelation. The stories and lessons are written with personal appeal to the reader. The only way to receive genuine trust and a blessing from this heaven-sent gift is to read with an *attitude of gratitude*. I have read the entire series through, in order, five times, and I can personally testify that each time I read Ellen White's writings I hear the voice of God's Holy Spirit speaking to my soul. I will never be the same, and in humility, I thank God!

The earmarks of the "remnant" are they "which keep the commandments of God, and have the testimony of Jesus Christ" (Rev. 12:17). The Scriptures define this testimony as follows: "for the testimony of Jesus is the spirit of prophecy" (Rev. 19:10). No wonder "the dragon [Satan] was wroth with the woman [the church], and went to make war with the remnant of her seed" (Rev. 12:17).

God's gift of guidance through last day prophecy, just like with all the Bible principles, will remain valid for all time—leading, guiding, counseling all the activities of God's work on earth through the church and its varied entities. The worth and value of God's guidance depends on our humble willingness to take heed.

Truly the gift of prophecy was—for these last days—*a very timely gift*.

Ellen White knew and accepted her mission, though often it was challenging enough to bring her to tears. The following quotations reveal Ellen White's passionate love for Christ, His Word, and her love and concern for people:

> "God has . . . promised to give visions in the *"last days"*; not for a new rule of faith, but for the comfort of His people, and to correct those who err from Bible truth" (*Early Writings,* p. 78).

> "As the Spirit of God has opened to my mind the great truths of His word, and the scenes of the past and the future, I have been bidden to make known to others that which has thus been revealed" (*The Great Controversy,* p. xi).

> "As the mind dwells upon Christ, the character is molded after the divine similitude. The thoughts are pervaded with a sense of His goodness, His love. We contemplate His character, and thus He is in all our thoughts. His love encloses us. If we gaze even a moment upon the sun in its meridian glory, when we turn away our eyes, the image of the sun will appear in everything upon which we look. Thus it is when we behold Jesus; everything we look upon reflects His image, the Sun of Righteousness. . . . To all with whom we associate we reflect the bright and cheerful beams of His righteousness. We have become transformed in character; for heart, soul, and mind, are irradiated by the reflection of Him who loved us, and gave Himself for us" (*The Faith I Live By,* p. 150).

> "The Holy Scriptures are to be accepted as an authoritative, infallible revelation of His will. They are the standard of character, the revealer of doctrines, and the test of experience" (*ibid.,* p. 293).

> "Jesus knows the circumstances of every soul. You may say, I am sinful, very sinful. You may be; but the worse you are, the more you need Jesus. He turns no weeping, contrite one away" (*The Desire of Ages,* p. 568).

Does It Pay?

Yes! It does pay to serve Jesus! The deep peace and security I personally receive from knowing and practicing my beliefs makes me joyfully eager to share my experience with you and others. My hope is that these next verses will feed your soul and mine and fill us with great longing! I think of this verse when I see outstanding beauty in nature: "Eye hath not seen, nor ear heard, neither have entered into the heart of man, the things which God hath prepared for them that love him" (1 Cor. 2:9).

I am comforted by this thought when I see other people's tears as well as my own and the reason for them: "And God shall wipe away all tears from their eyes; and there shall be no more death, neither sorrow, nor crying, neither shall there be any more pain: for the former things are passed away" (Rev. 21:4; see also 1 Cor. 15:51-55).

Without Satan in our midst, heaven will give us freedom from his temptations. The great controversy between good and evil will be over—praise the Lord! In my mind the greatest event of this time is the vindication of God: "Great and marvellous are thy works, Lord God Almighty; just and true are thy ways, thou King of saints" (Rev. 15:3), and His followers, by God's grace, are blessed for their obedience "that they may have right to the tree of life, and may enter in through the gates into the city" (Rev. 22:14).

I want to say like the apostle Paul at the end of my journey "I have fought a good fight, I have finished my course, I have kept the faith: Henceforth there is laid up for me a crown of righteousness, which the Lord, the righteous judge, shall give me at that day: and not to me only, but unto all them also that love his appearing" (2 Tim. 4:7, 8). And, this is my prayer for every reader.

How we should long to meet the One who has made our lives so meaningful and satisfying. Let's thank Him for these "exceedingly abundant" blessings far beyond our comprehension. "I go to prepare a place for you. And . . . I will come again, and receive you unto myself; that where I am, there ye may be also" (John 14:2, 3). And "so shall we ever be with the Lord" (1 Thess. 4:16, 17).

"Even so, come, Lord Jesus" (Rev. 22:20). ♥

We invite you to view the complete
selection of titles we publish at:

www.TEACHServices.com

Scan with your mobile
device to go directly
to our website.

Please write or email us your praises, reactions, or
thoughts about this or any other book we publish at:

TEACH Services, Inc.
P U B L I S H I N G

www.TEACHServices.com

P.O. Box 954
Ringgold, GA 30736

info@TEACHServices.com

TEACH Services, Inc., titles may be purchased in bulk for
educational, business, fund-raising, or sales promotional use.
For information, please e-mail

BulkSales@TEACHServices.com

Finally, if you are interested in seeing
your own book in print, please contact us at

publishing@teachservices.com

We would be happy to review your manuscript for free.

www.ingramcontent.com/pod-product-compliance
Lightning Source LLC
Chambersburg PA
CBHW070549160426
43199CB00014B/2430